The
Veil

and the
Victory

D1715221

The
Veil
and the
Victory

Anne Smerke

WINEPRESS WP PUBLISHING

ISBN 1-57921-172-0
Library of Congress Catalog Card Number: 98-89658

Dedication

This book is dedicated to Yvonne, my dearest friend and companion for twenty-eight years. She always understood my need for quiet hours and solitude during the writing of *The Veil and the Victory*. She is now at rest and peace with her Lord in heaven.

Acknowledgments

I thank the Lord for His help in the writing of this book.

I also thank Bonnie McNamara for her editorial help and for typing, proofreading, and placing the manuscript on her computer system.

Contents

Introduction

Clutching a letter in my right hand, I stopped as I came out through the front door of the building that was once the convent and my home. A peaceful quiet came over me. I glanced across the street at the high school I had attended forty-four years ago. A flood of memories swept before me. I brushed away tears as I still felt the love of my many friends, my classmates, and, especially, the Franciscan Sisters. They taught us well with patience and understanding, trying to bring out the best in us. I thought of the day I had joined them and had become a member of the Franciscan Order, forty years ago.

Here, on the top step to the convent, I had stopped when I was nineteen years old, turned around, and waved goodbye to the world. That goodbye included my parents, my four brothers and one sister, my relatives, and everyone else whom I loved dearly. The only ones present were my dear high school friends.

Now I felt the pain of separation as I had on that day. I squeezed the letter in my right hand, closed my eyes, and whispered a prayer to God thanking Him for what had been. I opened my eyes and looking across the street and to the left I saw the beautiful new convent that was built in 1944 to accommodate all the new sisters who had entered the convent by 1944. Next to it was the high school. How safe I had felt within those walls no matter what turmoil and unrest threatened the world outside. The large courtyard in front had many trees, a beautiful green lawn, and gardens of flowers that raised many "thank you's" to God as they lifted their branches and petals to their Creator. I felt so much gratitude in my heart for this beautiful home that had become my steppingstone to a better life.

Has it really been forty years? I asked myself. Something stirred in me so that I asked myself the next question. *What have I accomplished?* Through many struggles, worries, hard work, and tears I had managed to accomplish a few things, like becoming an accomplished music teacher, organist, choir director, teacher of catechism in grades 1–12, registered nurse, and a few other minor things. Next I wondered, *Is this what you set out to do?*

I had come here to serve God with all my heart and soul. What was missing? I had worked so hard—where had I gone wrong? Doesn't God honor hard work? All this hard work proves what? Ambition! Was I ever satisfied? No. Why not? I had been working for success and for the approval of others—the Community, especially. I was so successful! Whatever I was asked to do I had done in the best way I could and I had succeeded. For whom? For the Community. Success was important to them. A sudden thought propelled me back to my childhood again.

As a child I had heard our pastor relate a story about two women who were sisters, Mary and Martha. He told us the story had happened when Jesus was on earth:

There was a big feast, and Jesus was invited. Mary waited with longing to see Jesus, and when He came she forgot everything and sat down at Jesus' feet, drinking in His presence and the words He spoke. She listened with such devotion to everything He said that she forgot Martha and the dinner preparations! Martha was in the kitchen, busy as a bee, perspiring, flitting around hurriedly, trying to get everything done on time and annoyed that Mary was not helping her.

She finally stormed out to the other room where Mary and Jesus were and let Jesus know how dutifully she was working and how hard it was without Mary's help.

Poor Martha! She was suffering enough already, but she got no sympathy from Jesus. He reminded Martha with these words, "Martha, Martha, you are busy about many things, but Mary has chosen the better part."

What part had I chosen? I almost crumpled the letter in my hand when I realized the truth. Why had I chosen Martha's part?

I looked back at my home life. I always had great respect for my parents who taught me that my value and possibly my salvation were determined by hard work and personal goodness. Their examples confirmed this. When I entered the convent, the nuns reinforced this teaching. Our pastor at home frequently admonished the congregation in his sermons concerning attendance at Mass, praying the rosary, and working diligently to earn heaven.

I had not known that any denomination other than the Roman Catholic Church even existed until I was ten years old. A Lutheran minister and his family had moved into our hometown, St. Stephen, Minnesota, hoping to establish a Lutheran Church there. He was not accepted by the Catholic community. Within a month he moved to another town. We were cautioned and forbidden by our pastor to ever befriend or associate with members of any denomination other than Catholic. We were told that non-Catholics were heretics who did not want to obey God's Commandments or to work hard to earn heaven.

Not until after I had entered the convent did I actually meet any Protestant! I received my first assignment at age twenty-one. I was sent to Elk River, Minnesota, which was 75 percent Protestant and 25 percent Catholic. I was known as Sister Mary Jeannette. In Elk River I heard about Martin Luther—that he was a Catholic but had been excommunicated. Why? I had wondered. What driving force gave him the courage to break out from what he had always believed in and to proclaim his "new" beliefs about salvation? Had ambition and the need for recognition driven Luther? Or had his search for God been valid? Had Luther's discoveries caused the start of other denominations? I had resolved to find out. I knew it would be difficult since there were no resources among my Catholic associates, but I wondered which way is the right way.

When my three older brothers decided to become priests, the attention of my parents became almost totally directed to their welfare, health, and education. I was a girl, with no definite future plans. According to my parents, I would most likely marry, like my sister had. She had left home when I was four years old. She lived in New York and Oklahoma, seldom returning home.

Because of the great interest and concern for the future priests, my parents may have somewhat neglected my needs without realizing it. That feeling of unimportance, except while I was working, made me feel left out and used. I realized that hard work, obedience, and loyalty would make me acceptable to them. I became very competitive in my work. I organized my different jobs by allowing only so much time for each. I soon showed up my brothers by the amount of work I accomplished in less time than they did. I caught my brothers' and also my parents' attention. I refused to be a *nobody*, and this helped my self-esteem for the time being.

In high school I had continued to be competitive after one of the sisters helped me to see my abilities. This competitive spirit accompanied me when I entered the convent. I was on the lookout for persons in authority who would use me to promote others at my expense.

Please, God, tell me it isn't so! I thought at the entrance to the convent. This time the tears flowed from a contrite heart. How could I have mistaken ambition for serving God with my whole heart and soul? How could I have mistaken rules and regulations for the Word of God? I knew so little about the Bible and its contents that reveal the great love of God for each one of us and the promises of blessings and eternal life with Him to those who believe in Him and entrust their lives to His direction.

Where do I begin in living right? O God, help me do what I had set out to do; but I want to do it your way. (I felt like the Prodigal Son must have felt when he realized his mistake.) *Lord, I am sixty years old! It looks so impossible. Show me the way, for you know the way; you are the truth, and you are my life.*

I heard the door open behind me. I quickly wiped the tears away and turned around to face none other than the Reverend Mother. I smiled.

She asked politely, "Are you waiting for a ride?"

"Yes, Reverend Mother."

"Where do you plan on going?"

Without hesitation I answered, "On a long journey."

You see, she was the one who had handed me that letter from Rome I had been waiting for. It was the letter of dispensation granted by the Holy See, releasing me from my vows and my life in the Franciscan Community.

I again shook hands with the Reverend Mother, and with a new strength, confidence, and determination I walked down the remaining five steps to the sidewalk. I turned, waved to the Reverend Mother, and started walking.

The clothes I was wearing were my only possessions as I left my home of forty years. The day I had visited with the Reverend Mother, telling her of my decision to leave the convent, she had warned me of the financial distress the Community was experiencing—to the verge of bankruptcy. Today she had repeated "I am not able to give you any financial benefit as you leave. The usual amount is $500. I am sorry I cannot help you."

I relieved her by saying, "Reverend Mother, God promised me He would take care of me. I know He will."

I kept walking from my haven of safety into the unknown, leaning on the promises of God. *Lord, I am all yours. I place all my trust in you.*

Friends, it has been a long journey. Please join me as I look back at my beginnings, my well-intentioned attempts at a better life, my battles and wounds, my successes and failures, and finally, the awakening that led to a new beginning filled with love, peace, joy, and a happiness that comes only from above. This happiness lasts forever. It surpasses all that the world's riches can offer for a brief time.

We grow, bloom, and mature, as we are nourished with the Word of God which gives us life, meaning, and a foretaste of what God has prepared for those who love Him and seek to know Him.

CHAPTER 1

Humble Beginnings

From Slovenia to America

America! She is the land of freedom, of plenty, of golden opportunities. No more starvation, poverty, or petty wars.

This great news spread all over Europe by those who had been to America and returned to rescue their families from wars and oppression. My father had just completed his four years' training in the German army (although he had not served in actual combat) and left Slovenia in 1896. But he and his friends had completed their training; they were not AWOL.

Life in the German army was Spartan and oppressive. My father was tired of the meager daily menu that never changed. Breakfast was one cup of black coffee; the noon meal consisted of thin bean soup (one helping), and the evening meal was better—one helping of bean soup which contained more beans than the noon meal had. His only salvation from starvation was picking chestnuts and cracking them with his teeth and eating them as they found them during their rest periods in the hills. Any place on earth, my father reasoned, had to be better than this! When he heard the great news about America, he convinced some of his army training buddies to go too, and they all agreed it was time to leave Slovenia.

Sailing the Atlantic in 1896 was risky. Ships had very poor accommodations, and the trip was long—the crossing took fifty to sixty days. Passengers were packed into all quarters of the ships. Comfort was not a priority, and seasickness was common. While rooms were available, they were small and poorly equipped. Only the rich had furniture in their rooms. Many passengers slept on the floor or on benches provided by passengers. Ships had no provisions for sick people or medical emergencies. Each passenger cared for his own baggage. Ocean travel during this time was a far cry from travel in modern ships today.

My father left Europe from Slovenia with high hopes and great faith in God's protection and provision for the people. He left behind his three sisters and his parents, who feared going on such a dangerous voyage. People who left Slovenia received help from the Church. The Catholic Bishop of Slovenia in Ljubljana was contacted by the pastor of my father's local parish to make arrangements for transportation and relocation of his people in the New World.

The Bishop of Slovenia contacted the Bishops of St. Cloud, Minnesota; Cleveland, Ohio; and Pittsburgh, Pennsylvania. A list of names was given to the American Bishops through a responsible person on the ship. Upon landing in New York, the Slovenes decided which city to move to.

Many Slovenes settled in these three areas. The Bishops in America were contacted and everyone was accounted for as they reached the American shore.

My father had no relatives here, so he was free to go where he pleased. He had only acquaintances, like Jake Petrich and his brother. Jake was one of my father's army buddies who came over on the same boat as my father did. Jake had been to America already and had returned to Slovenia to help other Slovenes who wished to emigrate because he knew Eveleth, Minnesota had mining jobs.

My father chose Cleveland. Jake, my mother's brother, also chose Cleveland initially. He and my father worked in a winery for a while. Not long after, the Alaska Gold Rush shook Cleveland! My father did not waste any time. Another eager young man hoping to get rich boarded the first train to Alaska. My Uncle Jake decided to ride as far as Eveleth, where he would work in the coal mines.

Soon after that ship sailed for America, my mother also set sail from Ljubljana with a large group of men and women seeking the American dream. She was only fifteen. Her brothers and one sister joined her. Their destination was Eveleth to

Agnes Petrich, Anne's mother, about 15 years old, standing upper left, with her sister and sister's children. In Eveleth, Minnesota, about 1904.

join their brother Jake. When they arrived in Eveleth her brothers had jobs waiting for them in the coal mines, and my mother was spoken for as a housekeeper for a Jewish family. Uncle Jake had provided for these jobs.

Mother and Dad Meet

My mother was happy and enjoyed her work and got along famously with her Jewish employers. She was able to be with her brothers frequently. Two years later she met my father for the first time. His gold supply seemed satisfactory in Alaska, so he came back to Eveleth, where he knew he could get a steady job in the coal mines. He had come back from Alaska with ten large nuggets of gold. One night five of them were stolen as he was riding the train back to Eveleth. He fell asleep and awoke to find five nuggets instead of ten. He felt bad, but he asked Jake to get him a job in the coal mines. He was hired the next day.

Uncle Jake, who was already married, said to my father one day, "John, it's time you settled down. I want you to meet my sister Agnes. She works for a Jewish family. I'll take you over to meet her." My father agreed.

After supper they went to the home where my mother worked. She would not unlatch the screen door because Uncle Jake had a stranger with him. They were introduced through the screen.

Evidently my mother was not too impressed with John. She merely stated, "I have work to do—they are meeting here tonight to pray together."

This did not intimidate my father at all. He had five nuggets of gold, and he was going to put them to good use. He returned home that night, unable to sleep. So he spent his time thinking, planning, plotting how he could get Agnes' attention.

Years later he would tell us children how it was love at first sight. He called the courtship of my mother a "golden victory." He was well aware of the fact she was playing hard to get. Only he didn't figure how hard. He waited until Sunday morning and gave her time to get home from church. (One usually made good resolutions of kindness, goodness, forgiveness, and mercy toward everyone at Sunday Mass.) He took along one nugget to make a good first impression. A nugget of gold in those days was impressive to any woman. He knocked on the screen door, which he noticed was locked, and soon the inner door opened.

"Hello," he said, and to his astonishment Agnes answered using his name.

"Hello, John," she replied.

He proceeded boldly, asking if he could come in. She declined. Startled, he tried the next move. "Look what I brought you," he said, showing her the nugget.

She glanced down at the nugget, but the screen door remained locked. She merely answered with a guarded smile saying, "Nice" and "Goodbye."

He was crushed. This was not going well at all. He decided to go check with Jake to find out what he had done wrong. Jake was waiting for him, eager to hear how things were progressing. After my father unloaded his first defeat, he looked bruised and heartbroken.

Uncle Jake laughed. "John, she's very shy. I know she loves you. I know my sister. Don't give up! You keep talking to her. Visit her, and remember to give her time. Above all, let her know there are more nuggets," Jake said jokingly.

This was all my father needed to hear. He thanked Jake for the encouragement and went home in high spirits, determined and willing to improve his patience. He realized he needed to slow down and that she was worth waiting for.

My mother was brilliant and shrewd, with a pleasing personality. She had a strong will no one could weaken. Once she made a decision, no effort could change her mind. Each one of her six children had to learn this, one by one. She was also brilliant in math. She had only one year of grade school in Slovenia, but she qualified as a math teacher, a psychologist, and a psychiatrist, and she knew what to do in any emergency. If we couldn't figure out a math problem, she could—and without paper and pencil. She taught us how to figure it out using good logic and common sense. We were never allowed to miss school or church services no matter how carefully we plotted to get out of them.

My father saw all these qualities in her and knew he had a gold mine to fight for, not just a few nuggets. The second night he went to see her, his efforts were better received. He brought an extra nugget, and it worked! She opened the screen door. But again she decided how long he could stay. The third night he brought three nuggets and received a cup of coffee. The fourth night he decided to bring all five nuggets. She was warming up now, but his small voice inside said, "Be patient." On the fifth night she opened the door, she brought him coffee, and they sat down and talked. They spoke Slovenian, the only language they both knew.

He entertained her with his stories of his farm in Slovenia, the slavery inflicted by the Germans, and the trip to America. He talked about the Alaskan Gold Rush and his experiences working in the coal mines. She shrewdly surveyed him as he talked, taking mental notes of everything he said and how he said it. My father was really restraining himself—he checked his progress in patience and said, "Well, I better go now. I have to get up early tomorrow. I'll see you soon."

Things were going so well, but he knew he had to wait for the right moment. He even waited an extra day sometimes before seeing her again to control his impatience.

When I was in my teens, I marveled at my father's self-control. For instance, Catholics then were very dutiful to the restrictions of Lent, each fasting for forty days and sacrificing some indulgence such as smoking or eating chocolates to strengthen the inner man and to repent for sins committed. My father smoked a pipe, cigarettes, and cigars daily. Starting each Lenten season with Ash Wednesday, he had one cup of coffee and one piece of toast for breakfast, a full meal at noon, and one-fourth of a meal in the evening with nothing to eat between meals. In addition, he put his cigarettes, pipe and tobacco, and cigars up on a shelf. They came down forty days later on Easter Sunday. He never complained about it.

Only later did I realize what an influence my mother was on his life. She *was* a gold mine. Four weeks after my father and mother had met, my father decided it was time to ask her to marry him. Agnes' behavior toward him had changed completely over that short time. He felt they understood each other. Both were hard workers, and he respected her for who she was and what she stood for. Sunday Mass was a must for her—something he had forgotten frequently. He made resolutions and changes because of her goodness and straightforwardness, her honesty and simplicity. Having observed these virtues in her, he was ready to propose marriage.

They went to church on Sunday. My father asked her if he could come and spend some time with her in the afternoon. She welcomed the thought with a pleasant smile and assured him it would be more than all right with her.

My father had planned it well. He arrived all dressed up in his best clothes and offered her a present—a bag of five shining nuggets, one bigger than the other. It was a sunny day. Agnes took the gold in the sunlight. They lit up her face as she rolled them around in her hands. Then it came.

"Agnes, will you marry me?"

With no hesitation, she said, "Yes."

My father had won but only after some changes in character and hours of soul searching to meet the challenges of the gold mine he had found.

And so it was that John Smerke and Agnes Petrich were joined in holy matrimony in the Catholic Church in Eveleth, Minnesota, in June 1905. They settled in "Chicken Town." This was the part of Eveleth where everyone raised chickens. Mother enjoyed this. Dad continued working in the coal mines, a dangerous underground job. The miners never knew if they were walking on solid ground or on an excavation under their feet. Many men lost their lives in these poorly constructed mines. Trains were not used in the mines then. Donkeys hauled the coal out of the mines.

The Move to St. Stephen, Minnesota

On July 7, 1907, they were blessed with a daughter whom they named Mary. Catholics named their children after saints or the Blessed Virgin Mary. Three years later after Frank was born on May 30, 1910, Mother and Dad decided to move to St. Stephen, Minnesota, where they could buy a farm, raise cattle, chickens, and pigs, and sell produce from plowed land. They traveled by bobsled driven by two horses in temperatures of thirty to forty degrees below zero. This was a 110-mile trip.

In Minnesota, winter can last from September to the end of May. Frank, only ten months old, was safely tucked in Dad's heavy winter coat pocket to keep warm during the move.

They arrived in March 1911. St. Stephen was a small village consisting of a small bank, two grocery stores, a saloon, and a Catholic Church. About two hundred Catholic Slovenes, including Mother's younger brother, John Petrich, had bought up the farms around the town. Mother and Dad bought a farm two miles south of town.

There was only one church in town—a Catholic Church. Everyone was Catholic. My parents were devout members, brought up in Slovenia with rigid discipline. We learned that God was above every king or president on earth. God created the heavens and the earth. He also gave us the Ten Commandments to obey. If we wanted to get to heaven, we had better obey His Ten Commandments because He sees every move we make. Everything is under His command. He knows our every thought, word, and deed.

We knew about the devil too, that he was the enemy of God. He wants us to do the exact opposite of God's Commandments. We had to make up our minds whom we would serve, God or the devil. I was not taught about the devil's activities in the world. I thought he was in hell. We learned that God was also just, and on Judgment Day we will have to answer to Him how we chose to live: serving Him or the devil. Daily Mass was very important, but attendance on Sundays was an obligation. If we missed Sunday Mass with no valid excuse, we committed a mortal sin. We were told that if we died without confessing our mortal sins to the priest, we would go to hell.

A small sin, called a venial sin, constituted a lesser punishment. We were taught that if we died with venial sins not confessed, we were destined to a stay in Purgatory. I never quite understood this part. I grew up fearing God. I resolved I would keep His Commandments and my attendance at Mass would be flawless. I remember when I was four years old I started attending Mass daily with Mother. When she couldn't attend, I would feel guilty. This did not happen very often in summer when the weather was nice.

Later when I was in school, all the children attended Mass first, and then we went to school. My brothers and I walked one and one-half miles to school in rain, shine, or weather of thirty to forty degrees below zero, the typical temperatures during most of the winter. We were there every day except for three weeks in September. It was very difficult to convince Mother we were too sick to go to school. We became resilient thanks to her. We had to be thankful we had a chance to go to school.

Life on the Farm: World War I

Births of Joseph, John, Anne, and Tony

Our house of four rooms had no insulation. A pot-bellied stove kept it warm during the day and evening, but after we went to bed and the fire burned down, we woke up to an ice-cold house. The fire was restarted to begin a new day. There was a barn for the horses and cattle that came with the purchase of the land.

As time passed and the family grew, our parents added on to the house and the barn. As machinery came, a shed, granary, corn-crib, and smokehouse for homemade sausage were added. Dad also built a large pen and houses for the pigs.

On October 6, 1912, Joseph was born. John arrived March 31, 1915. World War I had begun seven months earlier, and many young men were called to duty, leaving a shortage of workers in the fields. The mothers and daughters had to take over working in the fields. On May 22, 1918, six months before the armistice, I was born. Mother had been working hard during this pregnancy, skimping on food so the children would have enough to eat. Times were hard.

From birth I was a very small baby, sickly, underweight, and not appearing likely to thrive. We lived fifteen miles away from St. Cloud, a larger town of about four thousand, where a doctor was available. He was one of the few richer people who could afford a car—a Tin Lizzy as they were called. He was called to come and deliver me because my mother had been in labor for forty-eight hours, and everyone was worried for both mother and child. The so-called midwife, who was not trained in midwifery, insisted the doctor be called. This was the normal routine; only in question-able situations was a doctor present for delivery of babies.

Eight years later my brother Tony was born with the same doc-tor present. By that time doctors attended deliveries more frequently.

My first year was an exhausting one for Mother. She did not recover well from my birth. She was weak and tired and needed much rest, so my sister Mary had to assume much of the domestic chores, including cooking, cleaning, washing and ironing as well as working in the fields. Farming then was grueling work with few comforts and little or no money. Gradually during this difficult time both Mother and I grew stronger.

At the same time another crisis developed with a neighbor who threatened my father. The neighbor resented my father's European immigrant status. The neighbor considered immigrants intruders. One day the neighbor's hatred overcame him, and he poisoned our cattle's drinking water. Our entire herd of twelve milk cows, ten calves, and two bulls died. The water was inspected, the poison identified, but no one saw the perpetrator do it. The man threatened my father's life as well. My father did not retaliate. He and Mother displayed God's law of love for one's neighbor to the furthest degree.

The case was dropped. My parents were devastated. They had to start over again. But no gold nuggets remained; they were used to pay for the farm and to buy the cattle, the horses, and the machinery to run the farm. But now five children had to be fed. The farm consisted of ninety acres: forty acres of plowed land for their crops of wheat, oats, corn, and potatoes, and forty acres of pasture with many oak and maple trees. Ten additional acres of meadow provided all the hay for the horses and cattle during the cold nine months of winter every year. My parents kept saying, "God is with us. He will help us get back on our feet. He never forgets us, but we must forgive our enemies and pray for them that persecute us."

My parents knew the basic principles of Christianity. Tithing was one of these principles my parents followed without fail. When we had no money, Mother would pack two dozen eggs, a fresh loaf of bread, and a ring of homemade sausage and take them to the pastor. They never went to church empty-handed.

In the evenings after all the chores were completed, we entertained ourselves by playing cards, making games of our own, or listening to our parents reminisce about life in the "old country." Mother and Dad always added to their stories thanks to God for bringing them to America.

They liked to tell of the beautiful mountains and deep valleys of Slovenia and of the picturesque autumns with bountiful displays of color as the leaves were ready to fall. Some stories were scary, like the ones about the people who died. The practice of embalming did not exist in those days. The coffins were all handmade by the families. When a body was ready to be buried, the coffin was nailed shut and lowered into the grave with leather straps. Occasionally, the noise of the hammering awakened a person who was still alive and who was then rescued from an untimely bed by knocking on the coffin lid.

My parents told about the sheepherding in the mountainous areas of Slovenia and about the people, who were all poor, living on what they planted summer and winter. The rich lived away from the small towns. Village stores were small and had some fruits and vegetables late summer and early spring. Essential everyday tools were available.

Some evenings, my brothers read books they had brought from the school library. They read by the light of an old kerosene lamp. Not even the nearby town had electricity.

At 9:00 P.M. we all knelt down to say the rosary together. My dad would kneel at the bedside in my parents' bedroom, and Mother stayed with us in the living room next door. My father led the rosary. We answered each Hail Mary and Our Father. About the middle of the rosary my father's voice would sometimes wane in strength and speed. He would succumb to weariness and begin to fall asleep. Mother would rush to his side, shake him to reality, and then try to tell him where he was. Every time, an argument ensued. This was how it sounded:

"Pa, wake up!"

"Oh, where am I?"

"You were leading the rosary. You fell asleep. This is where you left off." She would pick up the rosary and show him.

"No," he would say. "I said the Glory Be."

"No, you started it but you didn't finish it."

Pause.

"Oh, I'll just go on with the Our Father."

"No, you have to finish the Glory Be first!" Silence.

Guess who won! Maybe to save time, finish the job at hand, and get to bed, he gave into Mother's sharp and accurate memory that he had come to respect over the years. The argument usually perked him up to finish the rosary without a hitch.

My sister Mary, the eldest, left home when I was three and a half years old. She disliked farming. Her great ambition was to be a nurse. The Benedictine Sisters had a hospital in St. Cloud, Minnesota, only fifteen miles from our home, to which Mary applied and was accepted. To earn her schooling, she did all the domestic labor for the Flemings, a family in St. Cloud. A year later (1920) she was a registered nurse. She was hired by the Walker Hospital in Walker, Minnesota. She spent nine years taking care of the sick there. Her wages were ninety dollars per month. She met her future husband, Al Schramm, in Walker. Schramm was an aviator who flew mail coast to coast and who was close friends with both Charles Lindbergh and Will Rogers. He and Mary married and left for New York. They had three children, each of whom later pursued an education, as had their mother.

I remember the day Mary left. I cried so hard, feeling deserted by my only sister. She had been so good to me. I would miss her piano playing and how she curled my hair, took me to town, and taught me to swing higher on my swing, reaching the leaves on the tree branches with my feet. Now I had only three older brothers to deal with.

But by now they were deciding what to do when they grew up. All three of them decided to go to Crosier High School, college, and seminary to become priests in the Crosier Monastery. The monastery was located in Onamia, about fifty miles from home. The Crosier Order originated in Holland. The monks spoke Dutch and broken English. The Order had built a high school, college, and seminary for young boys who felt called to the priesthood. Many students joined the Crosier Order; others married and had families and were able to secure good paying jobs because of their solid education.

The Blossoming of My Music Career

Shortly after Mary left home I sat down at the piano and started playing single note tunes that I knew from songs my mother sang.

I was so excited when I could play a tune all the way through without a mistake. But I wasn't satisfied with that. I wanted to know how to read music and play it. I asked my brother Frank, who was home from high school, where middle C was. He showed me where it was on the piano, but I wanted to know where it was on the printed music. He told me that too. I figured out the rest through the following year.

Anne and her family (except for Tony) about 1922. Back row: John Jr., Frank, Mary, Joe. Front row: John Sr., Anne (about 4) and Agnes.

By the time I went to grade school at age five I was able to play a couple easy pieces from memory. When I realized that several first-graders took piano lessons after school, I ran home and asked my parents if I could take piano lessons too—and the cost was only twenty-five cents. My father was interested but told me it was impossible. I did not know then that weeks would often pass when no penny, nickel, or dime crossed our threshold. We were truly penniless much of the time.

Although the armistice was signed on November 11, 1918, when I was six months old, we were still recuperating from the economic ravages of war five years later in 1923. Money was very scarce. Our torn clothes were patch upon patch (but clean), causing many humiliations at school. Our shoes had to last more that one year even if they cost only one dollar per pair brand new. However, we could buy a ring of bologna for ten to fifteen cents, depending on the size. When the chickens were laying eggs, we were able to pay for the bologna and other small articles with eggs. They sold for eight cents per dozen.

Labor in the fields was mostly done by hand except for the horse-drawn mower that cut our hay. We did own a wheat and oats binder. Corn crops were cut by hand, and corncobs were harvested by hand. We picked potatoes on our hands and knees. The cows were milked by hand.

We had no tractor. Few existed. Only the rich could afford them. The hay had to be stacked and the oats and corn stored in bins for the winter months. The days from April until the end of October were ones of hard work for us farmers when I was growing up. I learned how to milk cows at age six. My dad let me start with the easy ones. I was so proud that I could help. I was sensitive to the financial problems my parents faced. Dad was never sick, but Mother was frail and sickly and was hospitalized several times. She was by nature a worrier.

When a family member was sick, I stayed by them until I had done everything I knew for them. I was empathetic, hurting with them and crying with them. My goal was always to make things better, seeking peace and joy as the end result. I wanted everyone to be happy.

I didn't really enjoy grade school. My shyness and nervous disposition caused me to stutter and feel self-conscious. I endured many snide comments about my worn clothing. The comments hurt deeply and caused me to retire into the shadows even more. But I held one trump card: I was an excellent ball player! Why not, with three brothers to teach me? I could deliver a curve ball that no one could hit. My batting ability exceeded that of all the other girls. I was light-bodied and able to run like a gazelle. No one could catch me.

These are some of the blessings that come from family. My brothers taught me the better side of life—enjoying myself and lightening the burden of so much hard work. I learned that there is a time to work and a time to play, a time to cry and a time to laugh. This made work easier, and I was beginning to develop confidence in myself.

My brother Frank was a clown, keeping everyone happy. When I was depressed he would lift me up on his lap and make faces until I laughed. He couldn't bear to see anyone unhappy, and he had the ability to cheer anyone up, no matter what the problem was or how down in the dumps someone might be. He was able to carry out this mission until he died in 1986.

My brother Joe was the serious one. He could not go to bed until every assignment and every problem was done and checked over twice. He also expected everyone to have his same attitude about rules and regulations. His serious outlook continued until much later in his life, and then it took an act of God to change him. In 1970, when tragedy hit the family, he finally got tired of being stern, legalistic, and authoritarian. He became more joyful, philosophical, and easy going. But we will talk more about Joe later.

John was a go-between. He had a dry sense of humor and a very serious side, especially in church affairs—rules and regulations. He was one part Frank and the other part Joe. They made quite a trio. While in high school they decided to each play their favorite instrument. Frank chose the four-string banjo, Joe the fiddle, and John the five-string banjo. I chose piano and stuck with it to learn other instruments. They all took lessons by mail and did very well. I learned the chords for keys of C, G, F, D, and A by this time.

The four of us played for all the parties on our farm. We never knew when the whole town would end up at our place for a night of singing, dancing, and games that involved everyone. We had a huge lawn—perfect for all kinds of entertainment. My brothers played their instruments close to the window so I could join them on the piano inside. We added an accordionist, and we became very popular. The party would continue until 2:00 A.M. or 3:00 A.M. We never worried about food and drinks because the guests supplied them all. Everyone had a good time, and there were never any brawls or fights. But what a letdown to get up at five the next morning! That never changed.

I was eight years old when my brother Tony was born. On February 18 at ten in the evening Dad called the doctor from the uptown grocery store, one of the three places in town that had a telephone. We children were ushered to the neighbor's house until Dad came to get us. Early the next morning we learned we had a baby brother and that his name was Tony. I was very excited, my brothers took it casually, and my father threw a party! My mother had made some tasty dandelion wine the summer before. This was the time to uncork it! My Uncle John came for the celebration, and after everyone had sipped a while there was no room for a bird to fly. (Slovenes use both arms to tell a story.)

When I graduated from grade school at age eleven, my older brothers were in high school or college. I was the only one left to help my father on the farm. Every year I had to stay out of school for six to eight weeks to help my father on the farm. This was no problem until my teacher, who understood farming and harvesting, resigned. The new teacher was reared in a big city. She had no understanding of or compassion for farmers or the realities of their lives. I was reported to the superintendent of schools for missing so much school. My father was called in to explain his lack of supervision of his daughter. Before we knew it my teacher had the whole school in an uproar. Dad explained the circumstances (in broken English) to the superintendent. He understood, but the teacher was relentless.

She would not help me make up the six weeks I had missed, and I paid severely for my absence. I was humiliated by her rigid, unbending attitude. One day when I couldn't answer a question in decimals and fractions, she called me "stupid." That bore a wedge into my pride. I battled with this "stupidity" for many years. I just knew I could never become anything worthwhile. I was stupid, so why try? I had no desire to continue school. By now I was satisfied with being a farmer the rest of my life.

Anne, 12, with her entire family in 1930. L to R: Agnes, Fr. Frank, Anne, Fr. Joe, Mary, John Jr., and John Sr. Lower left, Tony.

After I graduated from grade school, I was left alone with Dad on the farm for the harvesting because my brothers were all away at high school or college. Acres of corn had to be cut by hand and built into shocks over a wood horse. After the tassels were tied together on top, the wood pole would be pulled out from the wood horse and the wood horse carried to the next place for another shock of corn to be made. We normally had ten to twelve acres of potatoes to be picked by hand. My father dug the potatoes and I picked them and placed them in one-hundred-pound bags. Later these were hauled twenty miles by wagon to Rice, Minnesota, for sale. Every spring I tried to talk my father out of planting at least two acres of potatoes.

Needless to say I was unsuccessful.

Four years later our parish priest asked my father about my continued education. I was fifteen years old. My father and I had paid all the expenses for my three brothers in high school, college, seminary and ordination to the priesthood. Now Dad was confronted with the question of my education and the money box was empty. Due to his background and the times, Dad was not accustomed to seeing young women receiving an education and had not thought about it much.

He asked me, "Do you *want* to go to high school? We have no extra money. I don't know what to do."

I was brought up to love, honor, and obey my parents. I felt compelled to make a commitment. I would work for my room and board while I attended high school so he wouldn't have to worry about me. He was grateful and relieved. I was concerned about leaving home because Mother was not well.

Tony was in the fourth grade. No one remained to help Dad with the farm work. This seemed to be the time for my parents to retire. However, they remained on the farm until Tony went to high school at Crosier in Onamia, Minnesota, where my older brothers had been educated. Dad sold all his cattle and machinery and rented the land to our neighbors. With this money he had more than enough to pay for Tony's education—high school and college. Two years later he sold the farm.

My parents moved to town, only one block from the church. Tony married and settled in Portland, Texas. He started his own printing business and was so successful he was able to retire at sixty-two. He and Irene have three lovely daughters. Janet, the oldest, became a nurse, Joan became an iridologist after raising four children, and Judy joined her husband in the insurance business. Thus far ends my life on the farm.

CHAPTER 2

High School Years

In 1933 my parish priest enrolled me in an all-girl boarding high school run by the Franciscan Sisters of Little Falls, Minnesota, only thirty miles from my home.

St. Francis High School was an impressive three-story brick building. The main entrance on the north side had twelve steps, each twelve feet wide, leading to the large front door. To me it seemed massive. The only other tall building I had ever seen was the church in St. Stephen. I had never been to a big city before. St. Cloud, which was fifteen miles away, had only two- or three-story buildings.

As my parents and I entered the building we climbed another stairway which led to the first floor. To the right was a huge auditorium with a well-equipped stage for theater classes and other performances given by visiting artists such as singers, accomplished pianists, violinists, and glee clubs. The auditorium also served as a dining room for special occasions. I remember the banquet we served for Cedric Adams, the radio celebrity from Minneapolis. Miss Minnesota (six feet tall) was there, as well as many dignitaries. The sisters served the meal.

Classrooms occupied the rest of the first floor. Each one was bigger than my family's whole house. They were filled with student desks. The front of each classroom was reserved for the teacher's desk. Behind the teacher's desk loomed a blackboard as wide as the room. The ceilings were very high, and I wondered how the sisters or students cleaned them. At home I washed the ceilings by standing on a chair. At the end of the hall were stairways going down to the basement and up to the second floor. The music rooms, where the students practiced, were all on the second floor.

The basement had a huge swimming pool and showers. Swimming lessons were given every day of every week for all students. The classes were divided into groups of fifteen students each. We learned all the strokes, how to dive, and how to swim the length of the pool underwater. I thoroughly enjoyed this. At the end of the year we demonstrated all that we had learned, which was quite spectacular.

The rest of the basement consisted of a large chemistry lab and classroom as well as a Home Economics Department, where cooking was taught.

The down stairway from the first floor led us to the tunnel, which led to the hospital, the nursing home, the laundry, and the convent. The tunnel was well lighted and heated. Every year screams from freshmen on Initiation Night lingered for days. The seniors blindfolded the students and led them halfway into the tunnel, one group at a time. Then the lights went out, and wet, cold hands of seniors grabbed the new students' necks and bare arms until the terrified freshmen couldn't scream anymore.

The Music Department occupied half of the second floor. Next to the Music Department was the library. Adjacent to the library was the Assembly Room, where we studied days and evenings. One of the sisters was always present. Silence was a requirement in the Assembly Room.

A large library was accessible from the Assembly Room where we studied days and evenings. Silence was observed in these two rooms at all times. The sisters supervised evening study hours.

Dormitories occupied the third floor. Each student had her own bed and closet, which was spacious enough for clothes, extra storage above, and drawers beneath. The well-to-do girls, mostly from Minneapolis, St. Paul, and Duluth, usually occupied the eight private rooms. The third floor also provided a large recreation room, where we visited with one another, danced, sang, and listened to the radio. This was a special place for our parties and holiday affairs. We took turns decorating for the different occasions, always trying to outdo each other. Often, someone played the piano to accompany the singing of the favorite songs of that time. (Television was not available until the 1950s.)

Drab? We didn't think so. We learned how to entertain ourselves and to get our exercise at the same time by dancing polkas and waltzes. To me life in this school was a party every evening. It was an extension of our homemade fun on the farm. I was delighted with the new large family to which I now belonged.

Life-Changing Words

My science teacher was a singular person. I will never forget her. On the first report card day she kept me after class. Everyone else had received her report card. What had I done?

She picked up my report card and pointed to the B and said, "Anne, I saw your IQ test results. You are capable of A's and that's what I expect to see from now on in science."

Rome had spoken! She saw only A's from then on. She never realized what tremendous life-changing words she had spoken. I was finally convinced that I was not stupid! I could learn if I wanted to. I was in high school to learn—I was no longer on the farm facing a dismal future. I *could* be something more than a hay shaker's daughter.

My freshman year included sports and swimming. I excelled in both. Swimming classes were taught on a regular basis as part of the PE classes. I was chosen captain of the team in every sport. We played softball, volleyball, and basketball. We challenged the other teams. For the first time in the history of that school, we freshmen beat the sophomores, juniors, and seniors in all three sports. I don't know that we gained much respect from the elder students for this, but we sure did get a boost from the nuns! Their motto was "A team that works together can do anything!"

In my junior year I was given the leading role in the school play to be performed in January. I had a great desire to be in dramatics, but the principal discouraged me because I already had a heavy work load in school. I was also working for my room and board every day after school. However, it did not stop me from observing Sister Antonia coach the three-act plays. I was fascinated. She was brilliant! I learned that tone of voice, actions without words, stolen glances, facial expressions, and the use of hands made acting appealing and real to the audience. I took note of every suggestion and correction she made. Little did I realize that in five years I would be coaching actors in three-act plays on the missions.

My first three years in high school were an inspiration, a challenge, and a revelation to me. Now that I knew I could do anything I wanted to do, I wanted to do everything. Soon I realized it was time to start thinking seriously about my future commitment. I made great progress in music. I could not afford lessons, but I was allowed to practice daily. I soon became the accompanist for accomplished singers who came to visit their daughters or sisters in the high school. If visitors who performed stayed a couple of days, they were asked to give a program for the students in the evening. I was the only accompanist who could sight read, so accompaniment became my job.

My junior year in high school brought out the best in me. I matured, grew in self-confidence, and learned to interact socially.

In music I was inquisitive, daring, and interested in every phase of it. I belonged to the Glee Club as a singing soprano, alto, or tenor—wherever an extra voice was needed. Everything was fun.

My principal was astonished when she saw me playing first fiddle in the school orchestra. My friend Josie was taking violin lessons. Out of curiosity I asked her how she learned to play. She showed me the basics. She also gave me permission to practice on her violin. I compared the tones with the piano and figured out the spaces—it was simple compared to the piano. I practiced every day, and in two weeks I was seated with the first fiddlers in the orchestra.

I began to notice that I could introduce people without stuttering. As I gained self-esteem and confidence, my fears were disappearing. I could stand in front of my class and speak without stuttering or breaking down in tears. I was the happiest girl on the planet.

Because my parents taught us to thank God for everything we have and are able to do, I wept many times in thanksgiving for all the blessings I received. How generous God is. But I still feared Him. I still thought He was writing every error I made in that Big Black Book with my name on it. I could see God on Judgment Day presenting me my big book of sins I never atoned for. About this time I felt drawn to serve God in some special way.

The sisters were a good example to me. Their lives were devoted to attending Mass and praying together daily, teaching, nursing, housekeeping, and always helping others. Their conduct was impeccable. I scrutinized their every move. Their conversation was modest and reserved. Where did they come from? I wondered. How did they get that way?

Christmas Joy, Christmas Sorrow

Christmas was near, so I dwelt on going home—no classes for two weeks and attending Midnight Mass, which I loved. I came home two days before Christmas only to find out that my dear friend Johnnie, our neighbor boy, was very ill. He was the kindest, nicest boy in school. We worked together frequently on the farm. Neighbors helped each other freely in those days. Nothing could be done for him. He had spinal meningitis, a disease much feared and highly contagious. Doctors had little knowledge of its control in 1936.

Johnnie died the day after Christmas. I was devastated. How could God have allowed this? A week later my friend Joe died of the same disease. Two weeks later another classmate was taken from us. Two more followed. Because meningitis was known to be highly contagious, no one was allowed to attend these funerals, which increased our feelings of separation. Then another classmate was killed in a car accident. Would this never end?

Everyone held his breath in fear. Who would be next? Six strong young men passed into eternity. No young women were afflicted with the disease, but we were severely crushed by the losses.

The families of these unfortunate boys were grief-stricken beyond description. Johnnie's oldest sister became mentally ill. His only brother, Peter, wept every time anyone mentioned Johnnie's name for years after Johnnie's death. But this family grieved also for the other families who had lost loved ones of their own, sharing private and community pain. The professional study of grief and its resolution did not develop until another thirty or forty years in the future. The families tended to grieve privately, but this small town became closely knit because of the tragedies that brought such deep wounds. Only love and understanding could begin the healing process.

I went back to school with a heavy heart. Death and I had met, and the introduction was cold and cruel. How many days of life did I have? Despair came over me so strongly I felt my own life threatened. I became ill two weeks later. The sisters put me in the infirmary because my fever was rising. I went into delirium for two days with a fever of 105 degrees, and I was then hospitalized. When I came out of the delirium I was not able to swallow because of the pain in my throat. The doctor told me I had a large boil in my throat; a tracheotomy was considered although my breathing was not threatened. Isolation was advised. I wondered if I was going to die like the six boys at home had. Why was God allowing these strange illnesses to plague us? Didn't He care about us? What had we done wrong? My faith was shaking as well as my fevered body. So many questions and no answers.

I recovered slowly. Grief and illness put together can annihilate you if you don't have inner strength of faith in a God who loves, protects, heals, and provides for you. How I survived with none of the above is unknown to me. I felt so let down; I really wondered about God. My parents worried that I would not recover. My brothers were sure I was leading up to spinal meningitis. My illness started with a sore throat just like Johnnie's illness had. The boys' deaths still haunted everyone.

I know someone was praying for me because in spite of my depression and the unexplainable illness, I survived with very limited medical treatment. Antibiotics were still not available except in large cities. No one had a diagnosis for the boil in my throat. In those days lab work was not done to diagnose illness. Rest was the only treatment I had. I couldn't swallow anything, and injections of pain medicine were used sparingly. The illness and bed rest left me very weak.

Missing three weeks of classes worried me. I doubted that recovery would ever be sufficient to allow me to enjoy life again. The deaths of my classmates continued to depress my spirit. I brooded that maybe it was my turn to die. We had no counselors on the school staff, and people around me didn't seem to understand what I was going through. When tragedy struck, one was expected to get through it somehow, overcome it eventually, and heal gradually. Yes, you had to start all over again.

I survived, but it took three more weeks to recover from the boil drainage. I had a poor appetite, and every meal brought nausea and vomiting. Every morning the doctor drained the boil, but that was not enough. I thank the Franciscan Sisters for their kindness during this time; I know their prayers and those of my parents helped my recovery. The sisters encouraged me constantly, never letting me forget that I was going to get well and be strong again. They did everything possible to help me get well. I owed them my life because they had given me hope.

I returned to school and made the best of it in all my classes and soon caught up with the rest of the students. My junior year ended with a big question mark. I went home to work on the farm for the summer with Dad, but my heart was not in it. The loss of my classmates continued to be a deep, unhealed wound. My illness had done more harm than I had thought. Body and spirit were still wounded.

I wrestled with questions like "Is it worth living or trying to better myself? Death is right around the corner." I had no idea where all the pain was coming from, destroying my will to live. The illness drained me of all the strength I had, and I wondered if I would ever be able to climb that mountain to health again.

I wondered: *Whom do I blame? Who is doing all this to me? It can't be God; I can't blame Him, and He'll only add it to my long list of sins in that Big Black Book and condemn me on Judgment Day!* I had learned in catechism class that God is just. My mind was so tired of trying to sort this out. *Who will help me? Who can help me? Does anyone want to help me?*

Going to Mass every day wasn't any use. Praying the Our Father and the Hail Mary were no help, either. I no longer felt comfort in prayer. I felt like I was alone in a deep pit with no help. I had to get myself out of it. I started thinking of the sisters and the life they led. They didn't seem to have any regrets. But the convent looked so forbidding, so military. Everybody seemed to be doing the same thing every day. They taught the same classes day after day, year in and year out. They spent an hour every evening together as a group, which was the only time I saw them speaking to each other. They said prayers together—so different from the rest of the world. Everything was done within a certain time frame at a certain place.

Interesting, but I wondered what the point was. I was fascinated and frightened at the same time. Too many secrets! But I was drawn to them.

I was totally surprised when the high school principal asked me one day, "Anne, are you thinking about becoming one of us? Are you wondering about joining the convent?" I was stunned. How dare she ask me such a question? I never answered. I walked out of the room. Was she a mind reader? Did she have ESP or extraordinary powers? How had she known I was grappling with profound questions and considering convent life?

Family picture (except for Mary) at celebration of first Mass of Fr. Frank and Fr. Joe, in St. Stephen, Minnesota in 1936. L to R: Fr. John, Fr. Joe, John Sr., Agnes, Fr. Frank, Anne, and Tony.

I kept my distance after that. But I could not keep my mind off the subject. I went home for Easter vacation and visited my pastor. I wanted the whole scoop about nuns, and I got it.

The pastor said, "These are women *singled out* by God who set themselves apart from the world to serve God in a special way. They forsake their family and friends, and all the comforts of the world to lead a life of poverty, chastity, and obedience in atonement for their sins and the sins of the whole world."

This definition of nuns sounded good. Just what I had been looking for! Again I thought of the uncertainties of life day after day, illnesses of all kinds, and the distractions of the world.

When I told my parents about it, they were thrilled I was trying to make a decision about my future. A life consecrated to God! I read about St. Francis of Assisi. When I finished, I was convinced this was what God wanted me to do. I set my date to enter the convent on December 8, 1937. I was nineteen years old. Swallowing my pride, I went to my principal and told her my decision. She was happy for me and said she would arrange for an interview with the Reverend Mother, who was in charge of all the sisters. The convent was across the street from the high school.

The Reverend Mother interviewed me the next day. Despite my nervous state, the interview went well. She did not inform me of any internal rules and regulations—that would come after I entered. She asked me if my parents could set up a dowry. I wasn't sure what that was, so she explained it to me.

"Dowry—money, estate, goods as a down payment. If a religious leaves, this is returned to her. If she dies in the convent, the dowry automatically goes to the convent."

I told her we were very poor and had no money.

She accepted my answer graciously and said, "It is really not the important thing." The important thing was that I wanted to serve God. That concluded the dowry question.

The interview threw no light on the secrets of the inner sanctum of convent living. When a sister makes final vows for life, she becomes a "Bride of Christ" and receives a wedding ring, as a bride receives a ring from her husband in a traditional wedding.

CHAPTER 3

High School Years to Foley, Minnesota

The same day I decided to enter the convent, November 30, 1937, I found out that four other girls from my high school were planning on the same venture. We met and decided to make this step together on December 8, 1937 at nine in the morning. This was my senior year, and I had a fair load of subjects. I had difficulty concentrating on my schoolwork because I kept thinking about the major decision I had just made. Would I regret it? I knew my parents approved. Maybe my brothers would too. My sister told me a year ago she did not like nuns. Her experiences with the Benedictine Sisters during nurses' training had not been good. I shrugged off that opinion because I was joining the Franciscan Order. I had heard of the differences among Franciscans, Benedictines, Sisters of the Immaculate Conception, Sisters of the Sacred Heart, and Dominicans. Each had its own rules, regulations, and distinctive garb.

Franciscans wore brown garments, a large rosary, and a cord with three knots. The Benedictines wore black, and the Dominicans white. None of these details concerned me much then. That I would become a Franciscan seemed reasonable since that was the order I had known. I was grateful to the Franciscans for the opportunities provided me for an education and for my room and board. Unlike my sister, my experiences with nuns had been entirely positive.

I remembered too how kindly the Franciscans cared for me when I was ill. They encouraged me to excel in my studies. They helped move many mountains that had plagued me for years before I had met them.

They taught us many things like the fact that tragedies are part of life, and they will not remain tragedies but will become steppingstones to a life of victory. God is willing if we are. We need to refuse the temptation of self-pity when tragedy strikes and keep right on with life as conquerors. No matter what happens, we must grasp the bright side of life. To smile in the face of tragedy is a sign of victory. God is our best friend when difficulties arise.

The Franciscan nuns silently earned my respect. I saw how they set goals and determined to reach them. Their calm discipline impressed me. Everything was clean. Their motto was "Cleanliness is next to Godliness."

Dear Sister Rose! She was my supervisor when I worked for my room and board. No dust escaped her view. The halls in the nursing home had tiny baseboards. I spent many hours every week on my knees cleaning them. That job was as bad as picking potatoes on the farm. One day I skipped about ten feet of one side of the hall purposely because I was tired. I didn't get away with it. Two hours later I was called back from school to come and finish my job. Sister Rose was waiting for me. Silently she took me to the ten feet of unfinished business, stooped down, and swept her finger over the baseboard, showed me the dirt, and walked off without a word.

Silence during the demonstration of a neglect of duty says more than a sermon prepared from hours of study; it drives a nail through your conscience with the lesson you are supposed to learn so that it will last you for the rest of your life. (This lesson is sixty years old.) I remember it as though it happened yesterday.

Sister Rose never had to do that again. I learned to listen for her coming to inspect my work. The large rosary dangling from the cord around her waist was the signal. It made a distinctive rattling sound as she walked. She inspected silently.

We received few expressions of praise for a job well done, but we accomplished considerable work. I never heard the sisters talking with one another. They had their jobs to do, and their jobs were done well. The sisters were silent, concentrated, and consecrated. Their time was organized. I heard bells ring, but I never knew what they were for until I entered the convent.

The convent, across the street from the high school, was an old three-story building constructed fifty years before when the sisters first established their order in Little Falls, Minnesota. Next to it was the orphanage, also an old three-story building. Before I entered high school, the orphans had been transferred to St. Cloud, about thirty miles south of Little Falls. Sisters from this Order were assigned to care for the orphans in a new building made especially for caring for and training children. It was equipped properly with cottages, nurseries, and classrooms for the first eight grades. The old orphanage in Little Falls became the nursing home for the elderly.

In front of the convent and next to the high school was the chaplain's home. In 1933 only one chaplain lived there. He taught us in high school the basics of good Christian living every week. The whole school attended. Within a few years three priests were needed to care for hospital patients, the sisters, the high school girls, and the nursing home residents. These responsibilities comprised three full-time jobs for the three priests.

When I arrived, the nursing home was fully occupied with senior citizens. Many of us students worked there, either in the kitchen or on one of the three floors, cleaning rooms and halls and serving trays to the residents. All trays were served in the rooms since there was no large dining room. The trays were sent up on the *dummy*, a special elevator. I was grateful for our helper, the dummy, because it took down all the dishes and trays we washed after every meal from all three floors to the kitchen. Dishwashers then, remember, had arms and legs. We were the dishwashers. A sister supervised every floor before and after each meal.

In the back of the convent and nursing home, situated in the middle, was a huge laundry, which took care of all the laundry from the hospital, convent, nursing home, and high school. On Saturdays some of us students spent the morning and afternoon folding clothes, towels, and washcloths that the twenty-foot roller continuously spewed out to keep us busy. Three of us fed the roller and three others received the finished product from the roller. The six girls sharing this task had enough sense to be on friendly terms with each other always, no matter what happened. Some days I had to do the ironing or pressing of the nuns' habits and men's slacks and shirts by the hundreds. We had no time for between-meal snacks. We worked straight through from 8:00 A.M. to noon and from 1:00 P.M. to 5:00 P.M. The sister in charge was very strict. Everything went according to schedule with the big clock on the wall checking our progress to the minute. All the work was done before we left.

Postulancy, December 8, 1937 to August 12, 1938

December 8, 1937 was an exciting day for the five of us. The whole high school watched us leave the high school grounds that morning at nine as we walked across the street to the convent. We walked up the five steps to the landing, turned around, and waved goodbye. This was both a happy and a sad moment for us. The entire high school was a happy group of young women preparing for their futures. We were more of a family than schools are today. We were concerned about each other. We worked and played sports together. We competed and debated. We sang and danced together, and enjoyed one another's talents. Despite our competitive games, we experienced little jealousy or revenge. There was virtually no fighting or other teenage problems because we were taught by the sisters to be ladies. Perhaps it sounds hard to believe, but typical juvenile behaviors were simply not tolerated.

My dearest high school friend, Marion, waved goodbye to me, tears streaming down her face. She waited until I was inside and gave a last goodbye wave. I hurt to see my friend so sad. I would miss her, but I intended to make it up to her. Little did I realize how rigid the rules were until I was inside. The rules provided no chance to make up for anything.

We arrived at the Postulant Mistress' office, and after a pleasant welcome we were seated. She explained what our time as postulants would entail. She explained it well, in a strong voice and with a serious face. I remember her words:

> If you are going to live a life of service to God, you must leave all behind that is of the world. Your parents, friends, and relatives will no longer be contacted without permission from me. Your parents and family members may come to see you once a month, the first Sunday of the month. You may write to them with permission only. You will be assigned certain tasks that will be done before you go to school in the mornings and certain tasks after school hours. You will be assigned your rooms shortly, but before you leave this room I want you to know that *you own nothing*. Anything you are given to use is not yours but always referred to as 'ours.'

I took a deep breath for I could tell more was coming. She continued:

When you arrive upstairs in your assigned room, remove all your clothes and put on your new attire that is on the bed. You will no longer need any other clothes. You want to strip yourselves of the things of the world and live a life of total dedication to serving God and people. You will keep *silence* from the time you arise at 5:00 A.M. until 7:00 P.M. when we have recreation together until 8:00 P.M. Then we will go the chapel and say our evening prayers with all the sisters present. You will keep silence from then on and continue the same day after day. There will be spiritual reading during meals. When you go to school, you keep silence. You may not converse with your classmates. You are now going to your rooms and silence begins.

So this was the mysterious inner sanctum of Community living! Who on earth could possibly do this for a lifetime? How could I deal with all the regulations? I knew convent life would be different, but not this much. We went upstairs to our assigned rooms and put on our new attire as directed and came back to our mistress' office to receive further direction. We went directly to our classes and continued our daily program as usual.

As a postulant I wore a plain black dress and a black cape. A veil covered my head. This was my attire until August 12, 1938 when I became a novice.

The Postulant Mistress kept us moving along but not fast enough to keep me from thinking about my parents, relatives, and friends, especially dear Marion! We had so much in common. She came from North Dakota, and her parents were farmers like mine were. Marion was a sweet person, very caring and considerate. We had many discussions about farming because we both knew what we were talking about from firsthand experience. We agreed that there should be an easier way than farming for women to make a living.

About a week after one of these discussions, we were sitting on the back stairway, and I asked her what she thought of the nuns.

She explained that she liked them, some better than others, but that no nun could compare with Sister Immaculate.

"Why?" I asked.

She responded, "She's my aunt. She is the Mother General of the whole convent."

That revelation put Marion on a higher pedestal, and I grew an inch or two for just being her friend. I tried to compare Sister Immaculate and Marion but could find no resemblance. Marion was petite and Sister Immaculate was tall and round. Both were the same height. Sister Immaculate had an easy smile, displaying her perfect shiny teeth.

Marion was healthy with rosy cheeks, curly brown hair, and good posture. She was always well behaved. One day in the spring of our freshman year she asked me what I planned to do with my life. I told her I wasn't sure, that sometimes I thought of marriage and family but that I also wanted to be a nurse. I didn't know.

"What do you want to be?" I asked.

She said, "I want to be a cowgirl." That surprised me. But then she added, "I want to get married and raise a family."

From then on we kept each other informed whenever either of us had a new brainstorm. She went from married woman and cowgirl to ballet dancer and physical education teacher. I moved from nurse to actress and artist. I was happy with my music but had no desire to pursue it as a career.

Marion married and had a family, and I entered the convent.

My life as I had known it before the convent ended at the convent door. This was now to be my past. A new life was about to begin.

The night of December 8, 1937, my first night in the convent, was thirty degrees below zero. Each cell, or room, had a single bed and bedside stand, with a toothbrush and toothpaste, soap, and a glass. Each postulant had her own basin (not the modern kind that drains into the sewer) for washing water to use in the morning in her cell. I was wearing a long nightdress. The next morning I woke up to the bell, jarring and clanging like a cowbell, and put my feet onto an ice-cold wood floor. I reached for my wash basin to discover ice—one big chunk of ice that had time to form during the night. I hurried to the bathroom at the end of the hall. Holding on to myself, shivering, and clenching my teeth, I wondered if I should have foreseen this last night. When I stopped shaking, I trotted back to my room for another cold chill. Dressing on winter mornings would become a race against freezing to death. I felt better noticing the other girls were suffering too. How had I gotten into this?

We would have suffered less if we could have talked with one another. The big question began to dawn. If this were a sample of what was to come, could I stay? Silence compounded the pain. If only we could have complained to someone, we would have felt considerably better. Did this day have a name? Was it Initiation Day? Would we have more surprises? I remembered our Freshman Initiation as mild by comparison. Walking into a warm, dark tunnel would have been comforting right now.

For the rest of the day I never warmed up. Keeping warm became a major goal. How could I keep warm at night? Should I ask for long johns? Did they have any? No; the Postulant Mistress had made it clear that we had everything we needed.

The first chance we had to talk was at 7:00 P.M. the next evening. I longed to lash out about the frigid 5:00 A.M. awakening to a cowbell and the difficulty of praying at 5:30 A.M. to initiate a thaw. I had hardly grown up in a luxurious tropical climate, but this was offensive. Who stoked the furnace, anyway? But by 7:00 P.M. we were so eager to greet one another with *speech* that we forgot the icy introduction to convent living. Incredibly, no one mentioned it!

We learned later that the third floor was heated during the day but not at night. I noticed after about three weeks that the thirty minutes I needed to get up and wash every morning in high school had shrunk to ten to twelve minutes in the convent. I was getting used to the temperature. The winter temperature would often drop to twenty degrees below zero until November. Daily it would plunge to thirty or forty degrees below zero, with the coldest temperatures at five in the morning.

The Postulant Mistress held a daily rules and regulations class in which we learned more details about convent living. We were also informed about the length of this phase of our convent service. By August 12 the following year, we would enter the Novitiate, the second phase of convent life for Franciscan nuns, which lasts two years. During those two years we would go no place! We would spend all our time, night and day, on convent grounds, learning about the temporary vows we would take in two years and the final vows in five years. Our obedience would be tested in many ways. We would learn to live in *poverty,* and we would hope to make a choice: to give up married life and live a life of *chastity* for life or to leave the convent. The vow of *obedience* would prove our ability to live Community life. It also would be the *deciding factor* for the Community's acceptance of us or not.

On August 12 we would enter the second stage of the Community, the Novitiate. We would then be known as novices and receive the traditional garb of the Franciscan Order. The habit (garb) included the long brown wool dress reaching our ankles and a brown scapular of wool one and one-half feet wide and slightly shorter than the dress. This was put on over the head. A coif of white material covered the head and neck. Over this was added a white veil reaching the waist. The veil had a stiff bandeau that covered the forehead. A white cord came around the waist reaching two inches from the floor. From the cord was a large rosary, which hung on the left side to about mid-calf.

Novices, the women in the first two years of training, wore a white veil. After two years they would become professed religious making temporary vows of poverty, chastity, and obedience. Then they would receive the black veil. At the same time they would also receive their first assignment to some mission or school for teaching or nursing or other vocations.

In three more years, each sister would decide if she were called to this life or not. If she felt it was not her vocation, she could return to her home. If a sister felt she was called to live according to the rules and regulations of the Community, she made perpetual vows of poverty, chastity, and obedience. Vows were taken in a public gathering with the bishop of the diocese present. These vows were *binding until death.* Leaving the convent after taking perpetual vows would be totally contrary to church regulations and would be an insult to God. Vows, once made in public, were not to be broken.

In about a month, as we postulants became accustomed to the cold mornings, the prayers in common, the forever silence, and our daily chores, things started going more smoothly. We were a determined group. Nothing would stop us! My first before-school job was to clean the first floor hall and sweep the front steps. The first day I proudly took hold of the broom and began cleaning the hall. I started out well, but within a short time I retreated into my worldly way of sweeping the floor like I had done at home. I started whistling "Home on the Range" full blast! A tap on my shoulder only provided encouragement. I mortified my curiosity because I knew I shouldn't look to see who it was. I managed to whistle even louder. Then I saw two feet planted in front of me and felt two more taps on my shoulder from behind me.

Then came the dawn. A nun took me to a room and behind closed doors, where I received my private sermon on religious behavior and *silence.* Whistling was for cowboys. And so were guitars. So ended my renditions of "Home on the Range."

Christmas came and went rather quietly. My parents came to see me, and we had a wonderful visit. But the reminiscing reminded me of my friend Johnnie's death a year ago and the deaths of my other classmates. I wept easily and again felt that sense of impending doom ready to descend on our family. I felt secure by now in a protected environment; I had no idea that anything might happen to me. But I was concerned about my mother who was not feeling well and who looked so tired and somewhat lonely.

Tony was growing fast and was in the eighth grade. He took me aside and told me that Mom was not well. I hated feeling helpless. I knew I would not be allowed to go home to see my mother, much less stay and take care of her. We were not supposed to worry about our families. We now belonged to the Community.

All the restrictions about letter writing remained the same. I silently cried and accepted my fate, but it hurt so deeply. I loved and respected my mother. She had taught me all I knew about God and about living a good life. I remember her many warnings about keeping good company, reading acceptable books, wearing proper attire, attending church regularly, saying the rosary, and, above all, keeping the Commandments. She taught all of us through her example as well as by direct instruction.

But as postulants we were told to keep our thoughts on serving the Community and that God would take care of our parents. I learned later that my mother had been hospitalized for bleeding ulcers but was improving slowly. The news comforted me, but I felt remorseful in my inability to help her through this time of serious need as she had helped me in every childhood need. I tried hard to keep my mind on the Community and to be obedient to its rules and regulations, and in time it became easier.

January came in its true form—very cold with four to five feet of snow. The students were returning from Christmas vacation to face the dreaded midyear exams. I will never forget the day of the algebra test in Room 105. The room temperature was perfectly comfortable when we walked in. After we were seated, we started writing the test. Suddenly I felt dizzy, and a very cold chill gripped me. Then my whole body began to shake uncontrollably. The intensity of the shaking caused my right knee to jerk upward and hit the bottom of my desk. The pain in my knee was so intense that I screamed. The shaking became more like convulsions. I was nauseated. The sisters helped me back to my room at the convent and put me to bed. The shaking continued and the sisters piled more blankets over me. Nobody knew what was the matter with me. My temperature was 105 degrees.

I was transferred to the hospital next door, and the doctor examined me. My right leg was twice the size of the left one from thigh to ankle, and my right knee had swollen to three times the size of the left one. The nurse had given me 50 mg. of Demerol before the transfer. The drug made little difference; the pain was still severe.

The doctor made the diagnosis: "There is no doubt in my mind. This is a severe case of rheumatic fever." He explained what it was. It begins with a sore throat (strep), induces a high fever, and ends with inflammation of joints. It may also cause inflammation of the heart valves and scarring of the valve leaflets, which can result in valve leakage, allowing blood to flow backward. The only treatment for rheumatic fever in 1938 was Wintergreen oil on affected joints and Demerol for pain (antibiotics were still not yet available).

I was placed on strict bed rest for six months. After two weeks at the hospital I was returned to the convent and placed in a private room. The swelling was down and the severe pain was gone. I was allowed to study and write my midyear exams. The postulants brought me my daily assignments. I finished high school with the rest of the class and graduated from high school *in bed* at the end of May 1938. By this time I was allowed to get out of bed for a total of one hour per day. I recuperated quickly after that.

My biggest concern was whether I would be accepted into the Novitiate on August 12. Nothing was said. The silence about this important question scared me. Finally, in July I was called to the Mother General's office. She was very kind but did not hesitate to tell me that she did not think I was strong enough to take on the rigorous schedule and work load of the Novitiate.

I'll never forget her statement: "You can't be sick all the time, and it would not be fair to the rest of the sisters." She also stated that she would make her final decision by August 5.

If I ever endangered my heart condition, it was on August 5 when I walked to the Mother General's office for my evaluation. My heart was pounding. I was ushered into her office, and I sat down at her bidding, waiting for the ax to fall.

She smiled and said, "You certainly are a determined person! Your strength seems to have returned, and your conduct has been admirable. I am willing to let you enter the Novitiate."

I knew better than to show any emotion (like jumping up and screaming "whoopee!"). I quietly said, "Thank you, Reverend Mother," bowed, and walked out. I was so tempted to dance my whoopee dance down the hall but restrained myself again. It was worth all the restraint I could muster.

The other nine postulants were waiting. Grinning from ear to ear, I walked through the door, raised my right arm, and we all said "Whoopee!" silently. They were so precious. Throughout my illness they had showed such concern, and now they shared this triumph with me. We were a family. This good news brought new life and strength and hope, topping it all with indescribable joy! God had opened the windows of heaven again and poured out His blessings upon me, and I felt like there was not enough room in my being to receive it. I wanted to dance, sing, and clap my hands. This joy was out of this world.

Yet I knew that if I acted out my feelings I would be ushered out the front door. This puzzled me. Didn't God want us to be happy? Why couldn't I show my happiness and help others to be happy? Did God only accept somber faces and hard-working hands?

Well, so be it for now, I decided. The truth would surely creep out sometime in the future.

Novitiate Days, August 12, 1938 to August 12, 1940

Advancement Day

The convent was in a hustle and bustle as the sisters prepared for the August 12 celebration. This was a yearly event. It was the feast of St. Clare, the founder of the Franciscan Order for women. This day was chosen for advancing postulants to novices, novices to temporary professed sisters, and temporary professed sisters to perpetual profession. The perpetually professed sisters made their vows for life in the Franciscan Order of Sisters on this day. Sisters who spent twenty-five years of perpetual profession were honored on this day. Golden (fifty years) and Diamond Jubilarian (seventy-five years) Sisters were especially honored on this day also.

We ten postulants would become novices for two years in which we would practice living in poverty, chastity, and obedience, keeping silence as indicated in the rule, praying the Office with the professed sisters, and working in various departments. The Office was a collection of psalms and prayers we would say three times a day with all the sisters. Novices did not work in the hospital. Our job assignments would be laundry, convent cleaning, and garden work. No novice went to school or took music lessons in those two years. We would be separated from the world. We would have no novels, no newspapers, no radio, and no television (it had not been invented yet). This period did turn out to be a challenge. But I told myself that if all the sisters before me could do it, so could I. We were, indeed, a determined group of young women.

The Bishop of the St. Cloud Diocese came to the August 12 event and was the celebrant, with two assisting priests, at the celebration's Mass. When it was time for us to receive the habit, he and his assistants faced the congregation. The Bishop was seated on a special chair and received each postulant separately. The Postulant Mistress and the Novitiate Mistress helped each postulant dress in the brown habit, the cord with a rosary, the cross, scapular, coif, large white collar, bandeau, and white veil. A crown of thorns was then placed on the veiled head of each postulant. We wore the crowns for the rest of the day.

The Bishop prayed over each one of us and ended by saying, "And from henceforth you shall be called Sister Mary _____." We all had to change our names because in leaving the world, we were to leave *all things*, even our names. All the sisters received the name Mary in honor of the Blessed Virgin Mary. For our second name, we chose three possible names, from which one would be chosen for us.

Anne, age 20, enters the novitiate for two years on the annual Feast of St. Clare Day, August 12, 1938, and receives her new name: Sister Mary Jeannette. Note crown of thorns.

When the Bishop prayed over me, he finished with, "And from henceforth you shall be called Sister Mary Jeannette." Of the three names I had selected, I had been hoping for Jeannette because of my father John, and my brother John. (Frank, Joseph, and Anthony were already taken.)

My parents and brothers and many people from St. Stephen were there for the celebration. My sister was unable to attend. It was a glorious day! Joy and happiness covered the entire convent grounds. We postulants were so happy to have survived those terrible, death-defying cold days. That triumph only made us more confident that we could face more difficult days in the next two years as novices.

My parents, especially my mother, deeply respected the sisters as well as all priests. I remember my father remarking with pride, "I never dreamed of such a big blessing—three priests and a sister." My mother did not need to say anything. Her tears of joy and her hugs did all the talking.

The novices who had already passed the two-year test were also honored at this service. They exchanged the white veil of the novice for a black veil, which indicated their willingness to take temporary *vows* of poverty, chastity, and obedience. Now they could be assigned to a mission with two or more other sisters (one being the designated superior). These sisters were sent for nurses' training, dietary or food supervisor training, music study, or teaching instruction (to eventually teach children in grade or high school).

Our great day of celebration ended. Our time of testing was about to begin. For the last two months we had been stretching our imaginations as far as we had dared! We had conquered so much so far, but what else would there be?

NOVITIATE LIFE

The heavy habit we wore was a test in itself. It had tested us mightily even on that hot day we first received it, and it continued

to do so. The big collar was always in the way; the bandeau and the veil prevented our curiosities from straying; the noisy rosary hanging on the cord always announced our approach. These were challenges we did not get used to in just a day or two.

As postulants, we had often been forgiven mistakes because we hadn't known any better. As novices, we knew better; therefore, more was expected from us: strict adherence to the

Father John Smerke, OSC at his ordination in 1939.

daily routine, silence, regular prayer, promptness, respect, diligence, acceptance without excuses, restriction to campus all the time, limited visits and letter writing, and receipt of no telephone calls! Our superior, the Novice Mistress, took all calls.

Our letters, incoming and outgoing, were screened. If our parents, brothers, sisters, or relatives came to see us, we were not allowed to eat with them. This rule was especially painful when my priest brothers came to visit. They were insulted, and so were my parents. But this was a part of the training to help novices realize what it meant to leave behind *everything* dear, familiar, and precious. Our wants, desires, and attachments would daily be stripped away. In their place was empty space for God to fill.

Most of us wept occasionally from this draconian environment. I spent considerable time trying to make sense of such rigid discipline. We tried to understand that what we were asked to do was right in God's eyes. I wondered if God had suspended the Fourth Commandment in convents. How could I not honor the parents who had brought me into the world, sacrificed for me, fed me, and taught me the ways of God in the first place? Why could they not share my life anymore? We could not divulge anything. Unanswered questions loomed. My parents loved me and wanted to know how I was doing. Was I happy? My brothers were priests in a monastery, but they were not restricted as severely. I said again and again, "It's the rule. Different orders have different rules." But I did not understand. We were instructed not to question the why of anything. We were told that later, when we were more in tune with God, we would understand. This mortification was supposed to lead to perfection, which was pleasing to God.

I bowed my head in obedience and carried on as best as I could, but I doubted the possibility that I or my sister novices could attain perfection even if God provided us with another 150 years to strive for it.

Our first year of novitiate training was one of obedience. I was well prepared in this virtue by my parents and the rigors of farm life, but I still fell short. At home I could at least occasionally ask *Why?* Or, *Couldn't I do it this way, then it wouldn't take so long?* I tried it once. I learned one does not question the commands of one's superiors. Yes, that is *commands*. One was to obey as commanded. No questions; no discussions.

My superior asked me, "Would you ask God *Why?* when He told you to do something?"

"No," I answered.

"As your superior, I take His place. So do not question my orders," she replied.

I didn't—not audibly. I did, however, pray frequently, "Lord, I want to serve you as perfectly as possible; please help me to understand."

My efforts at obedience were improving, I thought, when my superior told me one hot summer day to open a window in the dining room and let some fresh air in. I bowed in obedience and did as I was told. I then kept on scrubbing the floor next to the dining area. My superior came in, took one whiff of fresh air (she thought), let out a sick moan and asked loudly, "What stinks in here?"

I got up from my bent knees and almost yelled the same. As soon as I stood up to her height, I could smell the same dreadful odor. I rushed to the open window expecting to find a dead cat when to my surprise I saw two large cans of garbage with no lids right under the open window.

"Don't you ever look to see what you are doing?" asked the exasperated nun.

Just then another novice came through the door with a pail of soapy water, tripped on the small carpet, fell down, and sent the pail flying into the dining area, flooding half of the dining room! She saved my day. I turned around and the superior was gone. The two of us sat down and laughed freely. What a relief!

The cemetery for the sisters was about two blocks from the convent. The road leading to it was kept clean by the novices. Beautiful fir trees shaded the road. The novices also planted flowers every spring on the graves of the deceased sisters. One beautiful spring day my superior told me to go to the cemetery and plant verbena on three of the graves. I got full instructions on how to plant and space them and how many seeds to place on each grave. She also told me to clean all three graves and to see if any other graves needed my expertise. She gave me the package of seeds and checked again to see if I knew which graves to work on. I did well. I was proud of myself. I went; I planted; I came home. I almost forgot about my new experience until that evening at recreation.

One of the novices was telling our superior what she had been asked to do in the kitchen that morning. The cook told her to bring the recipe book. Then the cook showed her which cake she was to bake. The novice told the cook that she had baked one or two cakes at home, so she was quite confident it would be "a piece of cake." The recipe called for two cups of coffee for the recipe doubled. The novice busily gathered all the ingredients and proceeded to mix, blend, fold, and beat. (We had no electric blenders or mixers to work with.) She poured the batter into a large pan and put it in the oven for the required time.

She watched the clock carefully, and at the exact appropriate time she took it out of the oven. To her astonishment the cake was flatter than a pancake and strange in color. The cook looked at it and asked the novice what went wrong. The novice told the cook how she had made the cake, just as the recipe stated. She said how hard it had been to mix the batter after she poured the two cups of coffee grounds in.

The cook laughed and said, "Sister, you were supposed to put two cups of cooked coffee in, not two cups of coffee grounds!"

Everyone laughed then, but not on the next day when we novices had to eat it! (Our vow of poverty forbade us to waste anything. Even a piece of thread was to be used until it was so short you couldn't sew with it anymore.)

After the short lecture on poverty, my superior asked me in front of all the novices, "Sister Mary Jeannette, you had a new assignment; did you have any problem?"

I proudly answered, "No, Sister." My big bubble of pride was destined to blow up in my face soon, for these novitiate days were known for self-inflicted humiliations.

She went on to ask, "What was the name of the flower you planted?"

While everyone stared at me, I frantically tried to remember that name! Ah, I had it. I smiled graciously and answered, "Oh yes, I planted those *vermin* like you told me to." The minute the word *vermin* passed my lips I knew my bubble of pride was about to erupt. I received no commendation for entertaining my sisters, believe me!

I started noticing how big the little mistakes were getting and how important it was not to make them. Mistakes were definitely a sign of imperfection that was not to be tolerated. More and more as these incidents happened; I felt guilty and fearful, believing I was actually sinning every time I made ridiculous mistakes. Was the price of working for God the loss of all the fun and joy I remembered from home? Didn't God want us to be happy while serving Him? Our superiors seemed to be teaching us that our tasks looked terribly wrong if they weren't done perfectly right.

QUESTIONS AND MORE QUESTIONS

We had been told the novitiate experience would be difficult and that some of us would not be able to take it. Then why was I complaining? Many times I had to rebolster my stubborn Slovenian nature to stand up straight and tall and take it on the chin with a smile, conquering that feeling of defeat. I had to give myself a talking-to in times of despair instead of feeling sorry for myself.

My second year of testing gave me courage. Looking back at the first year, I felt like a conqueror. I was standing tall on top of the heap of mistakes I had made back then. I had made steady progress. I was going to make it now. I missed my music, however, and like an answer to prayer, my superior told me one day that she would like to show me how to play the pipe organ in chapel. I was delighted. She explained the stops on the two manuals and the foot pedals. I understood her explanation, and with that she told me to try it and left me. I tackled the task with glee, and in one week I was playing for Benediction services. Soon, it was my job to select the music and play for many of the Masses. What a boost!

From there on, life had new meaning. I was allowed to practice a couple times per week. Now I had something to look forward to. The weeks and months started to fly—and I was wishing they wouldn't. In a few months I would leave the Novitiate and join the professed sisters, who had already taken the vows of poverty, chastity, and obedience years before. Was I ready to make temporary vows for three years? Was I ready to go to school if that was what they decided for me? I hoped they would send me to school to be a nurse. That had been my desire ever since I was a little girl. I took care of not only my brothers and parents at home but also every cat, dog, calf, little pig, chicken, or bird that was hurting in any way.

Maybe I would have to go to music school for piano lessons. The sisters were sent to Catholic schools run by some order of sisters. Some went to Duluth to study music at the Benedictine School, others to Winona, Minnesota, to study music with another order of Franciscan Sisters. The candidates for nursing were sent to Breckenridge, Minnesota. At this time our Order of Franciscan Sisters started to expand in the areas of nursing and music. The Community had acquired several small hospitals in the St. Cloud Diocese, and some of the old hospitals were now being used as nursing homes.

I remember well the three-story nursing home in Breckenridge, Minnesota. Many of the young sisters who did not go on to school worked in these two nursing homes. Where a sister was assigned, what kind of work she was preparing for, and when she went were all decided by the Community Board. Unfortunately, the need for money was considered more important than the sisters' inherent talents, and much unhappiness and discontent followed. Obedience was very difficult for sisters who happened to be the victims of such mismanagement, which in effect dictated the sisters' future occupations.

The usual preparations were being made for August 12, 1940. Postulants would become novices and senior novices would profess their vows of poverty, chastity, and obedience for three years. The vows were made in public before our relatives, friends, Community members, and our Bishop of the Diocese. In the next three years we would determine our futures—vows for life or departure from life as a nun. I had five days left before taking temporary vows when I began to wrestle with even more questions.

The progression from postulancy to novitiate to temporary vows to final vows for life seemed fair enough. But how would one grow in maturity, independence, and responsibility? I wondered how this approach could be healthy. The vow of obedience kept one very humble. Jesus was meek and humble, and I truly did want to be like Him. I couldn't question my superior's decisions, so when was I to use my brain? If I wanted to stay out of trouble, I must always say *yes*, whether I agreed or disagreed with the command. But was that normal? God gave me a brain to use, why shouldn't I use it?

I asked my superior, who was supposed to help me understand and answer my questions. She smiled and asked me, "Why do you find that so hard to understand? It's simple; obey your superior without questioning her command, for she takes God's place here. When you obey her, you are obeying God."

70

My next question was, "So then she never makes a mistake?"

"I think you are having a problem with pride," she answered and dismissed me.

I wasn't too happy about that answer. However, I had to admit she had a point. I was glad I had a chance to talk to her. She was kind and sincere, and she spoke with the authority that was given her. She listened with patience. No argument ever occurred, but her final statement always ended with an exclamation point. It was so final. To argue was pointless. I wrestled with my pride, and I battled with my Slovenian stubbornness for the next few days before I made my decision to make temporary vows.

I told the Lord, "I want to serve you in a special way," and I determined that I would work hard on my pride.

Temporary Profession, August 12, 1940 to August 12, 1943

PROFESSION DAY

Profession Day finally arrived. Our group of ten novices was still together after receiving many commands, corrections, humiliations, reprimands, and explanations! We had all shed many private tears as our pride had been wounded and our hurt human nature had fought the self-inflicted thorns brought on by self-pity.

Our two years as novices had been only a taste of how weak we were, not physically, but spiritually. We had no idea how prone to sin we were until we had been tested. And I, for one, had thought I was pretty good. I knew it would be difficult to eradicate self-pity, stubbornness, and laziness from my nature. I believed it was possible. One week of intense self-examination had put me into the proper attitude needed to move onward in service to God in the Franciscan Order. That Slovenian determination was challenged once again to banish despair and depression and to forge ahead.

August 12 was always a big day in the Franciscan Order because St. Clare, who was celebrated on this day, was the first follower of St. Francis of Assisi. St. Francis of Assisi left all his possessions, a promising future as a rich merchant, and his life of debauchery to give everything to the poor and to follow Jesus. He had stripped himself of all worldly goods so he could freely give of himself to others. He had wanted no attachments to impede his mission to profess Jesus to the world. He was the example we Franciscans chose to follow in our quest for a spiritual life that led to eternal life with God in heaven.

Never had an August 12 been rainy or unpleasant. August 12 was always a bright and cheery day, and this one in 1940 was no exception. The Bishop was there to hear each one of us novices make our profession of temporary vows in public. These vows would be in effect for three years. The day was spent visiting with relatives and friends. Congratulations and good wishes and blessings flowed all day long even from those who could not understand our choice of vocation.   The uncertainty of our first assignments in the community, unprotected by the massive walls of the convent that had sheltered us for the past three years, hung like a cloud over each of us all day long. At times I was gripped with fear and at other times bursts of excitement took over. Which emotion reigned depended on which assignment I imagined to be given to me.

FIRST MISSION ASSIGNMENT: ELK RIVER, MINNESOTA

Finally, at the end of Profession Day, after all the visitors had left, we who had just made temporary vows were called to Reverend Mother's office. We must have looked frightened for she asked us all to sit down. She gave each of us our assignments, starting with the oldest and moving down the line to the youngest. I was number three. The first was assigned to dietitian school. The second would study to be an x-ray technician. I waited for the ax to fall, and it did.

"Sister Mary Jeannette, you will go to Elk River. We have started a new mission of three sisters. You are going to teach piano lessons, lead two church choirs, and teach catechism classes from 1st through 12th grades. Sister M. will help you with the catechism classes and church history. Your superior will be Sister M. Rose."

I couldn't move. I was so shocked I couldn't say anything. My feet went numb; my ankles got hot; my knees went cold. My hands were ice-cold; my cheeks felt flaming hot; my heart was pounding so hard that I couldn't hear another word that might have been said.

Teach piano lessons? I had never had one! What was a piano lesson like? I could see myself sitting on a chair, like an impostor, next to the piano bench, a student sitting on the bench and glaring at me for half an hour, waiting for me to say something intelligent about how to tackle that wooden monstrosity they call a *piano*. The vision sent chills down my spine.

Sister Rose my superior? Horrors! I knew every minute of every day (forever?) would be spent dusting endless nooks and crannies of the house that hadn't been dusted for the last twenty years. And not only the house, but the church too. That was part of the agreement with the pastor. My head hurt.

Lord, please help me. I can't do this. I remember only too well how many times I had to re-dust the baseboards on the second and third floors of the nursing home when she was in charge.

I remember saying to myself, *This assignment is a mistake.* How fortunate that we don't know what the future holds for us. This was only the beginning.

Our Community of nuns was feeling the crunch of the Depression, as was the rest of the nation. Up to this point, the nuns had lived on the donations of the Catholic people of Little Falls and possibly some well-to-do relatives, if any. When this Community had separated from the original group at Belle Prairie, Minnesota, the sisters had to go out begging for food and supplies needed for survival. Now that was no longer necessary, but the Community was still struggling to send some of the sisters to study music, nursing, dietetics, x-ray, and anesthesiology to qualify them for their work according to regulations of the time.

Thus I became a prime victim of the times. There were no state inspections to disqualify those teaching without college education or certification. If one succeeded without higher education, the state did not inhibit that person's work activity. This was a time when people could earn enough to support a family on their talents and labors to the best of their abilities. Money was scarce and labor was cheap. Many rose to the situation and many failed. Talented people were often spoken for—and used.

The Franciscan Community was in the midst of this turmoil. God favored them in their struggle by sending many young women to them who were seeking the "better life." One year they were blessed with twenty new members. The usual yearly rate of new aspirants was between ten and twenty. Soon this Community would need larger facilities to house the growing family of sisters. These were desperate times for the Franciscan Community as well as for poor people with growing families.

I was not aware of these realities until years later. Information about the economic conditions of the Community was available only to the administration. The sisters were effectively cut off from knowledge about basic truths of the world. We had no access to newspapers or radio. From our viewpoint this was altogether reasonable, since we understood ourselves to have entered another reality as we entered the convent. Unlike persons who are involuntarily separated from normal events and information, we renounced the visible world and embraced a life of service and spirit. We had professed our willingness to walk in poverty, chastity, and obedience.

My musical talent and ability had been well noted by my Novice Mistress when she introduced me to the pipe organ. She never asked me if I had had any lessons. That was taken for granted because she and all the sisters had attended many high school programs in which my musical ability was displayed. The truth of the matter was simple—I did not know what a music lesson was. To play the piano or organ is one thing. To teach music to someone else, especially a child, is another.

Two days later we three sisters were packed and ready to leave for Elk River. The Reverend Mother came along. When we arrived, the neighbors came out to welcome us. The house was unlocked, so we went in. Immediately to my left I saw the piano room. I shuddered and went on. The home was lovely. There was a nice dining area with a round table. The house had two bedrooms, one with one bed and one with two beds and an adjoining bathroom. The kitchen was pleasant and well lighted. From the kitchen one could go out onto a screened porch. Later, we often sat out there in the evenings to visit in the spring and summer.

The Reverend Mother walked out on the lawn in the back, and we followed her. We visited for a while, and then she reached in her pocket for a five-dollar bill, handed it to my superior, and said, "Here is five dollars to start with." She then turned to me and added, "Sister Jeannette, you will have to supply the rest of the money for food with your piano lessons."

I felt the weight of that statement. What if no students would come for two months? If they did come and take one lesson, would they ever come back? Then what would I do, and where would I start? Where would I get teaching books? I had noticed with that quick glance at the piano room that nothing else was in the room besides the piano. I managed to find the courage to ask Reverend Mother where I could get material to start teaching. She told me to ask the music teacher at the school in town; surely she could help me.

By this time the pastor came to welcome us, and the subject of music was dropped. The pastor was a kind, gentle person. He knew my priest brothers. That was helpful. He quickly ran through the daily duties that we were expected to perform, including the work of the sacristan. Mass would be said daily, and one of the sisters would have to prepare the altar and lay out the vestments for the priest to wear during Mass. After Mass, the vestments were to be put away. The pipe organ was to be played every day during Mass.

The pastor mentioned the senior and junior choirs. The children were to sing at daily Mass, which, in those days, was sung in Latin. The Sung Mass included the Kyrie eleison, Gloria, Credo, Sanctus, and Agnus Dei. The children were to learn the Gregorian Chant rendition of the Mass. Until then, they could sing English hymns. The senior choir needed to learn everything for Mass, funeral Masses, and Benedictions. So far, members of the senior choir had no training.

The teaching of catechism and church history would be done in the church and the two extra classrooms. All twelve grades would be brought from the public school by bus, by the pastor, for one-hour classes. The classes were large. We would be teaching children from five parishes. The money earned from teaching these classes would go directly to the motherhouse in Little Falls.

My brain couldn't take any more! I was glad he had stopped explaining. Goodbyes were said, and the superior, who was also a cook, started preparing supper. I went to the church.

Somebody would have to help me! I went up to the altar, knelt down, and stretched out prostrate on the floor, sobbing out loud.

"God," I prayed loudly, "you sent me here to do a job. I have no idea how to teach piano lessons. If this is your plan for me, then help me!" I didn't care if the whole world heard me. I was desperate. Then I got up and started for home, a half block away, feeling somewhat better already. This day had been one long nightmare, and sleep was needed but elusive.

One week went by quickly. I had already acquired three students for piano lessons. God was merciful! The first student had some lessons during the summer and brought her books. They were first-grade books. I took down the name and the publishing company and ordered five more. The next thing I did was to ask her what her teacher had taught her and how. She started with scales—from there on, the teacher was the student.

By the end of the first month I had twelve piano students. These were mostly first- and second-grade piano students. The books were a tremendous help. I was practicing scales and chords, arpeggios and dominant sevenths. I had played these in piano pieces all these years but I didn't know what they were. The students kept coming back every week, and that really encouraged me. I felt guilty enough taking their fifty cents per lesson.

I began to notice something by the end of the first month. All my life I had always associated with Catholics. Elk River, however, was one-quarter Catholic and three-quarters Protestant. I had never met a Protestant before. Out of my twelve students, eight were Protestant. They were very respectful, kind, and cooperative. The parents would always stop and visit when they came to pick up their children. I was impressed with both parents and children. These Protestants are beautiful. This reality was contrary to what I had been taught about Protestants. In my heart I felt a twinge of pain. Why didn't we all worship under the same roof? I believed that we needed to be at peace with everyone.

My senior choir, numbering twenty, was delightful. We met once a week in the evening. After a month of practice we already noticed a difference. Cooperation brought good results, and everyone was pleased, including the pastor. The junior choir was eager to learn. Children love to sing and these learned by hearing. Only a few knew how to read music.

The first month of catechism classes went well. The students' first encounter with sisters was one of surprise, awe, questioning, and testing. For a while some of them could not believe we were real. They asked questions like, *Do you eat? Why do you have your hair covered? Or don't you have any hair? What happened? Why are you dressed like that? Where do you come from? Why do you wear that rope around your waist?* They went on and on with endless questions. Only gradually did they accept us as human beings that eat, drink, think, sleep, wake up, and study as other people do. They finally understood that, yes, we too were born on Planet Earth.

These small, new missions were a new venture for the Community. Only three sisters carried on the work of teaching catechism and church history, music lessons, and choirs. One sister was the cook and sacristan. One of the three sisters was appointed superior to the other two sisters, observing the rules and regulations of the motherhouse. The superior was responsible for the obedience of all three sisters to the wishes of the pastor regarding teaching, sacristy work, music, and any other request the pastor might make. She was responsible for our prayer life and observation of the rules and regulations of the Community.

The first year at this new kind of mission was full of surprises. We had no mission to compare with since we were the first of this kind. The people were kind and appreciative and accepted us graciously. They actually thought that sisters could do anything and knew everything! That's why we had been brought there! We were trusted as though we were superior to them and possessed greater knowledge than they did, including spiritual knowledge. Some had a difficult time accepting us as normal human beings, with faults and imperfections and lacking knowledge in many subjects.

By the end of the first year I had forty-two piano students, and all were doing well. God had sent me the good ones, the ones who were teachable, who received instruction well. At the same time they gave me a new insight into music that fired my enthusiasm for playing the piano. With a new desire to study, I could pursue it to the highest degree of achievement possible.

I was grateful for the talent. I thanked God for helping me, especially now, because it didn't look like I would ever have my first piano lesson! So He sent me students who could help to inspire me—and they did.

At the end of the first year I found myself alone. My superior was transferred as well as my sister teacher. I stayed on and welcomed my new superior and sister teacher. This was a big change. These two were the exact opposite of the first superior and teacher. It didn't work out well. At the end of the second year, these two sisters were transferred, and I stayed on. By this time I was a nervous wreck.

My schedule was heavier every year, including the responsibilities of giving a three-act play with special music for Christmas, teaching even more piano students, visiting the sick, starting a 4-H Club at the pastor's request, and still following the Community's schedule of prayer and daily duties. I was becoming very tired. I finally succumbed to colitis, a dreaded illness in those days. The only treatment was bed rest and eating only heavy cream. I was fortunate. Without consulting a doctor, we were doing the right thing somehow, and in two weeks I was able to start working again with no recurrence.

An Experience with Death

Within the third year at Elk River, 1943, I became very ill again. I had been teaching catechism class at the church and was returning home, when suddenly I had a stabbing pain in my left side. I barely made it to the house. I opened the front door and collapsed. When I woke up I was in bed and felt like I was having a seizure. I could not control it, and the pain was becoming unbearable. My superior came in the room and told me she had called the Reverend Mother, who had said not to call the doctor, that it was probably the flu, and to give me two aspirins.

The only way I could ease the pain was to jackknife my left knee to my chin and hold it there continuously. The aspirin helped some. The next morning I could not stand up due to the pain. The pastor missed me at Mass and came over immediately. After a few words with the superior he went to the phone and called the doctor. In a little while the doctor arrived. After examining me he discovered a cyst the size of a grapefruit in my left side. He ordered me to the hospital where proper pain medication was available and where I would rest with proper preparation for surgery.

The Mother General was called to the hospital to give the doctor permission to operate. She would not consent to the surgery. I heard her telling the doctor that in only three weeks I would be making my Profession of Final Vows. The doctor explained to her that my condition was serious and the operation needed to be done right away. The cyst might burst, he explained, and I could be in great danger.

She would not consent. With that she left the hospital. The doctor came to inform me that he was scheduling my surgery for 8:00 A.M. the next morning. This was stated with such finality that I said nothing.

The next morning I woke up wondering what happens when one has surgery. *Would they wait until I was asleep? How could they be sure that I was really asleep if I had my eyes closed? How would they put me to sleep? Was I going to feel some of the pain?* In those days, nobody but the doctor told a patient anything, and I gathered he would rather not be questioned about anything, knowing he would have to face the Reverend Mother's questions when she found out he had ignored her orders.

My anesthetist was one of our sisters, a brittle diabetic. Thank God I didn't know what that was!

The time for surgery arrived. No preoperative medicine was given. I was taken by gurney, completely alert, to the operating room. Left alone with the anesthetist, we both kept silence dutifully, according to regulations. I heard the door open, and just as quickly a damp cloth was placed over my nose. I smelled ether. I felt like I was being smothered. All I can remember is that struggle to breathe and escape!

I opened my eyes. The room was full of people. A doctor was on either side of my bed, and an oxygen tank was at the foot of the bed. I recognized the Reverend Mother's voice to my left telling someone to go ahead and toll the bell (to indicate that an individual of that town or convent had died).

Someone spoke urgently to her just then, "No, Mother. No! She's awake!"

I wasn't sure what was going on, but something out of the ordinary was happening.

My doctor shook me. "Are you all right, Sister?"

I said, "yes."

The people started leaving the room, including the sisters, the Reverend Mother, and some of the nurses. The doctor and two nurses remained. The doctor gave orders to the nurses and finally left the room. Someone told me to stay quiet in bed for eight days, at which time the stitches would be removed if no infection developed. The nurse also told me she would stay at my bedside all the time.

I asked, "Did something go wrong?"

She said, "You are doing fine. Try to sleep."

No problem—I was gone.

When the prescribed eight days were up, the doctor took out my stitches. The incision was clean and healing well with no infection. He told me that I could get out of bed in two days. My appetite was good, and I couldn't wait to get out of that bed and walk.

After two days, I walked down the hall and met my favorite nurse, Sister Faith.

She walked back to my room with me, closed the door, faced me, and said, "Has anyone told you about the day you had surgery?"

I said, "No. Something happened, didn't it?"

She hesitated, then said, "Yes." She acted as though she were afraid to tell me. She continued, "I have to tell you."

I said, "What do you have to tell me?"

She started to cry. I waited. I was frightened. What horrible thing could have happened? I was feeling fine. She wiped away her tears and started telling me what happened.

The surgery went fine. I was brought back to my room and Sister Faith, who was recuperating from surgery also, was asked to stay with me until I awoke.

Sister Faith said, "I sat down on this chair by the window and started crocheting. Ten minutes went by; you were breathing normally; your color was good. I kept on crocheting. I looked up again, and your face was blue! You had no pulse; you weren't breathing. I ran to the door and screamed 'Help!' In a few seconds the doctors were here. All the nurses from the whole wing and everyone was working furiously to revive you, but nothing helped. Sister, you were dead!"

I stared at her in disbelief. I thought of the struggle that I had had when the ether was applied. But I went through surgery all right.

She said the Reverend Mother was called. "When someone said you were dead, Reverend Mother said, 'You know, Sister Amanda is dying of cancer up on third floor. Her coffin is ready.' Reverend Mother made the remark that since you are the same size, we might have to bury you in it. (This was after two hours of trying to resuscitate, but our doctor would not give up.) The other doctor said it was no use—you were dead! But Dr. F. would not listen. He grabbed you by the shoulders for the last time and pounded your whole upper body against the mattress. He would stop and start again and again."

Because Dr. F. had disobeyed the Reverend Mother's orders not to operate, he must have been highly motivated to keep me alive. He must have feared problems with his medical license. Cardiopulmonary resuscitation (CPR) did not exist then. Medical personnel did their best to revive people with oxygen and some type of stimulation. Sometimes these techniques were successful and other times they were not. The doctor had little to lose by continued stimulation and oxygen. He probably noticed some kind of responses that encouraged him to continue.

Sister Faith finished the story. "That's when the Reverend Mother told the man to toll the bell. And that's when you opened your eyes. Sister, you have no idea what a shock it was to see your eyes open and your face light up with a smile, after two hours of anguish while we tried to bring you back to us. Where were you? Do you know?"

I was numb. I did not know. I remembered that when I awoke I felt I had come out of a deep sleep, and that it was good. That was all. But I did remember asking why the oxygen tank was at the foot of my bed.

"Why didn't anyone answer me?" I asked Sister Faith.

"Because Reverend Mother signaled to us to be quiet. I had to tell you because I felt guilty thinking I neglected my duty and that was why you almost left us for good."

I answered, "I am doing fine and nothing will stop me from making my final vows next week." I told her how grateful I was to her for telling me and for caring so much. I assured her this information would stay between us and not go any further.

Evidently I would never be officially informed of the incident. Sister Faith looked so relieved. She left the room to go back on duty, and I sat down to try and figure out why this had happened. Again the ether came back to mind. I couldn't shake the thought of that struggle. Had the sister anesthetist (brittle diabetic!) given me too much? How could they know if it had been too much? What could they have done about it if it was too much? How was it measured? I had been exhausted from a week of intermittent intense pain, which had weakened me greatly. Would the usual dose of ether have been too much then? That nurse's license was on the line too. I felt bad for my doctors and the anesthetist and prayed for them, hoping they weren't burdened with the same guilt feelings that Sister Faith suffered from.

I thanked God over and over for sparing me. I wanted to serve Him in a new dimension—a life of poverty, chastity, and obedience forever, vows never to be dissolved.

Perpetual Profession

August 12, 1943 arrived. The most important August 12 for me was this one, above all others. I had been in the convent for almost six years. I took my final step and vowed a lifelong commitment of service to God. A near-death experience changes one's perspective. My desire for spiritual growth was intensified. I was hungry for perfect truth. The experience humbled me to beg for help in finding that truth. I needed enlightenment in that search.

I remembered my parents saying, "Jesus said, 'I am the Way, the Truth, and the Life.'" There it was: the answer. The answer is Jesus. But what did that mean for me now? Where would I find its meaning? I was trying so hard to do the right thing, but I felt like I was walking blindfolded. My destination was unknown; my reasons for the journey uncertain. I simply obeyed and hoped I was doing right.

Two days later I went back to Elk River. I resumed all my duties with renewed hope. I had miraculously survived another experience that was unexplainable. Why had I had so many experiences of this kind? What was following me all the time just waiting to trip me up for another round of the same depressing struggle to keep on living? I was recuperating beautifully. I told myself to forget what happened and keep on keeping on.

I shook off these questions with no answers and buried myself in work. Work was more than sufficient to keep me from pondering impossible questions. Our schedule did not change much except for a couple new ideas per year. My piano student program was increasing annually, putting plenty of food on the table. My piano recitals were well attended. My acquaintance with Protestants had blossomed and increased considerably.

About this time God blessed me with a piano student who was quite accomplished after twelve years of lessons. The timing was perfect because I was ready to study more in-depth and advanced material. I received the boost from God with gratitude and took advantage of every opportunity I had to practice more difficult music.

One learns so much by teaching! You share what little you know, but you get so much more in return to be used in teaching others more. It's a form of tithing and receiving. I didn't know much about tithing then, but by obedience I was doing it without knowing it.

Our cook, who had been there for about four months (our third recruit), had decided she wanted to leave the Community. She was free to go as she had made only temporary vows, but we were left without a cook, a sacristan, and a housekeeper. No replacement was available, so my superior and I took on her jobs plus our own and kept on as though we had done it all our lives.

For the next two years we still did the two-sister operation. But it was beginning to drain us. We noticed ourselves slowing down in many ways. We weren't feeling well most of the time, and we were tired all the time. We could see no relief, and we felt used and neglected. We had no hope of help. I was falling asleep during piano lessons. After regular, one-hour catechism classes, we were both losing our voices.

Early one morning my superior came to me and said, "Sister, I can't do it anymore. I am calling the Reverend Mother to tell her we just cannot continue like this. She has to send us help."

I agreed wholeheartedly. In two weeks we were both transferred to Little Falls (the motherhouse convent) for a retreat of seven days. At least a retreat would give our voices a rest and give us quiet time without interruptions and time to evaluate our work in the mission of Elk River. I had no regrets. I had worked diligently, accomplished the goals I had set for myself, and we had been able to send extra money from lessons to the motherhouse convent. My superior and I lived a peaceful, prayerful life.

SECOND MISSION ASSIGNMENT: FLENSBURG, MINNESOTA

After the retreat was over we received our new assignments. My superior from Elk River was sent to Fergus Falls, Minnesota, another new mission. My new assignment was to Flensburg, Minnesota. The same duties went with me. This was another two-sister operation. My superior at this mission would be my Novice Mistress, Sister W! After twenty years as a Novitiate Mistress, she too had received a new assignment that year.

My two years of novitiate training flashed before me. My memory began dragging me through all the foolish things I had done then that had brought humiliation upon me that was hard to forget. (I needed to be reminded every once in a while that my stubborn pride was still sitting determinedly on my shoulders, totally obscuring humility that should have worked through by now.) I wondered if she remembered me. Horrors! I remembered the *vermin*, the garbage cans, and the times I had asked questions I shouldn't have—especially about superiors. There was the time I wouldn't squeal on another sister . . . and on and on. I didn't realize I had such a good memory. I wondered how hers was! I envisioned some wild scenes in the near future.

I felt a tap on my shoulder. I turned around and there she was—my new superior. She greeted me with an assuring smile and said, "Sister, isn't this wonderful! You and I together on a mission! Isn't this great! I never dreamed we would be working together so soon. I am really looking forward to this assignment with you."

God bless her, I thought. I was amazed to see her in this frame of mind—totally different from her persona as our Novice Mistress. I replied that I was surprised too. "Do you think this will work?" I asked her.

She laughed as she said, "I have prayed for this to happen. To live on a mission of two is such a drastic change for me. I need someone like you, experienced in mission work and who knows how to work with children, since I don't. I was Novice Mistress for twenty years, and before that I never worked with children either."

I felt sorry for her. I only knew her as a stern superior who demanded perfection in every area of religious discipline, especially in the obedience of rules and regulations. It seemed to have been her duty to humble me at every opportunity. She was so different now that she was not in that position of authority. She had no idea what she faced as a superior on a little mission. What a change from the convent seclusion she had known, never dealing with people in the world she had left behind. Now, being placed back in this world thirty years later, the real world of totally different attitudes, was going to be a test of adjustment for her. I felt her fear of the assignment, her fear of the unknown. I admired her humility, her obedience, and her willingness to step out in faith and try, in spite of her feeling of inadequacy.

I knew that feeling. I sympathized with her. She deserved assurance, acceptance, and encouragement from me. I made it clear to her that I understood her fears, and I would be glad to introduce her to mission life. I shared my experiences at Elk River, my first mission. She was shocked. After a long discussion on mission life, we parted. She went to prepare for her departure to Flensburg. She returned an hour later with a smile and a much better understanding of what to expect. She was actually eager to get there and face her new challenge.

We left for Flensburg on a bright and sunny day. Our convent chauffeur took us there, helped us unpack, and left. We settled in shortly, then took a tour of the house and the church across the street. The choir loft was adequately furnished for a choir of thirty. The organ was small, not like the big one in Elk River. The music supply was small too, but it was enough to begin with.

We met the pastor as we came down from the choir loft. He was very happy to see us and said he would be over to our house later to talk about plans for the coming year. (We kept the rule of silence as we did at the motherhouse convent. The rule allowed us to speak when necessary in the performance of our duties, such as teaching, or when asked a question. We did not indulge in any unnecessary discussion.)

The pastor arrived after our evening meal. He was not a chatty person; he got right down to business. Our teaching of religion classes was similar to the Elk River program. My piano students were my responsibility entirely. Six students wanted to take guitar lessons. Some wanted Hawaiian guitar lessons, and others wanted whatever was available.

Here came another challenge—could I learn to play the guitar before having to teach it? I borrowed a Hawaiian guitar from a student for one week and learned how to play it. Then I borrowed the Gibson guitar from another student and learned to play it also. The next week we had our first lessons. The students worked hard and progressed quickly. I put them all together as a class and by Christmas they had quite a repertoire for the Christmas program. They surprised everyone. We were thrilled to see young students so ambitious.

The Christmas program went well. Parents filled the auditorium and were delighted, naturally, to watch their children perform. The hit of the evening was the six guitar students. The audience was completely surprised by their playing. The applause was enthusiastic, but the guitar students finally ran out of encores. Happily, the excitement of the program carried around the entire town.

Sister W. and I worked together very well. She was the sacristan and a very good one. All the time at the convent she had wanted that job but never had it. I told her she deserved to play an important part in the first mission. Everyone respected and loved her. At the end of each day we shared many good laughs.

Our return to school after the Christmas holiday was ushered in by a blizzard. The first day of school had to be canceled; Minnesota snowstorms bring considerable snow and last three to five days. They are beautiful to watch from one's home but dangerous to travel in. Many people lost their lives in these blizzards. We were always careful to have a good supply of food on hand from before Christmas until about the first of June. Yes. One year, we had a three-day blizzard from May 29 through May 31. That same year we had to light the furnace on July 4!

On January 10 I came down with a bad cold. I lost my voice and was unable to teach. It was subzero weather. For one whole week the thermometer would not budge from forty degrees below. After four days I was feeling better and my voice was much improved, so I went back to teaching. After the second day of teaching, I came home with a severe sore throat, an earache, chills, and a fever of 102 degrees. My superior took me to the doctor, who in turn hospitalized me. I again lost my voice, but this time it was gone on an extended vacation.

On the third hospital day, the doctor wanted to know how much talking I had done on that day. I told him not much. He decided to restrict visitors and limited my speech to whispering. He said my throat looked worse than when I had come in to the hospital.

Two days later he came in to tell me, "No visitors! No talking! No whispering!" (Antibiotics were still not available.) I don't know what medication they were giving me, but I was getting worse instead of better. I couldn't eat because it was hard to swallow and I had no appetite. I was losing weight fast. No company. No radio. No newspaper. (Television had still not yet been invented.) All I had was a prayer book and a rosary.

The days were long and the nights were no better. I couldn't sleep. I was becoming depressed from isolation and lack of mental activity. I knew I was going to die and join my classmates because I heard the doctor telling the nurse in the hallway, "It's two weeks since Sister Jeannette was admitted. She's worse, higher fever, no appetite, much weaker, and depressed. She'll never make it! If she does survive, she will never be able to speak again. I have never seen such an ugly-looking throat."

I was unable to find any reason for hope. I was still in the hospital two and a half months later. It was almost April. I was weaker, still running a fever occasionally, and more bored by the day, with little hope of complete recovery. I was only twenty-six years old. What kind of future did I have to look forward to? I was ready to die. Why live? Death was constantly after me to give up. How easy it would have been to give up. The struggles of recuperation were sadly familiar to me. And I was sixteen pounds lighter, which did not help. If only I could have enjoyed the air outdoors for an hour a day, I would have had something to live for. In those days, if you were hospitalized, you stayed indoors until you were discharged to your home.

May has always been my favorite month. One of the first days the Reverend Mother came to see me. She told me she had to make a decision concerning me. She did not think I should return to Flensburg. She would make her decision after I recovered. I was still unable to talk and, therefore, deprived of visitors. She informed me that Sister J. had been teaching in my place and would continue until summer.

By another week's passing I was feeling stronger, and hope was returning. The next morning I woke up believing something was going to happen. When the nurses brought my breakfast tray, with the usual greeting, I answered them, not with a whisper but with an audible sound. The nurse and I looked at each other in disbelief.

The nurse said, "Oh, I must go tell your doctor; he's at the station. He will be so happy!" She was gone immediately. Soon nearly every staff member crowded into my room.

My doctor said, "Save the next words; we don't want you to lose it again!" He wrote out new orders to fit the occasion. At first I was allowed only a few words during the day, after which my throat was examined. If no redness appeared, I could continue.

Twice my speech had to be halted. I knew when I had said enough because I would get very tired.

For all these six months in the hospital, I was confined to bed. Finally, the doctor told me I could get out of bed a little at a time. My knees and ankles buckled with the first try. Exercises were started. In a couple days I was given a wheelchair with a walker attached. I was allowed to decide whether to get up and start walking. In those days, physiotherapy had not been introduced yet as a part of the recovery program. I wanted to get out of the hospital badly. My appetite improved from the exercise and strength began to return to my muscles. My heart rate was most often around 170 as I eagerly worked on getting up and sitting down repeatedly. They couldn't get me back to bed, and I begged to rest in the wheelchair. They were accommodating. I would fall asleep there many times throughout the day.

After three weeks of this struggle, I began to walk. What a thrill! It was July. I prayed to be strong enough by August to return to work. Where would I go this time? Would I lose my voice again? My recovery was good, as long as I was careful not to laugh or talk too much.

THIRD MISSION ASSIGNMENT: ST. FRANCIS HIGH SCHOOL

August 12 came again with all its festivities. We had a new Reverend Mother by now, elected by the sisters. She had been my principal at the high school all four years I attended. She called me to her office on August 13 to give me my new assignment. She was very kind and understanding. She had thought it over for some time and decided to keep me at the motherhouse in Little Falls until I was stronger. I would be teaching music lessons at the high school until I was able to go back to any one of the five small missions. What a relief! I was still having difficulty walking stairs the first month. Gradually I gained strength and was able to enjoy life again.

I stayed at St. Francis High School for two and a half years. I felt I had accomplished a lot while there. Again I was the accompanist for all programs and occasions. Twice I accompanied opera singers.

I also accompanied the thirty-five-member glee club, which toured every year. The last year I was there, they were entered in a competition with five other glee clubs in the state of Minnesota. The competition took place in a huge auditorium in Minneapolis. The piano was located in the middle of the auditorium. Every chair of the fifteen hundred-capacity facility was filled. Glee clubs were seated in the bleachers. When our turn came to perform, I walked to the piano and prepared my sheets of music in proper order while the singers came down and stood in their places. The rendition of the first number was done superbly.

The second number began with my piano introduction. The first line of the song had just been sung when somebody opened the door from the outside to the auditorium. All my music sheets took to the air and flew all over the audience. This sudden interruption by man and Mother Nature left me in a dilemma! Playing songs from memory was not something I had planned for. I knew the melody and I did the best I knew how. Meanwhile, a group of people from the audience gathered up the scattered sheets of music and put them back in order. Mercifully, one of these people was a music teacher. The judges were so kind. They called a ten-minute intermission so we could collect ourselves and our sheet music.

After all six glee clubs were heard, we had another intermission while the judges made their decision. In only five minutes the decision was announced. "The winner is St. Francis High School!" After the applause died down, the voice of the announcer came on again. "And let us not forget the brave nun at the piano! Sister, well done, you passed the real test of an accompanist. Congratulations!"

FOURTH MISSION ASSIGNMENT: MORRIS, MINNESOTA

In July 1957 I received my next letter of obedience (convent vocabulary for a transfer). The Community had established another mission at Morris, Minnesota, which included a grade school taught by *our* sisters. I had a chance to see Morris Grade School the day I received the assignment.

The school was a two-story building with a stage and auditorium in the basement. Two classrooms and a library occupied the first floor for grades 1–4. The two classrooms on the second floor were used by grades 5–8. The junior high school choir and band practiced in a large room on the second floor.

When I saw the word *band*, my mouth flew open, and I said, "Here we go again! I've never played a band instrument, have never worked with a band, and we never had a band in our home town of St. Stephen."

The most elementary information about bands was unknown to me; for instance, what specific instruments comprised the band? Where would I start? I continued to mutter to myself when one of the sisters walked by, stopped, and asked if she could help me.

"You look like you received some shocking news."

I told her the news was worse than death.

She asked again, "Can I do anything to help you?"

I said, "Yes, go tell the Reverend Mother I just died; tell her to find someone else to send to Morris, Minnesota!"

We laughed and she reminded me of her unthinkable assignment of the previous year, how impossible it had seemed, and yet how well it had worked out. She consoled me and comforted me, like I had consoled and comforted her then. She left with the words "It's your turn now."

A Monsignor, who is second only to the Bishop, was in charge of the parish along with an assistant priest. The church was quite large to accommodate the eight hundred parishioners. The balcony for the choir loft at the back of the church held at least forty choir members.

I was delighted and surprised to see the beautiful pipe organ to accompany the choir. It beckoned me to sit down and play. The majestic pipes were standing at attention in perfect arrangement.

I sat down and began to acquaint myself with the organ, the rich tones blending their perfect pitches, weaving wondrous melody. In the excitement, time was not. An hour seemed to pass in a few minutes. The music carried me out of time's dimension. This was so exciting. The temptation to play one pompous piece before I left was too strong. I chose the Wedding March. I pulled out the stops and started playing. How exhilarating! As I finished playing, I closed my eyes and kept listening for the lingering sounds floating around, gradually decreasing and finally disappearing into eternity. I felt numb. I did not want to open my eyes. I wished to remain in this awesome, delightful peace that came over me. Now, in this place, rebellion did not exist.

Suddenly I burst into uncontrollable weeping, realizing my ingratitude to God for the gift of music. He had blessed me so

abundantly in Elk River, bringing me to this level of achievement and mastery of the pipe organ, piano, and much more. Was this the same God I believed was writing all my sins in the Big Black Book, sentencing me to a thousand endless years in Purgatory, hoping my relatives and friends would pray me out?

I felt as though someone else was with me. I looked around and saw no one. Three words were coming at me: "Give thanks. Obey." I spent another

Sister Mary Jeannette (Anne) in traditional garb in 1950.

five minutes thanking God for all His blessings, especially music. My success at Elk River was still a puzzle to me, but my fears of this mission assignment were now gone. Somehow I expected the same miracles to happen here at Morris.

In the Catholic Church it is uncommon to speak of miracles happening in the present. It was commonly believed that God had performed miracles in New Testament times so people would believe Christ was God in His time, but that today this was no longer necessary. To me, my Elk River experience had been a miracle. And this day I felt I had an encounter with the True God while I was sitting at the pipe organ. But with whom could I share this? Could a person claim that God had spoken to him and yet not sound presumptuous? Would God speak to ordinary people?

I left the choir loft with a delighted heart, feeling that burdens had been lifted, as though I had been to an accelerated retreat. I had a new attitude of expectancy that good things would come. From somewhere came the certainty to keep all of this to myself. Musicians, as well as artists, were likely to be strange, I had heard.

I arrived at the house and took a tour of the kitchen and dining room. Then I wanted to see the music room. The superior opened the door with a smile and announced, "This is the music *department!*" This was unbelievable. Eight piano rooms. She then explained that some of the students didn't have pianos at home, and they practiced in the music department after school from 4:00 to 6:00 P.M., "while you are teaching at this piano," she added, pointing to a beautiful Mason & Hamlin grand.

I didn't, and couldn't, say a word while I tried to envision the noise of eight pianos being played at the same time, probably in eight different keys, and my piano playing in another key, accentuated by sour notes coming from each practice room! *Wait,* I thought. I shuddered, imagining what this would do to my sanity. *God help me.* I envisioned my nerves becoming permanently frazzled.

My thoughts were interrupted by my superior's timely remark, "You will start with eighty students two weeks from now!"

"God bless them!" I said, with complete sincerity.

Fresh air was the only necessity right now. We went outside and sat silently on a bench in the shade for a while, just breathing. I waited dutifully for the next ax to fall.

My superior broke the silence with a smile and said, "How much do you know about working with a band?"

"Nothing," I said.

She thought for a while, then patted me on my shoulder, adding confidently, "You will do just fine, Sister." Oh how I needed to hear that.

Trying to move from panic to practical problem solving, I asked, "What instruments do they have here in the band?"

She answered vaguely, "Oh, about ten or twelve." She didn't know which ones.

Moving ahead bravely, I asked, "Do you know who can help me get started?"

She answered quickly, "The man who supplies the instruments for our band was a band instructor. Surely he would be glad to help you. Stay here. I will call him right now."

With that she left only to return in a short while to let me know he would come over in the morning to help me get started. Silently I prayed "Thank You, Lord."

Supper had little flavor that evening. I went through the motions of feeding my body, taking for granted my mouth was still in the same place. Dazed, my thought processes refused to function effectively, I flitted from one problem to another nervously, accomplishing absolutely nothing. My first day in Elk River had been a cinch compared to this. I went to bed wondering what other surprises might show up the next day.

After tossing and turning my precious hours of sleep away, I was aroused by the faithful 5:00 A.M. cowbell. I was hoping yesterday was just a bad dream, but reality set in quickly as I bounded out of bed, asking God to give me courage to take charge over my fears, to face the day's events with faith. Today had to be an improvement.

I arrived at the chapel in time for prayers, meditation, and Mass. Breakfast was welcome. I needed strength to face this first day in Morris. The band director came at 9:00 A.M. He was a gray-haired man with years of experience teaching band. For the last ten years he had supplied schools with band instruments and assisted teachers with band instruction and by teaching students. I was a new challenge.

First he had to get over the fact that I had no band experience. Then he asked me when I had to start teaching. My answer closed off his voice box. I waited and prayed while he got up and started pacing the floor. *Dear Lord, I hope I didn't ruin him for life. Time is so precious, make him talk to me! I need his help so badly*, I prayed.

After his tenth round of pacing, he finally cleared his throat to request a drink of water. I excused myself and returned with a glass of water, noticing that he had fully recovered. I quietly said, *Thank You, Lord, and please help us both.*

We started down toward the school. He asked me again, "Two weeks from tomorrow? That's impossible." I had no enlightening words to offer; in fact, I had no words to tell him that he wasn't helping. He knew I needed encouragement, so he added, "Starting with nothing, I'm ready to bet you will be the best band director around!"

I smiled and answered, "Sir, with your help and God's help, I know I can do it. I am depending on both of you."

The band room was set up for practice. He took the baton from the music stand and handed it to me with the words, "I pray that you will become the greatest success in band history, and I truly believe you will!"

I received the baton and answered, "With God's help and your guidance, it is done." This small, spontaneous ceremony caused both of us to feel stronger and more confident. He picked up the trumpet and began to teach me.

He was an excellent instructor. I wasted no more time whining but let my willingness to obey be the springboard for God's help to conquer what seemed impossible. One instrument after another, all ten of them plus bass drum, snare drums, and Glockenspiel, was handed to me, analyzed, and explained as to how it worked, what the fingering positions were, how to produce good tone, and how to avoid improper handling. Every detail was accounted for. Two weeks went by too fast. I was ready. He was only able to come five days to check on my progress. I practiced on every instrument until I could play simple tunes and produce the best tones. I felt much better by now and quite ready to tackle a new dimension of my musical ability. My instructor was very pleased, giving me enough encouragement to launch into the unknown trials of this new adventure. My last day of freedom was near.

By now I'd discovered that the band consisted of fifty-three students, ranging from grades 3–8. Twelve were third-graders. No student could enter the band unless he had completed one full year of piano lessons. How ironic that the band director (me) did not fill this requirement.

My first meeting with the band was scheduled for the first day of school. Every member was there, old and new. I tried to match players with instruments (names would come later). I explained the seating arrangement. Everyone except the twelve new members came equipped with instrument and music they had learned, which helped. I had my baton and the leader's book. It was time to prove I had learned sufficient skills to lead a band.

I selected the simplest piece and asked the older members to play it under my direction. One could see that the instruments had been on a three-month vacation with their owners. This was, naturally, what I had hoped for. Yes! I could teach them. They could learn from me. For a while, I drilled them as well as the choir members. The exercises showed up their weak spots, endurance abilities, and willingness to accept correction. By the end of practice, I had plotted out my plan of instruction. New students got their schedules for private lessons in the evenings. The general atmosphere was upbeat and cooperative. I was delighted.

My piano students came according to the schedule I had made out the week before. By the end of the week ten more people had applied for lessons. One of these new students had only four fingers on her right hand. She insisted she could keep on with piano lessons if I would guide her in changing her fingering. I decided to help her. Every piece of music needed to be reworked. This teenage girl had admirable determination, cooperation, and a brilliant mind. By the end of the year she participated in the recital. To everyone's amazement her technique was so smooth no one would have guessed she had only four fingers on her right hand. By now she was able to take over the task of adjusting the fingering. She soon became one of my top students.

By the end of my first year at Morris, I did not have enough time to teach the 105 piano students. The town was very musical and supportive of the band. I had to request an assistant music teacher. The three choirs, senior, junior, and children's, were doing well. I had exhausted myself trying to do everything. My health suffered from this schedule, and my body communicated this to me with fatigue, insomnia, and two stomach ulcers that took a long time to heal.

I had to take some time off to regain strength, baby my ulcers, and get used to my new diet: forty-eight ounces of cream per day. By the end of my second day on the diet I missed using silverware. I insisted on using a spoon to consume the cream. On the fourth day, three bowls of gelatin per day were added—a pleasant change. The cream didn't taste so bad then. On the fifth day, Cream of Wheat was added to the diet, including all the forty-eight ounces of cream. Now it was worth living again, and I felt much better. My superior believed I was well enough to start teaching again.

My assistant music teacher arrived that same week, giving me hope. I was too soon back to the usual schedule, but the new helper had to be shown the ropes even if she helped with only piano lessons.

Six weeks into this routine and I was back to cream. I tried to heal the ulcers with the former regimen; it didn't work. As any fool could see, what I needed was rest. My work load was just too stressful. I ended up with bleeding ulcers and had to be hospitalized for two weeks. Talk about a slow learner.

The doctor assigned to me was a total stranger. He was very concerned about my health, noting my small frame, underweight condition, pale color, and extreme fatigue. He wanted to know what kind of work I was doing and how much. I told him I was teaching music at Morris. He wanted all the details.

After hearing my schedule, he stared at me for several moments, and said, "Does your Reverend Mother know how much work you are doing?"

"Yes," I answered.

He thought for a while, then paced the floor. He finally stopped in front of me and said, "You go tell your Reverend Mother she has no right to kill you." With that comment he left the room. Apparently he knew nothing about convent life.

I wanted to hug him. He understood! If only I could have one minute to say what I thought. If only I could have time to recuperate from one illness long enough to be sufficiently strong to tackle the next work load (which I would expect the motherhouse to lighten). It should have been clear to those in authority by now that my load needed cutting down.

The next day he came to see me, he had his senior partner with him. He asked me to repeat my work schedule from dawn to dusk, including every detail, to his partner. I repeated the schedule: arise at 5:00 A.M.; attend one hour of Community prayers, Mass, and break-fast; teach until noon; attend noon lunch; teach from 12:30 P.M. to 6:00 P.M.; attend thirty-minute supper, one hour of prayers, and one hour of recreation; retire at 9:00 P.M., except on Tuesdays and Thurs-days when I had choir practice from seven to nine in the evening.

Now the senior doctor stared. Then he asked me, "Do you re-ally like teaching that much?" I remembered my vow of obedience and hesitated to answer. He noticed and kindly reminded me that he admired our Community and the good we were doing. (How could he say otherwise since our Community owned this hospital, which was an obvious goodly source of income for him.)

I remembered God's commandment, vow or no vow, that God's laws came first. So I told him the truth, that I never wanted to teach anything. I wanted to be a nurse.

"How long have you been teaching?"

"Piano lessons, thirteen years and classes of catechism,(ten years)."

Then, to my embarrassment, he asked, "How much schooling have you had in music?"

I said, "None. I have yet to take my first lesson."

"How much schooling have you had altogether?"

"Grade school and high school," I answered.

His face turned red and the next words came out like thunder. "Then you have no right to teach at all!"

Pause. "Tell your superior or Reverend Mother that she is be-ing very unfair to you, making you teach music without preparing you for it and also depriving you of the joy of becoming a nurse, a beautiful profession, which God has called you to. Do all the mu-sic teachers teach without preparation?"

I had to answer honestly, "No."

Then he said kindly, "Please, Sister, for your sake, I hope this teaching misery is over for you." He too did not understand con-vent life, especially the vow of obedience.

The doctor went on to make me well aware of the health consequences if I did not speak up.

Two days later I was discharged from the hospital. I made my decision to obey the doctor, come what may. I arrived at the motherhouse, made my appointment with the Reverend Mother, and waited to be called. I went to the chapel, the only safe place, and stayed there. Where else could I go? Nowhere, but to God. But how or what to pray was unclear. I had misgivings about my conversation with the doctors. Had I done the right thing? All I could say to God was, "I'm sorry, please help me." I knew I would be in trouble if I said something to Reverend Mother and in worse trouble if I said nothing. This stress was not healing my ulcers. Conflict like this forced me to wonder to whom I had made my vows.

Two hours passed before I was called. I went slowly, trying to postpone the encounter as long as I could. The Reverend Mother was waiting at the door when I arrived. I survived the interrogation about my health quite well. The obvious question then came, "And when did the doctor say you could resume your work?"

I hesitated, and my mind went blank. Finally I realized the doctor never said anything about going back to work. He wanted me out of teaching music. I answered her with his statement in my own words. "Reverend Mother, he thinks I shouldn't be teaching music. It's too nerve-racking and is probably the reason for all these ulcers."

Quickly came the anticipated response: "Who does he think he is telling my sisters what kind of work they should be doing? You go back and tell him to mind his own business. He can run his clinic, and I will tell my sisters what to do. And you go back tomorrow and continue teaching music *and be happy*." With that she dismissed me.

Thank God it was over with. What was the point in arguing? My effort had been fruitless, as I had thought it would be. I learned a long time ago in the Novitiate that you do not question authority's decisions. This Reverend Mother refused to send me to nursing school before. She would never change her decision. Because she had never been ill in her lifetime, she could not understand illness and how difficult it was to work when not feeling well.

A DEATH IN MY FAMILY

That same year, on April 10, 1960, our pastor in St. Stephen called me, stating that my mother was very ill. She had suffered a massive stroke and had been admitted to the hospital in St. Cloud. The prognosis was poor. He advised me to get permission to come home at once.

When I arrived at St. Cloud Hospital, run by the Benedictine Sisters, my three priest brothers, my father, and my brother Tony greeted me. My sister, Mary, was unable to come from New York. We all went to my mother's bedside. Sister Rosaria, the nurse, explained my mother's condition to me and added, "Her blood pressure has been 300/100 ever since she was admitted, but she has a strong heart. She has not regained consciousness, and the prognosis is poor. She is not in pain. I am assigned to her care, so all of you can take some time to rest. I will call you if there is any change." We all took advantage of this opportunity to rest.

About nine in the evening we were called to her bedside. Her breathing was difficult. We started praying the rosary as was customary. We were halfway through when I looked up at her. I saw her take her last breath and quietly, peacefully slip away into eternity. She was sixty-nine.

She was buried in the St. Stephen cemetery on April 15, 1960. The day was beautiful and sunny. Snow lay on the ground, but the sun provided warmth to the quiet surroundings. The only music one heard was the warbling of the birds in the trees announcing the reunion of a faithful soul and her Creator.

Dad's Decision

After my brothers returned to their places of duty following the funeral, Dad made a big decision. My parents had been married fifty-two years. Dad missed Mother so much that after one month of living alone, he moved to Fort Wayne, Indiana, to live at the Crosier Monastery, where my brother Father John then ruled as Prior of the Crosier Fathers.

Before Dad left, I helped him with the remaining details at his home and helped him pack his suitcase for the trip. I was greatly relieved that he would be taken care of and that he would be close to the family during his last years.

Dad lived at the monastery for five years. His life with the Fathers was a healthy and active one. My father was in chapel every morning at five, saying his prayers. He stayed in the chapel for Mass every day, ate breakfast with the priests, and then went out to take care of the chickens and the gardens. He also did yard work and whatever else needed to be done. He was an example of faithfulness and obedience to the priests, so much so that they all hated to see him leave.

Five years later he returned to his house in St. Stephen and continued the same routine plus a visit to my mother's grave daily. Now he was spiritually fortified to be back at home. He wanted to have something to do. He asked the mayor if he could help at the grade school we all had attended, across the street from his house. He was hired as a fireman at age eighty-two. He did a wonderful job; the children loved him, and he enjoyed them. He would often tell us how much fun he had with the children. He was never sick as long as I knew him. Although quiet, peaceful, and caring, he was also strong, healthy, and hard working. To me, he was a prince.

Return to Morris

Immediately after helping Dad leave for the monastery, I returned to Morris the next morning and continued my work as music instructor. The band members were especially glad to see me. We made up for lost time.

The Monsignor came to listen to the band a month later and decided that they should march in the Legion Parade a month from then. Several high school bands would participate in the event, but Morris Grade School would be the only one of its kind. We were honored by the Monsignor's confidence, but he did not realize how much extra practice would be required.

Half of the fifty-three-member band was composed of third- and fourth-graders, whose little fingers required considerable stretching to reach some notes. But my band was so excited about the parade, it would have been cruel to raise any opposition.

The sisters were upset because it was against Community regulations for a sister to be leading a band in a public event. I knew that, but who would be brave enough to tell the Monsignor? My superior and I both realized this was his last wish, since he had been recently diagnosed with cancer. Neither of us could bring ourselves to say anything because he was so concerned about the children all the time, trying to give them every opportunity offered by the public schools. This was the crowning point of his devotion to the children.

My problem was easy to define. My band needed a bandleader to lead them while marching in the parade. Bands need leaders to signal when to start playing and when to stop and keep marching. As a sister, their leader in practice, I was not allowed to lead a band in a public parade. The Monsignor did not want me to hire any bandleader from town. I had to find someone who was associated with the band and would be willing and able to take the responsibility. The band could not perform without a leader. I felt I was carrying a heavy burden by myself. Again I went to my place of refuge—the church. Here was the quiet and peaceful space where I could think, and I knew God was present there. Sitting in the pew, I relaxed, holding my head in my hands. I began to remember the nightmare I'd had the night before.

My band was marching in a parade and ready to play. Their attire was exceptionally beautiful. But their instruments refused to play no matter how hard the students tried. After much embarrassment and much booing from the crowd, one of my eighth-grade band members appeared. He was a baton twirler. He took his place in front of the band, twirled his baton, turned around, signaled, and led the band. The instruments began to play. There was my answer! *Thank You, Lord.*

I flew out of the church, thanking God over and over for answering my prayer, and landed at my superior's door at the school. My knock brought her to the door unusually fast. When she saw it was I she said, "What's happened?"

Breathlessly I said, "I have the answer!"

"What answer? Calm down! You aren't making any sense."

I told her about my nightmare and that after praying about the band, I had realized that the nightmare was really my answer, scary as it was.

She merely said, "Well, that is a possibility."

Not much enthusiasm, I thought. There was no time to spare, so I left her standing there while I went to look for my boy who would solve the band problem. Class or no class I knocked on the seventh- and eighth-grade door.

The sister in charge was not pleased about the interruption, stating "Couldn't this wait?"

My answer was "No." I walked in unceremoniously, unannounced, retrieved my baton twirler, brought him out of the classroom, and asked him if he would be willing to lead the band.

"Yes!" Paul stated emphatically. He said he would do anything to beat the high school band. I arranged to meet with him after school.

The Legion Parade was unique because this was the first time the Morris High School allowed competition between grade schools and high schools. It was a favor extended to the Monsignor since his serious cancer condition was common knowledge. No one feared a grade school entry! I have not heard of this happening anywhere else.

I was so happy when my half-past-three piano student canceled. Paul arrived after three and I took him through the paces of leading the band. A one-hour phone call to the kind band leader who had introduced me to all the band instruments the year before gave me all I needed to proceed with the fulfillment of Monsignor's wish. I followed his instructions closely. Paul realized the importance of keeping time with the baton and step and the importance of the signals he would give. He was, mercifully, a quick study.

By the end of the week he and the band were ready to perform for me on the school grounds, marching and playing at the same time, alert to the signals from their leader, Paul. Only three weeks remained for practice, and this first effort, which was far, far from perfect, increased my fears.

During supper that night, the subject of the marching band came up. The sisters were still opposed to the whole idea, and having heard the first practice that afternoon, they were more than negative.

"Do you expect God to work miracles for you just so you can show off your band?" one sister asked. If they only knew how I had prayed against this.

Before I could think or say anything, the next words I heard were, "It's going to be a flop, an embarrassment." No encouragement was heard. In my heart I knew it would turn out all right.

Improvements were actually happening the next week. Fingers seemed to stretch farther, tones became clearer, and notes played on pitch. The band members were faithful in coming to practice. They accepted Paul and worked well with him day after day without complaint.

The day of the Legion Parade was perfect, beautiful and sunny. At 10:00 A.M. all the bands were ready to start marching. I issued last-minute instructions, which included a prayer for help. They were ready for the challenge. The boys wore white trousers and shirts and light blue capes. The girls wore white skirts and blouses and light blue capes. They all wore white shoes and tall, round blue hats with pompons. Sunlight played on the shiny instruments, making them sparkle. With heads high and instruments in position, the children, marching in perfect step, and their instruments were a splendid sight.

People lined the streets three and four deep for the length of the town (one and one-half miles). Our band was third in line. I had found a good viewing spot in a J. C. Penney building, watching through the windows. I was so proud of them. As they approached the Penney's building, they began playing at the signal from Paul. It sounded unusually beautiful. The crowd went wild with joy, pride, and astonishment. One could hear the *Bravos!* clearly. Never had I heard them play like this.

As they passed, the crowd demanded a repeat performance. Paul had caught my eye when the band had reached the Penney's building and had waved to me with a big smile. (A little out of character, but easily forgiven!) So now again, he turned around and looked up at me for approval for the encore. I smiled and nodded. He didn't lose a step. He turned to the band and gave his signal, and the band played on. I cried with joy and relief.

Again God had mercifully stooped low to help us out. He was on our side. I noticed Monsignor across the street; he looked so happy. He sat on a special chair close to the street where the bands marched by. I could see him wiping tears off his face. His dream had become a reality in this afternoon's performance by St. Mary's School Band of Morris, Minnesota.

At the conclusion of the parade, everybody stayed quietly in place until the winning band was announced.

"And the winner is . . . St. Mary's Grade School Band!" said the booming voice over the loudspeaker. Chaos and joyful noise erupted, with screaming, yelling, and cheering. People danced in the streets, overcome with pride "for those brave grade school kids!" The children deserved praise and pats on the backs because they had exceeded all expectations, including mine. Now they would look forward to the free trip to the state fair, granted by Monsignor. His dream had come true.

The excitement of the day was winding down slowly, although the cooling down process took a while. The band members came to me as a group to thank me for helping them win, but I had to admit they had done it. I could teach all day, every day, but it was up to them as a group to perform as well as they had. They displayed a loyalty to their school, reflecting what children can accomplish when aided by their faith.

Uniforms were carefully hung up and instruments were put back in their cases, ready for the next practice. I surprised them by giving them a week off. They had put in many hours of practice over the prior two weeks. They deserved a rest. I was so proud of them. The sisters congratulated them. With little visible embarrassment from the tears streaming freely down his face, the Monsignor embraced each band member. He then made them even happier by giving them a three-day weekend.

What a perfect day, I thought; *what a miraculous day*. The Monsignor died six months later.

I went home weeping with joy and thanking God for being so good to me in everything I did. I thanked Him for bringing about this triumph. I went directly to my bedroom; I was exhausted. I lay down and went to sleep immediately.

Hospitalization

Someone was shaking me awake. She kept repeating, "Sister, please wake up!" I opened my eyes and saw the panic-stricken face of one of the sisters.

She asked, "Sister, why are you moaning and groaning like that?"

I moved to get up and felt a sharp pain ripping through my abdomen. I fell back, vowing not to move again. The sister ran to get the superior.

I said to our superior, "Sister, it feels like I have some more ulcers. I think it would be wise to see my doctor." She agreed.

In two hours I was back in the same hospital, with the same doctor, and in the same room. I was in constant abdominal pain, plus there was pain in my head with the dread of the inevitable questions I knew would come. How would I explain this repeat performance, this proof I had not followed the doctor's orders?

A nurse gave me an injection for pain. What blessed relief that was. I welcomed a full night's sleep with no pain.

Morning came too quickly. All I wanted to do was sleep. In case the doctor would want x-rays and/or lab tests, I had no breakfast. I was told to rest until the doctor came.

The words, "Why are you here again?" woke me up. The doctor led a short question-and-answer session, followed by a few abdominal punches and a short lecture that ended with "I have to perform a surgery, then I will be back because we have a lot of serious business to discuss."

I prayed the surgery would be successful and that I would be fully awake for the serious business discussion. I appreciated my doctor who was direct and to the point.

He returned in four hours. He smiled and pulled up a chair saying, "All right, Sister, my surgery went well; I've made my rounds, let's talk."

My answer to the first question was "Yes, I had a talk with the Reverend Mother."

"Then why are you here with two more bleeding ulcers?" He gave me no time to answer the question. He continued with "I think I'd better write a letter to your Mother Superior. Maybe she doesn't understand why I think you should give up teaching music. If I may, I would like to write her a letter explaining my orders. What do you think?" I agreed. He went on, "I will also tell her you have to take two to three months off from any kind of work, and I want to see you in one month."

I nodded in approval. He added that he would show me the letter first.

His tone of voice had mellowed in the course of the conversation. Perhaps he was beginning to understand the superior/inferior relationship of convent life. I breathed a sigh of relief, hoping and praying that my future could be resolved peaceably.

RECUPERATION

Two days later I was discharged from the hospital and returned to Little Falls to recuperate at the motherhouse. What a welcome change! Spring was my favorite time of year, and where else could I find a more peaceful, restful atmosphere in which to recuperate? What a change this was from the hustle and bustle of the past year. One felt God's presence and peace in the motherhouse surroundings. All nature was giving thanks to its Creator. The birds warbled their loveliest melodies, the flowers displayed their richest colors, and the verdant grass lavishly carpeted everything. Trees lifted their branches, praising their Creator. How free nature is, and how grateful!

I remembered to thank Him for His goodness and blessings. How quickly we forget who loves us beyond measure, gives abundantly, lifts us up when we feel alone in this world, and forgives us readily. He gave us each so much more to work with: a mind, a will, and a soul to know Him better. And yet, who gives Him the most praise? I was humbled and grateful for the time I had now to reflect and meditate on these important things. How easy it is to forget who makes all things, even the impossible, possible. How quickly we reach to grab the glory for our accomplishments, forgetting to thank and praise the Master of all our accomplishments, the one whose Glory made us.

A Bible verse came to my mind, one I had heard quoted by one of the priests: "I am the vine, ye are the branches: He that abideth in me, and I in Him, the same bringeth forth much fruit; *for without me ye can do nothing*" (John 15:5, emphasis mine).

This was the only Bible verse I remembered then. Rarely did any priest quote the Bible during a sermon. Similarly, we did not have Bibles in the convent. But this verse about the vine seemed easy to remember, and I wondered why I was reminded of it now. I didn't realize then how God was trying to help me on this day of rest and renewal. I dwelt on this verse much of the day; it would not leave me. Even then I knew how important it was to simply let go and let Him. And then, of course, that was all I could do. I longed for a spiritual advisor to whom I could pour out my desperation and confusion, a compassionate person who would set me on the right path, who would lead me to health and happiness but who would not judge me.

Despite unexpected success, the teaching of music had become such a burden. Daily the desire to become a nurse became stronger. But hope was elusive in my current condition of weakness and exhaustion, and simply returning to a normal state was a challenging goal. I remembered my current doctor, who had actually encouraged me!

During my one-month's visit to the doctor, he showed me the letter he had written to my superior. The letter said exactly what he had told me.

No mention of this letter's contents was ever made to me by my superiors. All I could do was pray, rest, and hope. I felt I should be doing something. I was used to working and keeping busy. The summer months passed slowly. I was not used to a slow pace.

Because of the rule of silence, I remained in my room most of each day. In the first two weeks I was too tired to join the sisters for recreation at seven in the evening or for regular prayer time. I slept much of the time. The isolation was not healthy. After two weeks, ready or not, I insisted on being with the sisters for prayers and meals and recreation. It was difficult but necessary for my sanity. The first month was the hardest. The recuperation period was in total opposition to my ordinary convent life. Hurrying to get all the work done in a particular time frame was my ordinary pace. Now the slowest turtle passed me up a month prior, laughing.

The future was so uncertain. Many a time my thoughts drifted back to the success of the past year and the joy I had shared with my band members and their parents. I recalled the successful piano recitals of 105 students, the loyalty and success of the choirs, the happiness we had shared on many occasions that were special to the community of Morris.

The people of Morris were so giving. They breathed love, peace, joy, and a contagious energy. Working with these progressive, high-spirited people was an inspiration to me. They were interested in music and supported it. No request or demand was ignored. If money was needed, the ladies would get together and prepare a splendid dinner. All the proceeds were applied to the needy project.

When we needed new capes for the band members, the ladies put on a dinner, bought material, and sewed new capes in time for the Legion Parade. The whole town typically showed up for these dinners. For the second dinner, people waited in line for two blocks. The cooks ran short on food three times, but no one became upset. The people who were waiting in line made trips to the store for more supplies! It was a family project, whether they had family members in the band or not. More than enough money was collected for the project.

The town was one big family. These were true Christians with admirable values who loved and cared for one another. They made sacrifices cheerfully with no thought of recompense. Their reward was a prosperous community, and rightly so. God does not forget His children; He blesses them abundantly.

Three months of rest helped me to regain my strength, healed my ulcers, and above all, gave me an opportunity to examine my conscience thoroughly. I weighed my life and assessed how I had solved past problems. I thought about my mistakes and their consequences and whether I could change anything. Submission to superiors was a tough challenge and one not easily understood. Many conflicts and misunderstandings resulted from this difficulty. I often thought that God became a bystander within this structure, instead of remaining the God who is Almighty, all-knowing, all-powerful, and all-merciful. The question of obedience occupied much of this solitary time. The question was not whether we should be obedient or not, but rather whom we should obey. Hours of future meditation time would be filled with this question.

The August 12 celebrations came and went as usual. We saw new novices, eager to start a new life, testing their faith and strength of character. The newly professed sisters proudly wore their black veils, having conquered the rigors of novitiate training for two years. Now they were ready for their first assignments. They stood happy, eager, and full of life. Some would be very happy with their letters of obedience, some would be surprised, and others would be simply shocked at what would be expected of them. Fervently, I prayed for each one to receive a special blessing that would help them to look to Him for help always and to depend little on people.

FIFTH MISSION ASSIGNMENT: FOLEY, MINNESOTA

My turn for a new assignment came about an hour after the novices and newly-professed sisters received their letters. I tried to be calm as I walked to Reverend Mother's office, but my heart was pounding so hard and fast I was afraid it would arrive ahead of me. Breathless I entered at her greeting and sat down, swallowing hard. The conversation about my health started and ended on a happy note. She was happy I had recovered so well. No mention was made of any letter from my doctor.

My new assignment was presented calmly and decisively. I would go to Foley, Minnesota, to teach music, direct and accompany two choirs, and teach catechism.

The Reverend Mother added, "I hope you will be happy," and dismissed me.

Was I disappointed? Yes, but I knew I had to be obedient. I left her office with a prayer for her and one for me. At times I felt resentful, but I would squelch it before any anger set in. By now I had learned it didn't help to feel sorry for myself. In my heart I knew that some day, through unknown paths, I would become a registered nurse. I had to be patient.

Teaching again. My stay in Foley, Minnesota was one year. I had a full schedule of piano students, one of whom later won a six-year scholarship to the Vienna School of Music. He came to Little Falls on his return from Vienna and gave a concert in his teachers' honor at St. Francis High School.

Teaching catechism and conducting and accompanying two choirs was a much lighter load than I had carried the previous year. I resigned myself to the assignment and enjoyed my work as well as the companionship of the two sisters with me.

The year passed quickly, and to my surprise, I was transferred to the little mission at Browns Valley, Minnesota, on the eastern border of North Dakota. The duties were the same. It was a small western town filled with happy, bighearted cowboys with guitars, singing songs or whistling tunes. They were so happy to do something for you. "Much obliged" or "God Bless" was often on their lips, and it always came from the heart accompanied by a big smile.

A RAY OF HOPE

During the summer our Reverend Mother was elected for a second four-year term. A year passed and I was summoned to Reverend Mother's office. I was being transferred again. This time it was different. The discussion began with music and ended with nursing. The Reverend Mother could not understand why I wanted to be a nurse. I told her it had been my dream since I was a child. I never wanted to teach anything, especially music.

She was shocked. "Why didn't you say anything?"

I said, "I did."

She admitted she found it difficult to understand why I would prefer taking care of the sick to teaching music, especially after all the success I had. She also felt that I would be wasting a God-given talent. After some discussion of the difficulties I would encounter in nursing, she made the statement, "I don't think you are physically able to handle a nursing career."

I dared to answer, "I haven't handled the music career so well either. I am getting tired of ulcers and the diet that goes with ulcers. Would you please let me try nursing?"

The next question came quickly. "How much college education do you have?"

I was surprised she didn't know. I replied, "I have no college education. I graduated from high school twenty-eight years ago." I finally told her I never had any private music lessons of any kind: not piano, organ, violin, or any band instruments. This was all news to her.

"When did you start thinking about a nursing career?" she asked.

I told her the desire to be a nurse was always there since I was a child. She thought for a while, then she told me I was excused and that she would call me when she had made a decision.

A ray of hope was beginning to shine for me. I left the office very happy and grateful to God that this encounter had been peaceful and might possibly be fruitful.

CHAPTER 4

A New Career

Sixth Mission Assignment: St. Ansgar Hospital, Moorhead, Minnesota

Two weeks later I was called to her office again. She had made a reasonable decision. The Reverend Mother decided to send me to St. Ansgar Hospital in Moorhead, Minnesota, to work as a nurses' aide until I grew stronger. The assignment would help me get acquainted with hospital work in general. It was too late to apply for nursing school, which would have been too much for me at the time anyway since I wasn't completely well. I needed to build up my strength and make sure this was what I wanted.

I was happy about the assignment. I had been hoping all these years that someday I would have the opportunity to take care of the sick, and here was the beginning I'd waited for. I was forty-three years old, and it was time to start. "Thank You, God," was on my lips constantly.

A week later I arrived at St. Ansgar Hospital. What a sight! It was the largest building I had ever seen. It would be my home for a while, where I would see my childhood dream come true. My excitement grew when I thought of what the building held within. Here the mercy of God shone through for suffering mankind through the efforts of nurses, doctors, lab technicians, x-ray specialists, and nurses' aides, all working together, bringing God's love and healing to His people. The building covered a whole block. I envisioned it as a place containing all that was needed to help people recover from illness and disease.

As I studied the immensity of the place, I could only see the people's genuine concern for ailing humanity with no room for show. The plain, massive structure was inviting me to join the ranks of devoted, caring professionals and to give of myself that others may live.

I was so excited when we finally drove up to the front door of St. Ansgar Hospital. My happiness had reached its peak when I entered the building and was greeted by the sisters who worked there. They were truly happy to see me so excited about nursing. They were also short of both aides and nurses. This was a new beginning for me. After a delightful lunch, two sisters took me on a tour.

25th anniversary of Sr. Mary Jeannette's class in St. Francis Convent, Little Falls, Minnesota, on August 12, 1962; back row: 4th from L., Sr. M. Jeannette.

We started on the first floor. It was customary to visit the chapel first, which was at the south end of the main floor. Next we visited the administrative offices, a large dining room, a kitchen, the emergency room, the laboratory, and the x-ray department. We took the elevator to the second floor, the medical floor, which had two wings—medical and pediatric. It also included the intensive care unit. At the end of the medical unit was a large solarium where visitors and patients could spend time together. The third floor was reserved for labor and delivery on the north wing and surgical patients on the south wing. Psychiatric patients occupied the entire fourth floor. This hospital was one of the few which had accommodations for psychiatric care in 1960.

It was time for the evening meal. When I arrived at the sisters' dining room, my new superior told me to see her in her office at eight in the morning, when she would give me my assignment.

The sisters lived across the street in the former St. Ansgar Hospital. We each had our own private room, which was complete luxury to me. I enjoyed the space, privacy, and furniture. The room was comfortable and peaceful. The day's excitement had used up my energy, and I was ready to sleep in my new room.

The next morning we arose to beautiful sunshine loudly announced by the local birds. I was eager to start the day, happy, and at peace with God. We attended Mass after our prayers together and our half-hour of meditation. My heart was so full of joy and thanks that I wanted to burst out into singing, but as it had years before as I was a novice wanting to yell, our rule of silence prevented me. Our superior must have sensed it for she rang the bell at breakfast and declared recreation, which meant we could talk. Immediately the room buzzed with talking, laughter, and cheery welcomes. I sensed instant acceptance brimming with genuine sisterly love. Already I belonged here. What a glorious new beginning!

After breakfast my superior took my arm and led me to her office. She was highly respected by everyone, which was easily seen by even a stranger. She was down-to-earth, gentle, understanding, accomplished as an administrator, but humble in her dealings with doctors and the nursing staff. She was an example to the entire hospital. Every command and decision was given with love. Peace reigned in that place because of her walk with God; consequently, the hospital thrived. The sisters were so happy, so willing, so dedicated. To me it was heaven on earth, and I was grateful to be there.

What a change to enter a superior's office without shaking. We conversed as though we were long lost friends recently reunited. I sat across from her desk.

"I understand you are recuperating from a bout with ulcers. Are you feeling well enough to start working, or do you need more time to regain your strength?"

She said it with such understanding and love that I almost cried.

I replied, "I am so eager to get started. I've waited so long for this opportunity. May I start tomorrow? I have rested enough, and I feel ready to work."

With a big smile she assigned me to work on the medical floor and gave me a light work load until I had a good orientation and had time enough to settle into my new environment. I could have danced for joy.

The next morning my superior escorted me to the medical floor and introduced me to the staff. Again that pleasant, peaceful, and loving acceptance greeted me. The nurses' aides were kind and glad to have a helper. All sixty medical floor beds were filled. The head nurse was delightful and ensured that my orientation would be complete in three days. The senior aide was well trained in orienting new employees. How different this was compared to my introduction to teaching music twenty-five years ago.

I learned quickly how to care for the patients, enjoying every minute of waiting on them. Never in my entire life had I been so happy. It seemed as though God had prepared the right place and the right people at the right time so I could enjoy this humble beginning of my long-awaited nursing career. I felt privileged to be a nurses' aide, and I knew it would lead to the fulfillment of my dreams.

The days and weeks went by so quickly. Effortlessly I bounced out of bed at 5:00 A.M. with the bell's first ring. I was the first sister in chapel for prayer, meditation, and Mass. I was the organist for all services, for which I was happy. Keeping up with my music was important but would definitely remain in second place.

For several months everything went well. We had a full house three-fourths of the time. Many of the patients were residents of the three nursing homes in Moorhead, Minnesota, and Fargo, North Dakota. (The Red River separated these two large cities.) Good rapport existed between the hospitals and nursing homes.

A SETBACK BECOMES AN OPPORTUNITY

One day, I was assigned to care for ten patients. I bathed an elderly gentleman in his bed. (All baths were bed baths; we had no showers.) After his bed bath, I was supposed to transfer him to the wheelchair. This was no problem, and he looked forward to this change of position. On this day, however, he lost his balance. I caught him and with my left hand on the seat of the wheelchair, he turned around and dropped himself into the wheelchair and onto my left wrist. I felt a crack and sudden sharp pain. An aide came by to give me a message just in time to help me get my left hand out from under the patient.

The damage was done. My wrist started swelling fast, and the pain increased quickly. I was sent to the x-ray department and then to the emergency room, exiting with a cast on my wrist and a note saying, "Sister is excused from nurses' aide duty for six weeks. She is to return in six weeks for follow-up x-ray before returning to work."

I was completely unprepared for this turn of events and became anxious as many questions began to destroy my hopes and dreams. I went to see my superior, praying all the way to her office that she would understand and not ship me home. She smiled when I entered her office and quickly looked at me with pity. I explained what happened, and she erased my fears by saying how sorry she was and how painful it must be for me.

"Did they give you anything for pain?" she asked. I told her it was already taking effect. Her next statement was like a blessing: "Six weeks may seem like a long time, but don't worry. I hear such good reports from everyone on medical floor; I already have a new job for you. I want to introduce ward clerks on medical and surgical floors to relieve the nurses of some duties that can be handled by personnel who are capable and trustworthy for such a responsibility. I think it will be a great relief for the nurses. You can learn a lot about nursing if you work as a ward clerk. Do you want to try it?"

I didn't hesitate to say "yes." No wonder everybody loved and respected her. Her concern for each person's happiness came first. This kept the wheels of prosperity turning. Everyone happy, everyone working together, no strife, God's blessing on the household.

The next morning I reported for work on the medical floor as a ward clerk. My superior came with me and explained to the staff the duties and responsibilities of my new job. I answered the phone, delivered messages for doctors and nurses, and transcribed all doctors' orders on all patients, which were to be checked and verified by the head nurse. I also took phone reports of lab results and x-ray reports, waited on doctors as they came to make rounds, accepted medications from the pharmacy, and did whatever else the head nurse would request. I was the first ward clerk in the Moorhead–Fargo area.

The first two days were spent getting acquainted with the new work area, meeting the doctors, writing med cards, etc. All these tasks I found fascinating, educational, and interesting. I drank in all the knowledge I could find. I was learning names of medications as well as their strengths, purposes, and adverse effects. I listened to the doctors discussing among themselves the problems of their patients and the treatments the doctors had used with success. Nothing in the world could have drawn my attention and held it for hours at a time like this—learning how to care for sick people—did. I was full of questions. Everyone wanted to help, including doctors, nurses, and technicians. It seemed too good to be true.

ANOTHER HOSPITALIZATION

Three years went by swiftly. I had become quite accomplished in my job. I learned as much as I could about nursing and all the departments, and I loved all of it. Nothing had replaced nursing as the most important goal of my life. However, it would have to wait a little longer.

The ravages of my music career continued to do damage. For several months my ulcer problem kept reappearing, despite my pleasant work environment. We also lost our wonderful administrator and superior and were sent a replacement whose views differed completely.

Our new administrator (and superior to the sisters) did not approve of my job as ward clerk. The many responsibilities I acquired were given to me because I had proven that I was capable of handling all of them accurately and professionally. She felt a licensed person should hold my job. I was fully aware from the first day of her visit to the medical floor that my job was in jeopardy. My hopes and dreams seemed to be crumbling fast. The Reverend Mother agreed with my superior and stated that I belonged in music, since I had no education in nursing. I was devastated.

In two weeks I became ill with bleeding ulcers. I was sent off duty by the nurse in charge because she could see I was in pain. I was hospitalized the same day. The upper GI study the next morning showed a huge bleeding ulcer. I fainted in the x-ray department. A quick history of my many ulcers left the doctor no choice but to operate. I was scheduled for surgery the next morning. It was successful. They removed 70 percent of my stomach.

My recovery was speedy with no setbacks. I was up walking five hours after surgery and from then on I walked up and down the halls several times each day. I had learned well from previous surgeries to get out of bed soon and to keep walking.

Ten days after surgery, I had permission to return to my job provided I would avoid lifting heavy objects. *Never, never*, I promised myself solemnly, *would I let another ulcer into my life.* Thirty-one years later, I am delighted to report that not one ulcer has developed since then. Praise God!

In less than one week I would report to the Reverend Mother's office in Little Falls. I dreaded this encounter and rightly so. I left quickly as it was obvious to me that a battle would develop between nursing and music. I knew the profession to which I had been called. I believed that God plants a seed of hunger in each of us for a specific type of duty to our neighbor (which is everyone) and that such duty brings us closer to Him. Then He blesses us as we obey His calling. We, in turn, become a blessing to those we touch in that calling.

Another chance?

I arrived at Little Falls within three hours and was ushered into Reverend Mother's office at her request. Before walking in, I called on God for help. Strangely, I had no fear this time. I was ready to pour out my heart and render all my feelings for my desired goal of nursing. I knew the desires of my heart now. They were not accomplishments and recognition of achievement. I was happiest when I was working as a nurses' aide, giving baths, emptying bed pans, taking temperatures, making beds, and cheering up patients. This is the lowliest job in nursing, but it is also the most rewarding and fulfilling.

I felt I was giving the best in me for others' total well being, soul and body. There was more of me reaching out to help them than I could give through any other profession. My rewards were to see them get well and to enjoy the peace and happiness that I felt in rendering these services.

I sat down facing the newly elected Reverend Mother. Sensing that a third person was in the room, I looked around, but no other person was there. I congratulated her in her new position and assured her God's blessing through prayer and obedience. We spoke briefly about my stay at St. Ansgar Hospital in Moorhead. That led up to my taking over the conversation. I was very calm, confident, and sure of myself, making final statements that could not be questioned or misunderstood for wrong motives (such as stating only what I wanted to do or sounding as though I were in rebellion). My motive was clear to me: I believed God's Will was for me to enter the nursing profession. I was surprised at myself. So was the Reverend Mother.

"So you are saying that all you want out of nursing is to be a nurse aide?" she asked.

I calmly answered, "Reverend Mother, I am merely pointing out to you that in working in the lowest position of nursing I found the real me, which makes me a happy, productive member of the Community. God planted this seed in me when I was four years old. I felt very guilty charging piano students anything more than a penny for a lesson because I knew less than they did. I had no preparation for teaching music. I only taught music because of my vow of obedience."

She then asked, "If you have been out of school for twenty-eight years, you will find it very difficult to study again. You are almost forty-eight years old. The older you get, the harder it is to study and remember. I don't think you could pass the State Boards at your age."

I replied, "I feel the call to nursing so strongly; I would like to try it."

"I will have to think about it. I will call you when I have the answer," the Reverend Mother said.

One week passed before she called for me. She looked very serious.

"I still feel this is somewhat irregular, but I want you to go to Brainerd [thirty miles north of Little Falls] to the LVN Nursing School. They are taking applications for the next class starting in the fall. If they accept you, you will be in that class. Are you sure you want to do this?"

"I want to do this more than anything else," I answered, trying to control my delight. A knock on the door told me my time was up. I thanked Reverend Mother and left the room.

The next morning I was on my way to Brainerd. At least twenty students applied for the LVN program. I waited my turn and noticed the names being called alphabetically. I took my time completing my paperwork as I waited for my name to be called.

This was progress. *Maybe in one year I will be a nurse already*, I said to myself. What a happy thought! What a miracle! Just then my name was called. Prospective students were being interviewed in four booths. Three women and one man were interviewing. All the interviewers were instructors in the LVN program. The woman in the first booth introduced herself by name and occupation. Each interviewer asked me what my occupation had been up to this point, why I wanted to change careers, and why I wanted to be an LVN as well as several questions testing my knowledge of medicine.

To my surprise, the first instructor said to me, "You should enter an RN program. You are capable of handling much more than an LVN program can give you. You may go to Booth #2."

I got the same response from the instructors in Booths 2, 3, and 4. I was happy they thought I could possibly become a nurse, but an RN? In other words, I was not accepted in the LVN program. I wondered how this would affect the Reverend Mother?

I was called into her office three days later. The report from Brainerd had come in. I could see she was puzzled with the report. She had called the LVN school to see what the problem was and why I was not accepted in the LVN program. She did not believe the answer she had received and brushed it off as some weird mistake. Thus, she sent me to the nursing home at Breckenridge, Minnesota, to take care of the elderly.

Two days later I arrived in Breckenridge, feeling truly depressed. Just when I thought I was getting close to becoming a nurse, it had all fallen apart. I was hoping the superior of this place would understand my reactions to this turn of events. She had been one of my catechism students in my first mission at Elk River. She joined the convent at Little Falls during her last year in high school. We had never been stationed together since she had entered the convent.

We met at the front door of the nursing home. She had come out to welcome me, full of joy at seeing her catechism teacher of years ago. I too was full of joy as I remembered her genuine interest in catechism and church history classes. I always felt she would someday consecrate her life to God and care for mankind in a special way. She glowed with love and concern for everyone placed in her care. I was one of those lucky ones now. New hope was building up within me as we embraced in sisterly love.

We visited as we walked the halls of what used to be the Breckenridge Hospital, a three-story brick building with at least one hundred beds. Every bed was occupied. The residents were full of joy as they greeted us. Love had conquered their disabilities and fears as they received the blessing of their caregivers. As we entered the recreation room, able residents were baking goodies for everyone's afternoon snack. The happiness in this place was amazing, and the joy of serving one's fellow man was contagious among all ages.

As we came back to the first floor, we entered Sister's office. She asked me one simple question. "Are you still thinking of becoming a nurse?"

"Yes, but it does not look good," I answered glumly.

Her surprised look made me continue. I left nothing out regarding the last year at Moorhead and the attempt to enter LVN school. She was surprised, puzzled, and disappointed with the outcome.

She asked me, "Do you want to be an LVN?"

I explained that while I always wanted to be an RN, I would settle for an LVN license if I could care for the sick. I told her this had been my heart's desire my whole life.

"Well, then you should be an RN."

Immediately her wheels were turning. Summer school was beginning. Wahpeton College, North Dakota, was offering chemistry and writing classes for people interested in this type of work. Sister enrolled me in both classes. She explained to me the need for both these classes if I wanted to be a nurse. The classes would also help me get used to studying again. I would also learn what I was capable of.

I took an aptitude test and was surprised by the results. I scored much higher in social work than I did in music. I could only look forward now—no looking back or giving up.

I attended my first class in twenty-eight years on June 3, 1966. What a joy! In the class were seventeen boys and me. The boys treated me with great respect. They got together that first day and asked, "What do we call you?"

I explained that my name was Sister Jeannette, but all they had to say was "Sister," and I would answer because I was the only sister there.

They said "Sister, welcome to our class." I was touched at their kindness. With introductions taken care of, they settled down to business. The instructor smiled at this gentlemanly greeting and added his own welcome. He then began class. After a brief explanation of the course outline, he stated that for the three-hour lab on Tuesdays and Thursdays we would be paired off to work at our experiments together. The boy right across the aisle from me, Lyle, was my partner. He was very helpful in lab. He was bright, and he was a gentleman. I learned a considerable amount from him because he could explain things in a way anyone could understand. Naturally I was grateful. Because of his kind help, my final grade was a B+.

My writing class was taught by a woman. This class was fun and beneficial. A couple of months later, I wrote an article on "Music for the Aging" for a magazine. A year later I received a letter from Ireland asking if they could use my article there for several geriatric and music magazines. The proceeds from the article were used to buy an electric wheelchair with specially made hand gears for a resident with multiple sclerosis. We also bought other equipment for special disabilities of the elderly.

During the time I spent caring for the elderly at Breckenridge, I also taught some music to a recovering alcoholic. He was an Irishman whose repertoire consisted exclusively of Irish songs. We performed twice on live television in Fargo, North Dakota.

In the last week of May 1966 my superior and I decided I should visit our new Reverend Mother Yvonne who had been elected three months earlier. Reports of my schoolwork, aptitude test, and success with the recovering alcoholic were sent prior to my visit. My superior had also sent my article, "Music for the Aging." The rest was up to me. In my heart I knew I could and would be able to master the subjects of the nursing program. If I could pass the chemistry test, I could do the rest too.

I walked into Reverend Mother's office with more assurance than ever before. Patience and perseverance are a good way to start. Eventually the strength and power of these two qualities will break down the wall of resistance. Reverend Mother Yvonne was pleasant. She told me she had received the reports from my superior, including a copy of the magazine article. She was very pleased. Then she expressed concern for my health. I assured her I felt better than I had for a long time.

Reverend Mother then said, "You are interested in becoming an RN. I want to make sure you are physically fit, since nursing is not an easy job and will make many demands on your physical and mental abilities. You will be asked to make quick decisions that will be matters of life and death. You will also be responsible for correcting others when you recognize their mistakes, even doctors. I just want you to be aware of this. You will have ample time to think about it. If you still want to be an RN, apply for enrollment right now. You can discuss these things more in detail with your superior who is an RN. She has years of experience."

What a breakthrough. I was elated, humming out loud, not caring who heard me. The rest of the summer was spent reviewing what I had learned as a ward clerk, including a great deal about medicines for heart disease, kidney and liver disease, stomach problems, and infections. I also knew about narcotics and their uses. I had transcribed orders for all the medications ordered daily, and if I couldn't figure out why they had been ordered, I looked them up. By the end of the first year I could spot errors on doctors' orders and bring them to the attention of the nurse.

I had also learned how to check blood transfusions. One day a nurse was ready to give her patient a blood transfusion. I checked the type and showed her the blood was the wrong type. The nurse who had brought it from the lab had accepted it from lab personnel without checking it thoroughly. I learned the importance of accuracy from that incident. And this is equally true in dispensing medications. How fortunate for me to have had this head start.

June and July 1966 came and went with the regular festivities. I could say, "This year I will start nurses' training." But where I would go was still unknown. I wasn't concerned, since I was still celebrating the fact that I had finally received permission to become a registered nurse.

My superior had called me into her office during the last part of May to discuss various nursing schools. She had come well prepared.

Within the previous two years, the two-year Associate Degree RN program had been initiated. Many LVNs could not afford a four-year RN program but wanted desperately to raise their nursing statuses. The three-year nursing program had been dropped and the two-year RN Associate Degree program had been approved. Many LVNs had entered this program. The first two years had proven successful with 92 percent of the students passing the State Boards. The graduates and the four-year grads had taken the same state board exams. (Some of the four-year grads had not passed.)

A new two-year nursing school known as the Associate Degree Nursing Program had opened in Hibbing, Minnesota one year earlier with great success. Another two-year school had opened in Minneapolis. I realized I might not attend any of these if the Reverend Mother decided on another one. I knew which one I would choose if I were given the opportunity.

After speaking with my superior about these options, I left for Little Falls the next day. Reverend Mother was eager to see me. We discussed the two-year program and then she asked, "Are you saying you want to take the two-year program?"

I said, "Yes, at my age I had better take the shortest route. I don't want to walk across the stage with a cane on graduation day."

She laughed. Then, to my surprise, she asked, "Which school do you want to attend?"

Without hesitation I said, "Hibbing School of Nursing."

This choice pleased her because she knew the Benedictine Sisters had a convent in Hibbing, and she was sure they would let me stay with them. She had been there at one time herself. She permitted me to check out some of the other nursing schools.

I went to Minneapolis to visit their four-year program and the two-year program. I discovered that basically the two-year program prepares graduates for bedside nursing, and the four-year program prepares for administration. Bedside nursing was what I wanted. But some inner voice kept telling me, "Go to Hibbing." That was my first choice anyway.

I had no problem being accepted at Hibbing Jr. College. What a difference between Minneapolis and Hibbing! Big city vs. small town. I love small towns, and I liked the people much better. So Hibbing it was. I would report to Hibbing College on August 25 for my first class. The Benedictine Sisters happily agreed with Mother Yvonne that I should stay with them while attending the nursing program for the next two years.

The summer of 1966 was spent at the nursing home at Breckenridge. Until 1963, the sisters were not allowed to drive cars. At the motherhouse in Little Falls, a hired man named Albert took the sisters wherever they needed to go. But as times were changing everywhere, many more missions were established which necessitated more traveling. Consequently, more cars were needed, and sisters would have to learn to drive. This was a perfect time for me to learn with the rest of the sisters. In one week I was a licensed driver.

During that summer before nursing school, I also went on another annual seven-day retreat in Little Falls. A retreat of seven days included wake up at five in the morning, silence for seven days and nights, regular prayers at regular times, conferences three times a day, and to bed at nine in the evening. The purpose of the retreat was to commune with God alone, without distractions of work, to examine the past year's mistakes regarding Community living and the keeping of our vows. The retreat was the opportunity to make amends and to receive new insight into a more selfless life and into more fruitful Community living. This retreat regenerated me with happiness, joy, direction, and a new peace.

Following the retreat was August 12, which was a new beginning for me. I had no regrets. The struggles I had experienced for the past twenty-nine years of convent life had earned for me the strength and courage to start climbing toward that goal which seemed impossible to others but necessary to me. *The goal which had eluded me for years.*

Nursing School: Hibbing, Minnesota

A week later, on August 19, 1966, I left for Hibbing, Minnesota. My heart was singing the praises of my Creator, trying to match all of nature reaching upward to heaven with all its majesty. The bus made numerous stops along the way, but we still arrived in Hibbing on schedule. The Benedictine Sisters, with whom I would be staying, met me at the bus depot. They were such a merry group that I felt at home even before we arrived at their convent. Opposite this two-story building was the grade school, the church, and the playground. School was over, the children had gone home, and the sisters were free for the weekend. They had prepared for a get-acquainted party.

First, I was led on a tour of the convent. It was spacious, private, and bright. Plenty of rooms were available for all the teachers to prepare for classes, correct papers, study, or make decorations for their classrooms. A library was on the first floor. The kitchen sister was from Ireland. She had a continuous smile, especially when she did the Irish Jig. The Superior was young, kind, and understanding. She was a teacher also. On the second floor, each sister had a private room. When I saw the room they had prepared for me, I was ecstatic! They provided me with the best of everything. Each room had a sink, a commodity I had never had before. The large recreation room had a television. The chapel was large enough to accommodate all twelve of us.

The supper bell rang, so we all went downstairs to the dining room. Our Irish sister had prepared a delightful, nourishing meal with all the trimmings and a big "Welcome" sign for me. We ate heartily.

After evening prayers were said in chapel, we all met in the recreation room. We visited for an hour; some played games, some watched television. I remember how we compared Franciscan Sisters with Benedictine Sisters. We Franciscans wore brown and the Benedictines wore black. We followed the Franciscan Rule according to St. Francis of Assisi, while they followed the Benedictine Rule according to St. Benedict. They were more lenient in the choice of work. They were less strict in some things. Otherwise, we all followed much the same routine. My choice of nursing over music was a source of great interest to them; we needed two recreation hours to finish that discussion.

Saturday was spent quietly with the Superior, going over issues such as the temporary schedule I had received from the college, where I would eat meals, and so forth. She, in perfect harmony with well-known Benedictine hospitality, was concerned about every facet of my stay. We found that the sisters' schedule would be almost the same as mine, which made it easier for everyone.

On Sunday some of the sisters took me on a tour of Hibbing, a typical town of ten thousand in northern Minnesota. It was only one hundred miles from the Canadian border. The winters, spanning from September to the end of May, were very cold. The thermometer frequently dipped to forty or fifty degrees below zero. No one was shocked to see a bear walk down main street. Rest assured, he walked alone.

Monday was registration day for the college students. Nursing students stood in line with the others. We bought books and other essentials, making sure we were fully equipped for all our classes. I could barely carry all my books, which were piled up to my chin as I walked out of the building.

The college was only two blocks away from the convent. I looked around to see if any other sisters were registering. I couldn't see one. But this did not disturb me at all. Nor was I bothered by being the object of numerous stares. Evidently, most of the students had not seen a nun before. I was so elated to be here, and I was more than ready to begin.

Tuesday morning was our first class. Our nursing instructor was a strict, serious registered nurse who had evidently experienced every kind of accident and incident that required split second decisions. She had a hidden sense of humor that surfaced every once in a while. We paid close attention to her, waiting for the humor to emerge. No one wanted to miss these rare gems of wit. We thought she was unable to show sympathy, but we soon realized that she had a heart of gold. She was approachable. She

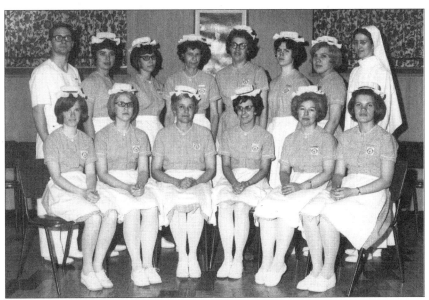

Hibbing School of Nursing, 1966. Sr. M. Jeannette in back row, far right. (Note updated head apparel.)

was a good listener and a good friend. She accepted us students just as we were. With no favoritism, she had time for each one of us. To me, she was the essence of truth, honesty, and sincerity as well as an excellent teacher.

Getting acquainted with classmates, fifteen of us, was fun. They treated me as one of the group. Many of them were interested in my life as a Catholic nun. Coming from different parts of the state, some had never been in contact with nuns of any kind, so they were interested in my attire and my choice of nursing. Soon they realized I was a normal human being, making mistakes like anyone else, and needing education because I do not know everything, just like other students. Many college students actually thought that nuns had a special connection to all knowledge.

Our instructors for anatomy, microbiology, physiology, chemistry, and English II were men, whereas women instructors taught all the nursing subjects. The nursing subjects included pediatrics, obstetrics, psychiatry, psychology, medical and surgical nursing, diseases, and pharmacology. Three extra but required classes besides these were given as six-week courses during the summer.

Sr. M. Jeannette's first year of nurses' training. Sr. M. Jeannette, smiling, at hospital desk.

The first six weeks were difficult. This was a period of adjustment to the schedule at home and at school. Besides learning how to study and divide my time among all the subjects, I noticed that I seemed to have fewer hours in the day. Often the hours ran out. One day I sat down to figure out how I could accomplish more in less time. I made some progress but was still unable to do everything necessary.

After an hour of trying to sort out the hours in the day, I began to sink. I nearly gave up. Had I taken too big of a bite this time? Was it really more than I could handle?

Some courses, like microbiology, required a lot of memorization, which took more time. *Who made up these names anyway?* I asked myself. Thank God I was good at spelling and pronunciation. Physiology, a study of functions of living organisms or their parts, a science of the vital processes of animals or plants, also included long names we had to remember. Anatomy also had difficult names to remember. I started to laugh at myself that night, so I put my books away and went to bed at one in the morning.

Five in the morning came too quickly. I had learned to pack my school bag the night before. This saved me a lot of trouble the next morning. All I had to do was quickly grab the bag and run.

After the first six weeks of school I felt much better about everything as I settled into the daily routine. I did well in my tests, which proved to me that I could master the subjects required for nursing. All the subjects fascinated me. Not one was boring because all were necessary to reach my goal.

My letters to Reverend Mother were joyful and positive. She was happy for me and was convinced by now that I could run this race. Her encouraging words lifted my spirits and washed away doubt. She spurred me on with new strength and determination.

From there on I had the attitude of a conqueror. How much we poor mortals need one another. A few kind words of love and encouragement can change your attitude, turn your life around, and help you grow. You reach a plateau and stay there for a while. Then later you move to a higher level. I felt like I was soaring from one level to greater heights. I knew these were inner changes wrought by God Himself.

Since I was four years old I had been running this race, coming up against many obstacles, but never giving up, until I broke through the barriers of opposition. I began to run faster as I saw time was running out, calling out to God more often because that was the only source left for me. He was the only one who understood me. He knew how to draw me to Himself through His love and mercy. On whom had I depended up to now?

I realized how blind I had been. Now He was opening my eyes to see Him leading the way, feeding me His grace and His strength for the last lap of the race. Just then a question flashed through my mind: what was the importance of running this race and winning? When I would finally become a registered nurse, what then? Would I be satisfied? What did I love more than caring for the sick on a daily routine? How would anyone know what I am thinking? Only one answer remained: God. I knew He cared.

Who had brought me through all the opposition, the struggles and illnesses? Not my Community; not my friends. No one could revive me after two hours following my first surgery but God, the all-powerful Almighty One. And after two hours, I should have been brain dead. But I wasn't. I could speak, recognize people, and move all my extremities. Who had taught me how to teach piano lessons when I had had no instructors? Who had given me the ability to teach without having taken any lessons myself? No one could have except God, who is almighty and all-powerful and who knows everything, especially our needs. Being obedient to my superiors, I could depend on God to supply the rest. This was my understanding at that time.

What a loving, caring, and generous Father! I have learned by now that He also wants me to share heaven with Him after I have finished my assignment here.

The telephone rang, bringing me back to the present. One of the sisters from Little Falls called. After some small talk, her voice took on a serious tone.

"I have some bad news about Reverend Mother," she said.

"What bad news?"

"She has been diagnosed with cancer," she replied.

There was silence on both ends. This was shocking news because Reverend Mother had looked so healthy when I had left in August.

She continued, "Reverend Mother has been looking well in spite of the diagnosis, which has been confirmed by a specialist. She needs all the prayers of the sisters. She requested I let you know."

All I could say was, "Thank you, Sister. Rest assured, she will be in my prayers."

The rest of the conversation did not seem important. We said our goodbyes, and I went to the chapel. I was so shaken with the news I found it difficult to pray. All the memorized prayers I had learned throughout my Catholic life seemed so empty and impersonal in a crisis like this. I felt so helpless. I wanted to personalize this prayer, no matter what it sounded like. I opened my mouth and started talking to God from my heart. The words came easily, to my surprise. I finished my prayer and left the chapel, feeling unusually good about having prayed that prayer. I felt such peace. That fear of God the Judge was not there. Instead, I sensed a beautiful closeness to a presence I could not see but knew was there. Could it have been God? I remembered my mother telling me, "God is everywhere. He knows your every thought. He is God."

The warmth of that intimacy lingered, and I did not want it to leave me as I was walking to my class. My thoughts were interrupted as I entered the classroom, but I determined to pursue this later.

My first year of training ended with this bad news: I had to stay at Hibbing for the required summer courses. The sisters kept me informed about Reverend Mother's progress. The news was encouraging. She was responding well to chemotherapy, even better than expected. I was relieved. Reverend Mother was about to continue as leader of the Community.

The summer months went by quickly for me. The weather was so accommodating; ideal for long walks after class every day. The sisters let me take care of some outdoor work, such as caring for the flower beds and doing some garden work. I recalled my childhood back home on the farm (without the tiresome chores of potato picking and hay stacking).

My second year of training started in late August. We continued our clinical work at the hospital with our supervisors in constant attendance. They were always there at our beck and call, instructing and performing every procedure once. The second time, we students did the procedures while our supervisors watched, approving or disapproving and correcting if necessary. Our hands often shook while we were being watched. The supervisors were very understanding, ignoring the shaking, guiding every move quietly and respectfully.

All the supervisors insisted on the privacy of the patient, verbal contact with the patient, explaining the next step before proceeding to start it, and being honest with the patient. We were also taught to be kind and gentle with every action. Every procedure was explained in detail, allowing the patient to ask any questions necessary to understand it before it was begun. The patient we were treating was always the most important person in our lives at that moment.

Each patient we treated was sacred to God. A sick person depends on the mercy of the one caring for him and, as a child of God, deserves to be treated with respect, dignity, and love. I loved every moment of this sacred duty to which I was called, treasuring every opportunity to learn how to help in every kind of illness, easing the pain, worry, and fear that it brings.

As much as I wanted to keep music out of my way while studying nursing, my past career came to light. The professor of music at the school happened to be from my hometown. His class met at 2:00 P.M. every day before one of my classes did. A number of my classmates and I came early one day and stood outside the door listening to the music students rehearse. The bell rang, and the professor and his class came out. We recognized each other immediately. He asked if I was teaching music in this vicinity.

"No, I am in the nursing class," I replied. This required some explaining. I tried to do it in one minute, as my class would be starting soon. That was all my classmates needed to know.

Soon we were having songfests while I accompanied on the piano and sang with the others. It was a lifesaver for all of us. Studies were tough that second year. We had many more exams, more papers to write, and precious little time to relax. All the students loved to sing, and I noticed the excellent baritone and tenor voices. We had good sopranos and altos too, outnumbering the two men in class. I introduced several numbers that were popular at the time in four-part arrangements. In a short time we learned all the numbers since all the students could read music. What a switch that was from thirty years prior when only the rich could afford to learn to read music.

By the end of four weeks, we had a varied repertoire worked up. One evening the new unofficial chorus was singing away when the door opened and our instructors walked in, applauding and demanding an encore. They had attended a boring meeting down the hall, and thinking it was Mr. Pappenfuss's class rehearsing, they decided to peek in and listen. They were overjoyed to realize the music was coming from the unofficial nursing class chorus! We sang all the four-part numbers for them, complete with some solo parts. The instructors were so impressed and delighted that they took us out for a treat.

But there was more to it than simply treating those poor, hard working nursing students. Already a conspiracy was afoot. Their minds were working overtime with this sudden stimulation from our surprise choral group. They requested we make public appearances as the only nursing program with a student choir. Several charitable campaigns were underway in the Hibbing area then. They were asking for donations for Crippled Children Care, Cerebral Palsy, and Mental Disabilities. The instructors asked if we would be able to perform in two weeks.

The students enthusiastically supported the plan. I wasn't sure we could get enough practice for three performances with our heavy schedules. Another nursing student played the piano very well, so I decided she and I could play at least two classical piano duets that I happened to have. I agreed to the deal if we had one public performance for all three charities. In two weeks the performance would be held in the college auditorium. The public was invited.

We gave our best for the three charities. People came out of curiosity and for the good cause. My choir was excited and delighted for the opportunity to perform. The concert was a huge success. We collected several thousand dollars, which was equally distributed among the three charities. The audience was generous and pleased with the performance, and the nursing program welcomed the good publicity. Our studies suffered a little, but the joy of doing something special for the children was worth it.

A week later we were studying obstetrics. After one week of study I was assigned to a mother who was due in two to three weeks. The husband would call me to come to the hospital when she was ready to deliver her baby. In the meantime, I accompanied her for her checkup at the clinic. The visit was an opportunity to get acquainted with my patient and to get her history. She was a mother with four children ranging from ages two to eleven. She was eager for her fifth child to be born. Her husband was devoted to the family and had a substantial income. The checkup was completed. Her blood test was normal, and the baby was doing fine. All we had to do was wait for the great day to come.

A week later my phone woke me up at 3:00 A.M. My patient was ready to deliver soon. She was on her way to the hospital. I came shortly after. The nurse in charge took me to the room, checked the patient's progress and the baby's heartbeat, and said, "She is all yours. If you want me to come, just press this button and I will be right in. She is only dilated to three centimeters, so it will be a while yet before she delivers."

Fifteen minutes later, I timed her contractions that were getting closer together, checked her, and determined she was six centimeters dilated. I decided to call the nurse because we were taught that after the first and second pregnancies, deliveries are usually more rapid. I wasn't taking any chances.

But the nurse wasn't coming and I had called three minutes prior. The patient's next contraction was long and hard. I couldn't wait. After that contraction, I got her on the gurney, wheeled her into the delivery room, and somehow moved her onto the delivery table when she started her next contraction. I barely had my gloves on in time to deliver the baby just as the nurse came in. She apologized for not getting there on time. She had been called to help a patient on the other end of the hall and had not heard the buzzer.

I was shaking considerably but grinning. The regular plan is this: the charge nurse is always present for a delivery, the doctor delivers the baby, and the student nurse is there to observe and learn. For this event, we practiced a new plan: The doctor was the last one on the scene, the charge nurse was unaware of the event, and the student nurse delivered the baby. The mother was doing fine. The husband just walked in to hear the newborn's first cry when the doctor walked in half asleep. I was grading the newborn's progress when I observed an abnormality. The baby had a clubfoot.

I heard the mother just then saying to her husband, "The baby is so beautiful, so perfect." Her words, "so perfect," wrenched my heart.

What a bitter disappointment she would have to endure as she faced the consequences of this abnormality. There would be monthly visits to the doctor, the removal of each old cast, and replacements with new casts until the foot was corrected. But thank God, he would be able to walk normally some day. I whispered a prayer for them, hoping the parents' faith would help them envision the miracle of total healing in the end and that their love would give them strength and patience until the healing was accomplished. They loved this child very much; that was obvious.

A week later our class arrived at Fergus Falls, Minnesota, to do our internship in psychiatry at the state mental institution. I dreaded this part of nursing because I knew nothing about psychiatry, which is the branch of medicine concerned with mental and emotional disorders. Most people knew only a little about it, but it was becoming more prevalent in the medical profession. Many people would not accept the reality of mental illness and the need for psychiatry. People tended to feel insulted if their doctor referred them to a psychiatrist because few people knew what it really meant. Today it is accepted by the majority of people and has helped many people live more peaceful, productive lives. In only the past twenty years, tremendous advances have been made in the areas of brain chemicals and the treatment of mental illness caused by imbalances in these chemicals.

We students lived in a two-story building about two blocks away from the main part of the institution. The mental hospital was a two-story brick building with a high wire fence around it. Doors were always locked, so we made sure we arrived in time for classes. We could go by tunnel, but it was spooky.

One rainy evening we decided to go back to our living quarters through the narrow tunnel. We noticed cells on either side separated by a thick cement wall. We could see into the cells through the wire fronts. Stopping to examine the interior, we saw stark relics of the past: restraints for the mentally ill consisting of iron ankle bracelets welded onto a cement block in the ground. We were shocked. Although the cells were empty, the reminders were crude and frightening.

We kept moving on when suddenly a man's head stuck out of a wall and leered at us. We jumped and wanted to turn back but decided to continue on. Our two men students assured us they would handle any problem for us. We passed the man who scared us. He sat on a stool in the far corner of the cell. He looked at the ground floor in front of him as we went by. No other specters appeared, and we arrived safely at our living quarters. Full of questions, we decided to corner our instructors in the morning before class.

We went to bed wondering if the man in the tunnel was confined to his cell and, if so, why. The tunnel adventure brought nightmares to some students and total insomnia to others. Daybreak was most welcome. We wanted answers.

Our instructors were not at all surprised at our questions when we told them the tunnel experience. Last year's class, of course, had asked all the same questions. We learned that in the late nineteenth and early twentieth centuries, before psychiatry, the mentally ill who were unmanageable were considered demon possessed. If other methods of control failed, patients were placed in these cells. These patients were usually strong men, although at times mentally ill women had to be placed here as well for the protection of the more subdued patients in the regular wards.

Now, with proper medication, the cells have no further purpose. The medication Mellaril was introduced in mental hospitals around the time of my nursing education (1950s to 1960s). The results were astounding. If they continued on this medication, some patients could even return to their families. Our instructors pointed out to us that the patients at this facility were less dangerous than people on the streets were.

The tunnel man? One of our instructors explained, "He's been here the past three years. His actions are somewhat strange at times but he is perfectly harmless. He is allowed to go about as he pleases. He has no one, not a relative or a friend, so he claims this place for a home until he can be placed in some other environment. His problem is he cannot take the responsibility of taking his medicine." The question and answer session was completed and we were satisfied.

We met every type of mental disability. We studied each patient, his or her problem, the mode of correction, and the medications used to help him or her cope with life. We were assigned several patients from different categories, and we wrote a case history of each. Our stay in Fergus Falls lasted six weeks and proved to be very interesting and educational.

Our internships of pediatrics, medical, and surgical nursing remained. Surgical nursing included operating room (OR) instruction. My days in the operating room were exciting. The first day of the one week I was scheduled to be in the OR was the coldest day of February—fifty degrees below zero. I walked the eight blocks to the hospital at 7:00 A.M., wearing three pair of heavy socks, two pair of slacks, two heavy sweaters, a heavy overcoat, three scarves, and a winter cap under my veil. My boots came up to my knees. The only visible part of me underneath the heavy layers was my eyes peering through a pair of glasses. Two pair of mittens failed to keep my hands warm. By the time I arrived at the hospital, I was seeing red everywhere. The sun's rays bounced off the pure white snow banks, nearly blinding me. No cars would start until later in the day.

The last lap, the eight stairs leading to the front of the hospital, was the worst. My boots were frozen stiff. Because ice covered the steps, reaching the eighth step took a while; I climbed the last two on my knees. I entered the hospital and sat down on the first chair I could find. One of the nurses came by and informed me that surgery had almost been canceled. Everything was frozen and the system had broken down, but the generator had just kicked in. The surgery would begin thirty minutes later than scheduled; the surgeons were scrubbing in.

I went to the locker room, unwound myself out of various wrappings, and went to the surgical suite. The patient whom I had cared for over the last five days was being prepared for abdominal surgery. She was an elderly lady in her seventies, feisty, fussy, funny, and alert. The surgeon decided that sodium pentothal would be too risky as her anesthesia. Instead she would receive a spinal tap, which meant she would be awake throughout the surgery.

For a spinal tap, the doctor inserts the anesthetic in the subarachnoid space in the spinal column. This deadens the body from below the diaphragm down.

During the surgery, the main surgeon asked the patient questions, which she answered readily. She appeared to be amazingly calm. Finally the surgeon noted she still had her appendix. He explained to her that it might be wise to remove it now if she wished. The matter was settled quickly. She responded clearly with, "Remove it." The surgery went very well with no complications. This experience helped me to decide in what part of nursing I wanted to work. My decision for now was bedside nursing on medical, surgical, obstetric, and pediatric wings. The emergency room fascinated me as a sideline.

During this time in 1966, the Franciscan Sisters decided to modify our apparel. We were allowed to retain the long wool dress (called habit) or to change to the short dress of the same material and continue to wear the veil. Very few kept the original habit. Within the next year, we were allowed to wear secular clothes as long as they did not offend modesty. These changes were quite a shock to some but welcome to the majority of sisters. Within a short time, the veil was also discarded. I welcomed the change wholeheartedly. Also, our names were changed to our baptismal names. I was now Sister Anne.

I was enjoying every moment of my two-year training, almost hoping it would never end. The college, the hospital, and the new group of sisters seemed to work together well. I was happy to be there. Classmates became dear to me, and instructors brought out the best in us. I was looking forward to Christmas, only one month away. This year I would stay at Hibbing, spending time caring for geriatric patients because this was my only opportunity for obtaining this experience. Our Community had several nursing homes, so I wanted to take advantage of this offer.

On December 1, 1967 five feet of snow covered the ground. The temperature had been forty to fifty degrees below zero daily. This morning warmed up, but by the afternoon a storm was brewing. Sleet and snow were predicted; the temperature was to turn very cold around midnight.

I remembered my father taking us along for our one and one-half mile trip to church for Midnight Mass on Christmas Eve. We did not travel by car or horse-and-buggy or sled; we walked. My father would walk ahead making sure the path was clear. Our whole family made this trek. In those days we still fasted from noon on—no food or water until after Midnight Mass and our slow walk home. By 2:00 A.M. we were extremely hungry. The feast of Slovenian raisin bread and homemade sausage, hot coffee, homemade doughnuts, apples, and popcorn lasted until half past five in the morning, when we did chores.

As I was remembering all this I could almost taste the delicious food we had. The nostalgia made me lonesome. I sat there reminiscing about those loving, caring, God-fearing years as we grew up on a small farm, which yielded everything we needed during those desperate years of the Great Depression. We learned to work for a living without pay, sharing the proceeds with one another, without envy for one another, not trying to excel to gain favor, but to contribute as much as we were able to give to the benefit of the whole family.

We were so happy on Christmas Eve when we found our stockings, which we had hung up, each bulging with an apple and two popcorn balls. Each child received the same. We had no toys. Nobody complained. I've never seen such genuine happiness since. We prayed together as a family before and after meals, said the rosary at nine in the evening, then went to bed with happy thoughts and peace in our hearts. Sleep came quickly as did chore time at 5:30 A.M.. We all rose at the same time, did the chores together, and ate together. We always knew where every family member was. This same love and care extended to our neighbors. If they needed help, we were there to help them. If we needed help, they came to our aid. Neither family expected any recompense.

I wondered why these values weren't promoted in the convent. What was wrong, and when had it gone wrong? Were the ways of thinking and living outmoded? Were they stupid, old-fashioned, and obsolete? Where were the happiness and the peace of mind that had made life so worthwhile and secure despite the poverty we endured at home?

All the rules and regulations of convent life did not bring the love, peace, and joy I had expected when I made my vows. The sisters could have been a real family; they were not. We called ourselves a Community! The environment in Hibbing reminded me, unexpectedly, of home. Already I dreaded leaving Hibbing after graduation in June. Did I want to continue the life I had so far in the convent? Should I even be thinking these thoughts? Vows were not to be broken. They were made for life. Who could help me?

My thoughts stopped there because I received a long distance telephone call. My brother Father John called from Onamia. Father John was stationed at a Catholic parish about thirty miles from home. Dad had called him and had asked to be taken to Onamia Nursing Home two days ago. That was interesting. My three priest brothers and I had tried for the last ten years to convince Dad to go to any nursing home he wanted, and Dad's answer was always a definite

"No; I can take care of myself." This was true, but he would at least have companionship and nourishing meals in the nursing home. He was now ninety-two years old but as spry as a fifty-year-old man.

Father John and I both wondered why Dad's sudden change of heart. We remembered how he had sacrificed everything twenty-two years earlier when he went to the nursing home in Little Falls with Mother, who had suffered a stroke one year be-

50th wedding anniversary in Little Falls, Minnesota. Back row L to R: Fr. Joe, Fr. Frank, Fr. John and Tony. Front row L to R: John Sr., Agnes, Anne in traditional habit, 1955.

fore their fiftieth wedding anniversary. He told us he had to go with her or people could say he had divorced her, which was not true. He was blessed for doing so—they celebrated their fiftieth in grand style with the three priest brothers at the altar for the Mass. Friends and relatives from three towns filled the sisters' chapel. It was glorious! After a beautiful dinner served by the sisters, my father wanted to dance. All his life he had loved to dance. All the ladies from the three towns lined up for their turns. He danced from then on until supper and after supper until 9:00 P.M. What a happy man and a wonderful dancer!

Now he was in a nursing home of his own choice. We were all happy about it. I was sure he had brought his harmonica along. He loved to play it and dance at the same time. He had such perfect rhythm. Father John assured me he would check on Dad every week and keep me informed. We were all relieved.

I returned to my studies as usual. There was no time to waste. I was looking forward to working with the senior citizens during Christmas vacation. They would be residents of several different nursing homes in the area. The hospital had one section reserved for these precious people, and if patients had to remain in the hospital for Christmas they would get special attention, I was told. Just like the patients at Breckenridge Nursing Home, they were very special, according to our instructors. Since geriatrics was not a part of our curriculum, I had to prepare for this on my own. Fortunately, the chemistry class I took in Wahpeton, North Dakota, saved me many hours of study. My credit had been accepted, so I had time for extra studies like geriatrics.

Less than a week after my dad entered the nursing home I received a call from Onamia Nursing Home stating that my father was dying. I could not believe it. The sister who called told me that he was doing so well until that afternoon. Around five in the evening he became very tired. He had been playing his harmonica for the residents. When the sister brought his supper tray, he asked her if he could lie down for a while. She assured him she would keep his meal warm for him. She checked on him an hour later. His breathing had become somewhat difficult at times but just for a short while. He woke up later when she came in, and he asked for something to eat. He said he was feeling fine. He ate everything on his tray. She told him he could stay in bed and rest as it was getting late. She checked his condition an hour later, and he was clearly in heart failure. The priest was called to give him the last sacraments. He was alert during this time but fell asleep again. That was when the sister notified me.

A snowstorm had raged outside all day and the predictions were not good. The roads were icy, and traveling would be dangerous. The sisters were so kind. They arranged for someone, a dependable driver experienced in Minnesota's unpredictable weather, to take me to Onamia. We left Hibbing at eight that evening. Snow was still falling, and the roads were icy. We drove four and one-half hours to cover 120 miles, but we did arrive safely.

I entered the hospital half an hour past midnight. The sister who had called me met me at the door. I could tell she had bad news for me. Dad had died a half-hour before I arrived. He went so quietly and effortlessly; like my mother had, he just slipped into eternity.

We went into the dining area. Sister had prepared a lunch for us before we came. She was weeping with me. She finally wiped away her last tear and said, "Your father was a saint. Everybody loved him dearly. I feel like I've lost my own father. When he came here, he was using a cane because ice was on the ground. He came by the desk and stopped, looked down one hall, turned and looked down the other hall, and said, 'Yes, this is a good place to die.' He had a smile on his face. Your brother did all the admission, and I took your father to his room. He was so pleased. He must have known he was going to die soon. He was a prayerful man, an example to us all."

I asked where Father John was, and the sister said, "We have been trying to reach him all day. He is supposed to be in Minneapolis at the Crosier House, but the storm was worse there than here. Don't worry; we'll find him. He must have stopped somewhere to wait for better weather. The storm is expected to clear by morning."

The rest of the family had been notified. Father John was reached at the Crosier House in Minneapolis the next morning. He was back to Onamia by noon to make all the funeral arrangements. I stayed for the funeral two days later. I felt so peaceful about Dad's death as I stood by his coffin remembering his faithfulness to God and his wonderful care and concern for his family. He looked so peaceful. I could see him walking through the gate to heaven. God stood there to welcome him with the words, "Well done, my faithful servant."

The church in St. Stephen was filled to capacity. My three priest brothers celebrated the funeral Mass. The parish priest delivered the eulogy, extolling the exemplary life of a humble farmer whose dedication was an example not only to his family, but also to the whole world around him. Everyone who knew him expressed the same sentiments.

He was laid to rest next to Mother who had died in 1960. I returned to Hibbing immediately after the funeral. The only member of the family who was unable to come was my sister Mary. She lived in Tulsa, Oklahoma. My brothers were all there, and I had a wonderful visit with each one of them. Another chapter of our lives had closed rather unexpectedly.

The Home Stretch

Making up missed classes was not difficult. My instructors and several classmates gave me notes on all the subjects. We were ready to start classes in pediatrics. After we would return from Christmas vacation, we would be assigned certain children to learn how to care for them, meeting the special needs of each child and his individual medical problem.

I was assigned a three-year-old girl who had just been diagnosed with spinal meningitis. Anyone with this diagnosis is immediately placed in isolation. The patient had to be in a room alone with no visitors except the doctor and the nurse. This disease is highly contagious. Isolation protects caregivers from the disease. The doctor and nurse caring for an isolated patient must gown in isolation attire, including mask and gloves, every time they enter the room. These precautions also protect the patient. Before leaving the room, the caregivers remove the isolation apparel, taking care not to contaminate themselves or their clothes. The bacteria may not be brought out of the room.

In this case, the mother was allowed to visit her child. She had to observe the same procedures for isolation. She was allowed only one visit per day because of her other children. The little girl missed her family the first two days, but after having such frequent visits from her total care nurse, that is, me, she began to call me "Mommy." I was gone on Sunday, my day off, and the next morning the nursing staff told me she cried for her "Mommy" all day. When I entered her room, she screamed "Mommy!" Everyone on the floor heard it.

Patients do tend to become attached to the one who cares for them. Nurses have to learn how to handle these emotional attachments. Sick children are more dependent than older patients are. My instructors took this opportunity to instruct the whole class thoroughly on this subject the next day. The little girl recovered completely and was taken out of isolation. Two days later she was discharged. Happily, she clung to her real mother all the way out and threw me a kiss. I was relieved.

We started our medical and surgical classes in late February. We were on duty at the hospital every morning doing our clinical studies of different types of patients. Afternoons were spent in the classroom, learning about diseases of the different systems of the body, various surgeries, and patient care before and after surgery. These two classes brought all our studies to a climax, and they were the most interesting. Medical and surgical nursing brought all the previous subjects to life by integrating all our learning up to this point. This made me more certain than ever that bedside nursing would be my specialty, my forte. We had no hours to spare, and the midnight oil burned nightly. The last three months of school passed quickly.

Now we began to think about graduation. I continued to have many doubts about returning to Little Falls to wait for an assignment in nursing. Perhaps because I entered the convent at nineteen, I was greatly affected now, at age fifty, by the school and the Benedictine environments. The Benedictine Sisters accepted me as I was. Without realizing it, I was becoming alienated from the Franciscan Sisters of Little Falls. I had matured almost overnight. I didn't know where I belonged. I had no time to ponder this question since my precious time was needed for studying. Our class had been recently informed that our two-year program graduates would take the same state board examinations as the four-year graduates. We studied even harder.

The first week in May I received a call from Reverend Mother Yvonne. She was wondering what day graduation would be. I told her it was set for June 6 at ten in the morning. She was making arrangements for a group of sisters to attend and bring me back to Little Falls the same day.

Before I could think or stop myself, I said, "What makes you think I want to come home?" *Let's settle this here and now,* I thought. *You might as well learn my true feelings for the first time. I am tired of this game.* These were the thoughts racing through my mind. I had no fear.

"Reverend Mother," I continued, "I dread the thought of coming home. I am tired of all the opposition to my being a nurse. I am tired of being pushed around as though I am a mental case and cannot think for myself. I have accepted the talents God gave me, and I have used them to the best of my ability. Above all, God had placed a great desire in me many years ago to care for the sick, and I am ready to do it. Is the Community ready to accept me in my new role as a nurse or not? After many humiliations, you allowed me to try what seemed impossible. I thank you for that, but I need the assurance of acceptance, or I will remain here until I am accepted. I have been treated like a decent human being here. I feel loved and accepted. I owe them so much for all the encouragement they have given me when the going was tough.

"Where was my Community these past two years? Are they waiting to hear that I flunked the course? If you cannot promise me a better life, more understanding from my sisters, and acceptance as I am, I prefer to stay here."

A ton of weight dropped off my shoulders. Incredibly, I felt no remorse in speaking my mind. No shame, no fear; I was cleansed.

For the first time in thirty years I was able to make a stand for honesty and truth. What had made me say all this? Was I losing it or was I finally coming to my senses? Suddenly I realized what humility was not. Humility does not mean letting people trample over you. No, humility is honesty; it is facing the truth about yourself and others to make things right.

Reverend Mother's voice was trembling when she answered. "Sister, how long have you been feeling this way? I know many of the sisters doubted your decision to become a nurse, but I feel they are changing their minds about your capabilities. You are so talented in music that your nursing decision was hard for me to understand too. Please give us another chance. I promise you I will stand by you and I want you to let me know the minute there is a problem. I am asking you again, please come home."

"If I do come home, where do you plan to have me work?"

"I had planned on starting you at St. Gabriel's Hospital here at the motherhouse. They have been asking for you and are eager to have you on the staff. There is a wide range of opportunities here for you to pick for your specialty," she replied.

I said, "I know I have a vow of obedience, and I can honestly say I have until now obeyed by accepting the most difficult assignments without complaining or arguing. But I feel used and manipulated, and if this continues I will have to refuse, to protect my sanity. I can no longer live under such trying circumstances as I have in the past and remain normal mentally. And if that would happen, of what use would I be to the Community? I understand that St. Gabriel's Hospital is run by secular administration entirely and not by the sisters. Am I correct?"

"Yes, that is correct."

"What about the departments?"

"They are also run by seculars. Only three sisters work at the hospital: one in the record room and two nurses on medical floor."

I answered, "I want to think this over and pray about it. I am glad I had this opportunity to speak out my true feelings. I thank you for your kindness in listening. This is the first time I have been allowed by a Mother General to defend my position."

She said, "I too am glad we had this talk. I hope and pray it will help you to make the right decision. I, for my part, will do all I can to make your future more pleasant. I will call you next weekend, for I am concerned. I had no idea you were so burdened, for which I am truly sorry. Please forgive me."

She was obviously sincere. I calmly replied, "Reverend Mother, I forgive you. I forgive all the sisters. But I cannot take any more of the same. This has to stop if I am expected to be fruitful in my work. I feel sisters should support one another in sisterly love, if we understand or not. God is still in charge, and He does not owe anyone any explanation. I am fulfilling His desire in me, and that makes me happy."

We said our goodbyes. I hung up the phone and took a deep breath. I could not believe I had said all those things. Effortlessly the thoughts and feelings had come out, as though I were reading them out of a book. Sensations of relief overwhelmed me. I was at peace. Finally, I was no longer carrying the burden alone, a burden of guilt for being unable to meet the demands placed on me. This burden had come with my first assignment in 1939. The weight of this burden had never left my spirit. It had pressed down on my happiness and severely damaged my health.

I realized the present Mother General was progressive. She did not try to sanctify the vow of obedience by using stern commands, forcing the inferior to submit, without any consideration of the inferior's feelings. This Reverend Mother did not sanction the practice of sending sisters into work positions with inadequate preparation.

The uncertainty and stress felt by sisters unable to perform their assignments brings fear and inevitably curtails spiritual growth. I saw a ray of hope for the Community with Reverend Mother's leadership. She realized that God was still in charge, above all leaders, and that leaders had to submit to God's direction in the lives of those entrusted to them. The only way a Community can exist and progress is through love for one another, and that love has to start with those in authority for each individual member. Love conquers all. A military type of leadership fails.

I felt the lightness, having cast off the bonds of many years. We finished the rest of the school year. Reverend Mother called as she had promised. She was happy to hear me say, "Yes, I will give you all another chance. I request the same for myself."

Graduation Day

Reverend Mother made arrangements for a group of sisters to attend the graduation and bring me home with them after the festivities. Only one week remained of nursing school. It was less painful now to think of the separation from my newfound friends. We prepared for the great day, a day of triumph for me. I had almost lost that dream, but God had provided perseverance to complete the program, to reach my goal.

The reality of graduation set in more clearly as we tried on our crimson robes and tassels and practiced our march to the auditorium stage. The two years of intense study had passed quickly, and some of us questioned whether we were adequately armed with what we had learned in such a short time. The responsibilities of a registered nurse are many and frightening, to say nothing of the state board examinations we had to face to prove our adequacy in this sacred profession.

June 6, 1968 arrived with abundant blessings. Rain had fallen the day before, cleansing the air and preparing the earth to display its beautiful green carpet of healthy grass. The skies were cleared of all the clouds to give way to the splendor of the sun's rays, promising a bright future to those who had struggled to renew their minds with timely knowledge of how to love and care for the sick and bringing restoration to suffering humanity.

The sisters from Little Falls arrived early in the morning. Two of my classmates were able to come, which was a pleasant surprise. The encounter was emotional, too, because years had passed since we had gone on different assignments. The Franciscan Sisters met the Benedictine Sisters, who showed their Benedictine hospitality and skills at entertaining. I was whisked away by one of the group to my room to fix my hair so I would look presentable for this exciting public occasion. I wore a navy suit with a white blouse and high heeled shoes.

All the sisters, both Benedictine and Franciscan, attended the graduation exercise. My sisters hugged me and whispered in my ear, "We are so proud of you." I was visibly elated. Seldom if ever was any day as great as this one. I have always remembered it vividly. Perhaps the longer one holds a goal, the greater its realization. Further, I could say goodbye to the past and start my new life as a nurse with good and happy thoughts and with no regrets.

As we waited for graduation to begin, it occurred to me that this would be the first graduation of mine I had ever attended! I missed my grade school graduation because my mother was ill and I had to stay home to care for my brother Tony, then two and one-half years old. Rheumatic fever prevented me from participating in my high school graduation. How laughable to wait fifty years for one's first graduation!

Huge bouquets of roses perfectly adorned the front and sides of the stage. The students looked at each other and smiled as the dignitaries walked onto the stage. No time was lost with the proceedings. Our major goal was to get our diplomas without tripping. We all wore high heels, so the cap and gown could be a trial. No one fell, our fears dissolved, and we all navigated safely back to our places.

After the graduation we were escorted to our main classroom where we were served our farewell dinner. All the sisters and relatives were invited to eat with us. Flowers, banners, and good wishes adorned the classroom. Our instructors had arranged this. Some musical entertainment by the college students followed the meal.

Then came the difficult part: farewell speeches from our instructors. Everyone cried. These instructors were special people. I remember each one clearly. They were truly dedicated individuals. They gave of themselves wholeheartedly and helped all of us understand that to be a nurse is a sacred profession which bids the best in each of us.

Final goodbyes were trying. The school asked us to keep in touch, especially about first jobs. The staff members wished us well in our exams in two weeks and gave us much hope for a successful nursing career. Our class had an outstanding record of accomplishments.

Classmates' goodbyes weren't so difficult because we would be spending two full days together in Minneapolis in two weeks, sweating over our exams.

Finally at five that afternoon we were able to part with our caps and gowns and return to our homes. The sisters served an evening lunch during which we had a chance to visit for the last time. They were all so happy for me. I tried to express my gratitude to the Benedictine Sisters who had taken such good care of me and given me the support I had needed so badly. We shared so many good laughs over the past two years, warmed by many bowls of hot oatmeal before bedtime when the temperature outside was fifty degrees below. We were still laughing when we said our farewells, easing a little the pain of separation.

Five Franciscan Sisters, three large suitcases in the trunk and large boxes of books and papers weighed the car down nearly to the surface of the road. Along the way, after driving through one of the larger cities, we took a shortcut to Brainerd. After one mile the shortcut turned out to be a dirt road. We were in the middle of nowhere, when we all heard a "pop" and said, "We have a flat tire." We couldn't see any houses, only trees and bushes. So two of us started walking down the road hoping to find some living being who could help us unload the trunk to find the spare tire. About half a mile down the road, a car came driving toward us. It stopped and the driver asked us if he could help us, since he guessed we had car trouble. We thanked him for stopping, and he drove us back to our car.

He had the whole problem taken care of in a short time. He refused to take any payment, adding simply, "It was my pleasure to help you ladies."

The town of Little Falls was asleep when we came home shortly before midnight. We were ready to join them in sleep after our day of excitement and surprises. The convent was darkened and quiet. I was shown to my room on the second floor. Peace and quiet were welcome and sleep came quickly.

Nursing

I awakened at the sound of the bell announcing to me that I was back at the motherhouse. Those two years at Hibbing seemed so short. The routine here had not changed: morning prayers, meditation, Mass, and breakfast. Silence during meals was still observed as we listened to the spiritual readings of St. Thomas à Kempis and others chosen by the Mother General.

After breakfast I made my usual visit to chapel, thanking God for the wonderful two years in training, my new acquaintances there, the graduation, my sisters, the Benedictines, and the safe trip home. A special prayer went up to God for the kind man who had changed our tire.

A tap on my shoulder made me look around. It was Reverend Mother. She looked so well in spite of her bout with cancer. She asked me to come to her office. I followed her as we walked in silence. After closing the door, she faced me with tears streaming down her face, embraced me, and said, "You can't imagine how relieved I am to see you home. I was so afraid we were going to lose you."

I smiled and said, "Reverend Mother, I am going to hold you to your promise. I am glad I am here, and I am looking at this with a positive attitude. I have you to thank for letting me follow my dream. I have no bitterness in my heart toward anyone; I am at peace now. This is a good way to begin my life as a nurse. I did not have peace until you showed me you believed in me and trusted me. Thank you for listening and understanding the night you called me. I kept my frustrations to myself all these years; it was time I got rid of them."

She agreed and added, "You have the right attitude and a big heart. You will do very well. I would like you to go to the hospital this morning to see the director of nursing. He will give you the schedule."

"That's music to my ears, Reverend Mother. I will go now."

The hospital was familiar to me. It was a three-story building. The main floor had a chapel, which was seldom empty. The administration had its offices to the right from the entrance. The emergency room was next and then the morgue. The dining room and kitchen were in the next section as well as a continuance of more offices.

The second floor provided space for the lab and x-ray departments, surgical suite, intensive care unit, and operating rooms. The third floor was known as the obstetric department, nursery, and delivery rooms. The units on all the floors were much larger than the ones in Hibbing Hospital.

I found the director of nursing who was also the anesthetist. He was the father of ten children and a very kind, helpful person. He was approachable and a person who put people at ease. I told him I had state board exams in two weeks but that I would like to get started. He was kind and thoughtful. First, he wanted to acquaint me with the surgical and medical floors, and possibly the intensive care unit. Medical and surgical patients would help me review my treatment skills. I was happy for this assignment.

I spent one week on the medical floor, then the next on surgical. This was a good test of my skills. Surgical floor had its thirty-eight beds filled all week, and the medical floor had almost the same. I prepared many patients for surgery. That meant inserting nasogastric tubes, starting intravenous infusions (IVs), doing catheterizations on some patients, and prepping incision sites. I loved every minute of this.

On surgical duty I also took my turn in private duty nursing. A three-year-old girl had been run over by a car twice. She was not breathing when she was brought in. Our new surgeon, who came the same day I had started working, did CPR upon her arrival and continued it all the way to the OR. She was revived and maintained well enough for the surgery. When she was finally brought to her room, she had two IVs, a tube to one kidney, another tube to her abdomen, a urinary catheter, an oxygen tube, and a cast on her broken left leg.

I was finished with my eight-hour shift on surgical floor when she was brought to her room. No nurses were available for private duty at that time, so I was asked to take over until someone could relieve me. This duty kept me very busy, observing every tube and its patency (continuous flow) or lack of it. Every detail had to be charted, as we had been taught. No one else was available, so I stayed the eight hours. I appreciated this opportunity to review what I had learned. My memory did not fail me.

The next day I reported to work on surgical floor again, and again I was assigned to private duty with the little girl. To my surprise and joy she was totally awake and alert. She smiled at me and asked if I would be her nurse. I assured her I would be with her all day. I asked her if she was having a lot of pain, to which she said "No." She was brave. As the nurse was getting ready to close her night charting, I went to the nurse in charge to give her the good news. This was my first experience with a case like this.

Just then the doctor came to check on the little girl. His first words were "Let's get her up in the chair today. It will take two people because of all the tubings. Be careful."

We did as ordered. She sat up for half an hour with no complaints and no nausea, asking when she could have something to eat. That treat had to wait one more day. She was satisfied.

The little girl progressed rapidly. Her tubes and tubing were removed two days later with no complications. What a trooper! In only one more week she was able to return home to her family, and I was on my way to Minneapolis to take my state board examinations and see my student friends.

The exams were depressing. More difficult than I had imagined. My classmates and I met after every exam and compared answers. We came to the same conclusion every time: we should have stayed home. The second day was even worse. We tried to cheer ourselves with comments about our bravery in having attempted the exams. After the last exam we left, tired and depressed. Next would be a three- to six-week wait.

In three weeks our test scores arrived. I sat down in chapel and waited for a while, trying to prepare myself. Finally I opened the letter and started reading the scores from the bottom of the page upwards. The last test was on psychiatry, the one each of us had expected to flunk. I was shaking all over when I looked at that score. I continued looking upwards and the rest of my scores were one to ten points less than my score in psychiatry.

Miracles still happen, I said to myself. I had passed those impossible exams! After thanking God for having helped me through this final stage of the nursing program, I went to tell Reverend Mother the good news. She was genuinely happy for me.

"Are you enjoying your nursing career so far?" she asked, with a twinkle in her eye.

"Reverend Mother, words cannot describe my happiness. I must see my director today. I don't know what he has to tell me, but I'm certain he will be happy to hear this great news."

She smiled and said he had been pleased with my work so far. "Keep it up," she said.

I assured her I would and left for the office of the Director of Nursing (DON).

He was waiting for me. Before he could say anything, I told him my wonderful news. I said, "I am happy to announce I am now a registered nurse in the state of Minnesota."

He grinned and said, "What perfect timing! I am now making you the charge nurse of surgical floor on the 2:00 to 10:00 P.M. shift. You will be responsible for our thirty-eight-bed surgical ward."

Laughing, I said, "You are joking, aren't you? We were told in nursing school that two-year grads would seldom be asked to take that position, especially in hospitals. Besides, I need more experience. This new surgeon is operating day and night, performing vascular surgeries, which I am not acquainted with. He is very aggressive, like the case of the three-year-old girl that was run over twice by a pickup." (*Lord, help me!*)

He answered, "Yes, and you did a great job taking care of her. Also, your work in ICU (Intensive Care Unit) was enough proof that you can handle this job. I want you to start your new job on Monday." This was Thursday. I didn't see how I could talk him out of it by Monday. Surely others would not agree with him, but his mind was made up.

I went back to Reverend Mother's office. Certainly she would agree with me that this is highly irregular. She did. However, this director was known for making good choices. She advised me to give it a try. I gave in.

This was unexpected; I didn't feel capable of handling the numerous split-second decisions a charge nurse would have to make in this job. For the next three days I prayed, "Lord, help me!" moment to moment, over and over.

What would my instructors say when they found out? "Only three weeks' experience, and she is already ignoring major instructions we gave the class repeatedly." I could hear them. Well, I had explored every possible excuse. What else could I do?

My vow of obedience applied to secular leaders as well as nun superiors. I had to try. That vow was not easy with me. During my music career I had reached into the impossible, thanks to that vow. I earnestly preferred to leave it out of my new nursing career. My desire was to be a bedside nurse. No titles, no power, no position. Did God expect this of me? Again I was reminded that our superiors take God's place. Many times before I had questioned this part of my religious training. Did they check with God before we were given assignments? I turned my thoughts to other problems to avoid becoming more confused than I already was.

I spent the weekend reviewing some of the surgical procedures, the preps, the postoperative care, and what problems to look for after surgery. After several hours I decided that I would learn most of my surgical care over time by the hands-on method. The staff would have to help me until I had more experience. "Nursing is all a matter of using common sense," our nursing instructors had told us repeatedly.

When I arrived on the surgical floor on Monday, I checked the list of surgeries done that morning. We had one amputee, two gallbladder surgeries, one appendectomy, and a vein stripping. All thirty-eight beds were occupied. The amputee had a heart problem. The appendectomy patient was an open and close case: he was full of cancer; the prognosis was about six months. He was forty years old with a family. In addition, two more surgeries were scheduled: one for 5:00 P.M. and one for 7:00 P.M. We were off to a good start.

Two LVNs and two nurses' aides worked with me. I had to get acquainted with all thirty-eight patients, but not now. We were swamped with postoperative traumas from the surgeries of the morning. The amputee began to bleed profusely. The family of the cancer patient came and wanted to talk with the charge nurse. They were in shock from the news they had not expected; they sought explanations and comfort. The morning's five surgical patients needed pain injections. Ten of the patients from yesterday's surgeries had IVs still running, which needed supervision, and all the medications had to be dispensed at 3:00, 6:00, and 9:00 P.M.

I said to myself, *Is there room for anything else? I am one person. Where is that evening supervisor? Maybe she can help for half an hour.* After all, I wanted to shout, "This is my first day!" I paged her. After my brief scream for help, she came running. She was incredulous at our situation.

I said, "Would you please start passing the medications, so I can start taking care of the patients? They need new bandages, repositioning, and so on. You know." She nodded and I took off with the surgical cart with all its supplies. I grabbed an LVN to help me and attacked all the problems on the way. Forget dinner. We had to settle down everyone first.

Finally, at about 9:00 P.M., we took turns getting a bite to eat. The patients were comfortable. They had received their back rubs and medications and were asleep or watching television. Visitors were gone. Now it was time to start charting because the night shift would be coming in one hour for report. I had to make sure I had marked down every narcotic I had given, the time and place it had been given, and the results. I also kept records of all the IVs; i.e., what times the bottles had been changed, what medications had been inserted into the solutions, and how fast they were running. The information seemed endless but important. All pain medications had to be charted, including the times given, the reasons for giving, and results obtained. I finally finished at 2:00 A.M.

What an initiation! Would every day, I wondered, be like today? The LVNs assured me some days were less hectic, but not many. This was the busiest place in the hospital. The two LVNs and two aides were extremely helpful. We became well acquainted during those eight hours. They made my burden considerably lighter in the following days. I was happy in my work, and I was helping people get well. I made sure they were comfortable and provided spiritual help for them.

The first year on surgical was gratifying. I was able to use all my knowledge and skills. I had wanted to do this for a long time. Additionally, I was learning about public relations with administration, coworkers, patients, and patients' relatives. Everyone becomes your brother, sister, father, and mother. Their concerns are your concerns.

That first year was also a tremendous learning time. No book in any library on earth can teach what hands-on experience does. What is learned this way is never forgotten. Immediacy energizes our minds when we learn while performing the task. I remember thinking, *It will be a snap this year. I have learned so much. I don't know what could happen that hasn't already happened.*

A couple days later I was summoned to the office of the Director of Nursing. I had no idea why, so I decided not to worry. I walked in to the office and to my surprise there he was, as calm and pleasant as he'd been a year ago when he had given me my first assignment. Next to him sat both the day and evening supervisors. I wondered if they were going to fire me, but they were smiling.

The director said, "Sister, I have been so pleased with your work on surgical floor and so have my two supervisors that you are our number one choice for evening supervisor of the whole hospital."

Dead silence followed as I stared at them with my mouth open.

Then he continued, "I know you like surgical floor, but we feel you should spread your wings and move on to your full potential." I will never forget that sentence.

I replied, "But this is too big a bite too soon."

"I think the bite was bigger a year ago," he answered.

Beginning to come out of shock, I was trying to comprehend the enormous responsibility of this job. I thought of the ICU and KDU (Kidney Dialysis Unit), and fear gripped me.

As though reading my mind, the DON began to explain. "The night supervisor will show you all you need to know about dialysis. The ICU nurses will acquaint you with everything in ICU. We expanded it this year to twice its size and equipped it with all the latest machines. You will enjoy it. You will be available to all units and departments on the 2:00 to 10:00 P.M. shift. You will carry a beeper at all times. The emergency room has been very busy the last three months. You will start all the IVs and blood transfusions. You will replace Mrs. Beam who is leaving us two weeks from today. You take a good rest now. If you have any questions, call me anytime, night or day. I know you will enjoy this job."

Still dazed, I shook hands with him and said, "I will try my best."

I welcomed my two-week vacation. I was happy about the new job because I was scheduled Monday through Friday and had weekends off. On surgical floor I worked ten days straight then one day off, all year round. This was indeed a welcome change.

The night nurse supervisor called me a week later to arrange to brief me on the KDU. She had taken the course in Minneapolis prior to the establishment of the unit at our hospital in Little Falls. When we met, she gave me a thorough explanation of the dialysis and acquainted me with the personnel. This was a lot to absorb in two hours, but she also gave me material to take home and study.

Similarly, the nurse in charge of ICU gave me a tour of the unit and all the equipment. She told me I would be informed immediately when a patient arrived so I could start the IV; medications could then be given promptly. It was important that the evening supervisor come quickly when notified. She assured me that I would have full cooperation in finding all that was needed in any emergency in ICU.

I knew all this would be a worthwhile learning experience just like surgical nursing had been a year ago. The obstetrics division and the medical nursing did not seem as challenging. Pediatrics was not frightening; children bounce back quite readily. Emergency rooms have their hair-raising episodes almost on a daily basis. ER is never boring and requires skill in triage. Intelligent observations have to be made constantly. A definite requirement is those skills needed in caring for minor injuries that do not require suturing. No patient can come to the ER without a call to the doctor for orders by the nurse.

A supervisor needs to know how to care for every type of patient. She must have good rapport with personnel and doctors as well as the public. This challenge would require all I had learned so far and the willingness to learn more.

My first day as supervisor was a pleasant one. Everyone seemed happy that I'd accepted the job. After receiving the report of all patients in the hospital from the day supervisor, I made my rounds to all the units.

At 4:30 P.M., I was headed for the dialysis unit to hook up my first patient for a treatment. The woman was a grade school teacher in her fifties. I looked at her lab reports. Her hemoglobin was 4.2. The normal hemoglobin count for a female is 12. I remembered when I had had a hemoglobin count of 9.4. I was weak, tired, and unable to work more than two hours at a time. How did these people do it? Dealing with twenty to thirty healthy students all day is enough for a person with a hemoglobin of 12. She slept soundly throughout her four-hour treatment. I watched her closely, and when I left her I made sure my helper did the same.

I was told this woman came for treatments so she could get a good rest three times a week. Dialysis patients have low hemoglobin because of red cell loss from hemolysis, or bleeding, and impaired production of red blood cells. This patient hoped for a kidney transplant. I prayed that day would come soon.

They had been correct in warning me of the multiple incidents, accidents, diseases, and lacerations that flooded our emergency room. The ER was the busiest place in the hospital. I spent several hours daily helping the nurse in charge. One day a call came from the ambulance en route to the hospital bringing in a young man in his twenties with a gunshot wound to his chest. He and his father had had an argument while filling the silo. As the argument worsened, adrenaline increased, and the deranged father picked up his shotgun and shot his son. The boy's wife heard the shot, ran to the silo, and found him in a pool of blood. She called the ambulance, while the father stood by and did nothing.

When the young man arrived at the ER, the young woman came running to me and cried, "Sister, please hurry, baptize him, he has not been baptized. He's dying; I don't want him to go to hell!"

I obliged while we were transporting him from the ambulance. I noticed a glass of water at the entrance, grabbed it, poured the water over his forehead, and said, "I baptize you, Jim, in the name of the Father, the Son, and the Holy Ghost. Amen," and continued to resuscitate him since he was still breathing. He opened his eyes, looked at me as though he wanted to say something, but smiled instead, and breathed his last breath.

I turned around and his wife was in the doorway sobbing, reaching her arms to me. I went to her and embraced her and held her without saying a word. Words seemed useless now. I wept with her. How does one console someone in shock, grief-stricken by the horrible death of her young husband, murdered by his own father? I prayed silently as I held her sobbing in my arms. She was a woman of genuine love. She wanted him saved. She knew his physical life was ended, but she didn't give up her desire to have him baptized. Her heart was bleeding, but it did not prevent her from acting on her purpose of baptism, her final act of love. She wanted God's best for him.

As her sobbing subsided, I took her to the waiting room, where we had more privacy. She was finally able to speak. She turned to me and said, "Sister, how can I thank you? I am so relieved! You baptized him. God is so good. I have prayed ever since we married that he would be baptized some day. I had been so worried. Why did it have to happen this way?"

She continued in a slow, steady voice to explain the father's intolerance of his son. The dispute was over religion, but God had the final say for his believer.

We were interrupted by the charge nurse, who needed to know about disposal of the body. The wife had gained strength in this short time and was able to perform the tasks at hand with dignity and respect. She handled herself with a new power that could come only from God. We said our goodbyes, but the bond established while sharing such grief gave me a new insight into the wide span of responsibilities which comprise the nursing profession, if it is truly a healing profession.

I have never forgotten that incident. It etched into me sensitivity to wounded hearts. The incident became a springboard in succeeding years to minister to the sick at heart, mothers with children caught up in drug addiction and alcohol, runaways, abusive husbands, and so on. Endless sorrow and misery—no more would convent walls hide these realities from me. I did not have to hunt for these problems. They came to me; they were everywhere. Sorrows became the fabric of the work place.

My first year as supervisor passed rapidly. I learned things every day. New experiences occurred every day. I was becoming familiar with the people of Little Falls and surrounding areas. I no longer came to work with anxieties about possible nursing situations; I was relaxed and in control of whatever circumstances might be presented.

One day I came to work and started my shift as usual. A new nurse was on duty in the ER. She had received only two days' orientation, so I needed to check on her frequently to see if she needed help.

About six in the evening, when everyone was at supper, I stopped in the ER to see how things were going. My beeper went off as I opened the door. The new nurse put the phone down and came running, explaining hurriedly, "A lady brought this two-year-old child in saying the child got sick this morning. The lady said she had to leave right away, but that the parents were on their way and would be here any minute. Would you please help me?"

Of course I would help. "Where are the parents?"

"I don't know. Ten minutes have passed already, and they have not showed up. I wish they would hurry. The child is congested, but she just sleeps. I wish I knew who her doctor is."

"What is her temperature?"

"One hundred and two degrees five minutes ago."

I had her take it again. The child's body was very warm. We started sponging with cool water and washcloths, but she was already convulsing. The nurse said her temp had risen to 103.8. I kept sponging and soon the convulsions stopped. The child opened her eyes just as the parents walked in.

I wanted information. I asked question after question, but the parents stood there, shrugging their shoulders, saying nothing, and apparently comprehending less. Finally it dawned on me. I said to the nurse, "Her parents are deaf and dumb."

She looked shocked. "Call Dr. Wilder. He is on call tonight."

I turned to the parents and said, "Dr. Wilder?"

They nodded and smiled. We were on the right track. We had learned in nurses' training that blind people marry and so do the deaf and dumb and that they raise families.

Dr. Wilder came in minutes. The child was improving. One could see the doctor and the parents knew each other well. The communication was established by writing notes. Soon all information was received and orders for medications were written. This crisis was over.

I quickly left for the delivery room to answer the message I had received after Dr. Wilder had appeared in the ER. Two mothers were ready to deliver at the same time. I went to the second delivery room.

One of the doctors was there, but not the second one. He did not get there on time, so I delivered the baby. These were happy days for me. I cherished them even more because I had to wait many years to enjoy them. What joy could compare to helping others in all the ways I had at my disposal right now! I resolved never to miss an opportunity to help alleviate the stress or pain of anyone who came across my path.

Two days later the day supervisor and I switched jobs. We were already blessed with two feet of snow overnight in mid-October. She lived nine miles out on a farm and had to wait for someone to open the road for her. The day shift did not offer the frantic pace I was used to. The doctors were available, the administration handled major problems, the pharmacist was on duty the whole shift, department heads were there, and I was looking for something to do. By one in the afternoon, the day supervisor relieved me. Since I had little to report, I prepared to go home.

As I was leaving by way of the ER, the doctor on call stopped me. He grabbed my arm and said, "Sister, would you please do me a big favor?"

"Of course, doctor, what is it?"

"I have a really sick eight-year-old boy in ER. He slipped and fell, hitting the edge of the sidewalk with his head. He has a bad concussion and has been vomiting ever since he came in an hour ago. I need you to accompany him on the ambulance to Minneapolis. He will need a lot of care on the way. Would you?"

"I am ready, Doctor. I will go."

In two minutes we were on the road. My first ambulance run! That hour and one-half to St. Mary's Hospital in Minneapolis was the busiest I had been all day. The boy started vomiting as soon as we took off. He was extremely agitated and, therefore, hard to control. I had to make sure his head was turned to the side so he wouldn't choke. At one time he was gasping for breath but recovered as soon as I administered oxygen. He did not exhibit any pain, but I could not give him any medication anyway because it would interfere with his examination and diagnosis.

Just as we stopped at the ER, the boy opened his eyes, looked at me, and asked, "Where am I?"

Before answering his question I asked, "Are you having pain?" He denied having any pain. I continued, "You fell and hit your head on the sidewalk at home. Your doctor wanted you to come to Minneapolis to be checked out by a doctor here, to make sure you are all right."

"Oh," he answered, while examining his arms and legs. Clearly he did not know what could be wrong, so he asked, "Do I have to stay here?"

"Only if the doctor thinks you should. We will find out soon. I will stay here until he decides." That seemed to satisfy him.

The ambulance door opened. I convinced the boy to stay quietly on the gurney while they took him to the examining room. After about two hours of x-rays and further examinations, the doctor said the boy could go home with us. He remained fully awake through all the tests and had no further nausea or vomiting. He felt no dizziness and answered all questions without hesitation. What a relief! He was eager to go home and so were we. To me this was an amazing recovery. His parents were waiting for him to come home. This was a happy ending.

We returned to Little Falls at 11:45 P.M. I checked in at the front office, and they were very happy to see me. No wonder—the night supervisor was unable to come in and her substitute was out of town. Would I? I was wide awake, so why not? Divine mercy was operating because it was a quiet night with no emergencies on any floor. I stayed busy helping wherever needed.

About this time, a new evolution had taken place in some Catholic communities. Sisters started living in small groups of five or six in houses near town. Some remained at the convent. Many of the sisters moving to small groups were working different shifts and different jobs. This gave them an opportunity to share in all the duties of small group living, which in turn provided a normal home environment. The convent routine of prayer, meditation, and Mass was carried out as closely as possible to maintain the unity of all groups. I was a part of the small group movement and truly enjoyed it. The five sisters that lived with me were delightful, sincere, and accommodating. I worked the evening shift and the rest worked the day shift. On our days off we would drive to Brainerd or St. Cloud, each thirty miles away, to do some shopping and thus spend time together.

Another change during this period was that each sister received twenty dollars per month to spend for whatever she chose. Times were changing in many ways, and most sisters seemed to adapt well to these changes. But some of the older sisters found changes difficult. A small stipend of twenty dollars went against the vow of poverty, some of the sisters felt. They believed this change was capitulation to the ways of the world and predicted a gradual breakdown of Community life.

Others saw this change as a matter of learning responsibility and accountability. Further, we saw that some aspects of Community, as it had been in the past, kept us from growing up and becoming adults. The world was progressing while we were regressing. We should be able to make the changes as well as the outside world did.

Was Community living a structure of the past? If God had called me to convent life, as I had been told, could He not call me again to a different type of mission life outside of convent living? I would have to follow His call as I had the first time, would I not? But our vows were binding until death! No one could answer this question without insulting God!

I could not get this matter settled in my mind. Was I worshipping a false god? The longer one serves in a lifestyle dictated by human beings, I realized, the more one becomes accustomed to those rules and becomes comfortable in that system. Once comfortable, one refuses to change. Without change, one becomes boring and lifeless, like a machine. A machine is good to use until it is worn out, then it is cast out and forgotten. A new machine replaces it. Is that all there is to life? This was unthinkable. My mother and father had spoken of God and heaven. Where had that teaching gone? Hadn't Jesus died on the cross to save us from sin and hell, so we could live with Him forever in heaven? If Jesus did all that for me, then I know He does not think I am a machine. I mean much more to Him.

I thought living here on earth should be more alive than I was experiencing. But what was the secret? I couldn't help remembering my first mission assignment in Elk River, Minnesota. The Protestant parents of my music students had something real and alive in them that had separated them from us. I recalled their joy, their peaceful approach to problems, and their positive attitudes in spite of illness and financial setbacks. How had they acquired such treasures? There was no use asking anyone in my neighborhood. I resolved to find out somehow because there had to be a better way to live to please God. I also wanted proof, not just someone's word. I prayed the prayers I had been taught. Did other prayers exist? How would I ask God for enlightenment besides, "Please, God, help me!"

At the same time, we were hearing about our new Pope. His name was Pope John XXIII. We also followed the proceedings of the Second Vatican Council and the outcome. These things were astonishing. Changes were taking place there also.

Pope John said, "Let us open the windows of our Church (Catholic) and let the Holy Spirit enter."

What did that mean? Who was the Holy Spirit? I learned that the Holy Ghost was the Third Person of God, but what did He do? What was so important about the Holy Ghost entering the Catholic Church?

Everyone spoke of Pope John as the Pope of love and humility. He was a well beloved, as well as very progressive, Pope. Although he lived only a couple years as Pope, he accomplished a great deal for the Catholic Church. He opened the door to a new freedom and life in the Holy Spirit, breaking down the doors of idealism without God's anointing. Persons who had made vows in religious institutions could now receive dispensation of these vows from Rome if they had valid reason for requesting the dispensation. The Second Vatican Council made many changes in the Catholic Church to its own advantage.

Thanksgiving was getting close. Much snow had already fallen to accommodate those who were going to Grandma's by sled. Everyone was busily preparing for the holiday.

My cousin in Eveleth wrote me a note saying she had seen my brother Father John, who was stationed at Hilman, Minnesota. She was worried about him because he did not look well. That evening I called him to make sure everything was all right. He answered and sounded jolly as ever. He told me it must have been a touch of the flu but that he was feeling much better. We planned to spend a day or two together at Christmas at his parish. I would play the organ for his Midnight Mass and help the choir sing. The next day we could go to St. Stephen, our hometown, and visit our neighbors on the farm. He seemed to be his old self, laughing and joking as usual.

After our nice long chat we said our goodbyes, and I mentioned I was planning to call our brother Tony in Portland, Texas.

I asked if I should ask or tell Tony anything for Father John. Tony was married, had three children, and owned a print shop. Father John sometimes bought some of his printing, but Father John indicated that he did not need any at this time. "See you at Christmas," we said.

I did not notify Father Joe in Nebraska or Father Frank in Texas. It wasn't necessary. I would tell my sister, Mary, in Tulsa when I called her before Christmas.

Thanksgiving was rather quiet at the hospital. Many patients went home for Thanksgiving, so the work load seemed easier. Everybody was hurrying around soon after, getting ready for Christmas. Every department did its own decorating and every day the noise level rose, while the excitement rose to a higher pitch too. The weather added a holiday touch with a blanket of snow two feet deep putting everyone in a spirit of happiness, anticipation, and giving.

On December 13, 1970 I was asked to drive three sisters to Minneapolis to visit their parents. We had so much fun window-shopping and enjoying the beautiful decorations of the big city. We arrived at one of the sisters' homes tired, hungry, and cold. Her mother had fixed a hot meal that we devoured with delight. We washed the dishes in return, sat down, and visited. We were having a grand time when the phone rang. It was ten o'clock. We were looking forward to going to bed.

The call was for me. It was the evening supervisor calling from Little Falls Hospital to tell me that Father John had been brought to the St. Gabriel Hospital in a coma. He had suffered a massive stroke. She told me it would be wise to come home at once. I was shocked. Father John was the healthiest of us all, the strongest and toughest. He was never sick at home. He was only fifty-five. *My favorite brother! He can't die!*

We left in a short while and arrived at the hospital in Little Falls at the stroke of midnight. The supervisor took us to his room.

179

He lay there so quietly, so pale, with eyes closed and no sign of life except shallow breathing. I stood there in disbelief. This wasn't happening. The doctor said he would not recover, but he could linger for days. The hospital provided a room for me across the hall from him so I would be close. I was heartbroken and in enough shock that I could not speak or weep. I sat down on the bed and stared at the floor. Was this a dream? Why John? It was a mistake. I could not understand. Why would God take a young priest in death when priests were so scarce? It made no sense. Why take him so suddenly? This was cruel and heartless.

CHAPTER 5

Coping With Grief

There were no answers. Several Crosier Fathers were there. They were as stunned as I was. Silence hung over all of us like a heavy weight, forbidding us to speak. Father Frank, Father Joe, and Tony were notified. I was asked to notify my sister, Mary, in Tulsa. She was shocked to hear the news and asked the same questions I had. Mary was ill with pneumonia. Father Frank was recuperating from surgery, and Tony, who was in Portland, Texas, could not come.

Father John Smerke, OSC.

Father John died three days later on December 20, 1970. Father Joe and I were the only family members at the funeral. He came from Hastings, Nebraska, where he was teaching. The only time I saw him was when he arrived on the day of the funeral. We went to the cemetery and stood together at the graveside during the usual prayer service. The snow was two to three feet deep. The day was cloudy with more snow in the forecast. Silence spoke loudly as we stood there. I remembered hearing someone say a scripture verse in which God says, "Neither are your ways my ways." What did He mean? I thought, *I know God knows everything. But why?*

God's Provision

I came back to Little Falls in the afternoon. The first sister I met offered her condolences and then informed me that Reverend Mother had died on December 21 and had been laid to rest in the sisters' cemetery at the same time Father John had been buried at Onamia. I had not heard anything in the past week about Mother Yvonne because of Father John's illness.

This shock also came with no preparation. Mother Yvonne had been my very dear friend through the past four years. She had allowed me to follow my dream to become a nurse and had stood by me as she had promised. Father John and she were my dearest friends on whom I could depend. Again the question *Why?* surfaced. They had been my spiritual mentors. They had believed in me, encouraged and inspired me, and had become vital parts of my motivation, success, and happiness. *God, why is this happening to me? What have I done wrong?*

I was a very private person and confided in few people. Sister Mark was a friend who could always cheer me up when I was down. God chose to take her three weeks later with no forewarning. She was found dead in bed, holding her rosary in her hand. She was only 60 years old.

My three dearest friends were gone into eternity! I broke down and sobbed my heart out. Although I tried to accept these tragedies, the anger overcame me. I was angry at my misfortunes, angry with God for having allowed them to happen, angry with myself for believing that God loved me and cared for me. My entire spiritual foundation was crumbling underneath me.

I decided the only thing I could do was to lose myself in work. This effort had helped before. I even asked my supervisors to add hours to my regular schedule. I did not want any free time. This was the only way I knew to deal with my sorrow.

The first week went by quickly. Helping those who were dependent on me gave me relief from the pain of my grief. How long would I have to live like this? How long would this method work?

The second week I realized I was alienating myself from the sisters and crawling into the deep recesses of misery. In the evenings I came home exhausted, choosing to say little or nothing to my sisters, and spending most of my time in my room to avoid sharing my misery with the sisters' peaceful, fun-loving recreation. Expressing myself was virtually impossible, and I would burst into tears if anyone said something kind and understanding.

The following weekend, as an act of kindness, the sisters asked me to drive them to Brainerd, thirty miles away, to do some shopping. A change of scenery, they hoped, would help me. We left for Brainerd early in the morning and, despite my grieving status, had a wonderful time shopping, arriving back home in Little Falls late that evening.

Snow had begun to fall about suppertime. One of the sisters had to go to a meeting at 8:00 P.M. I offered to drive her there because the roads were becoming icy underneath, with snow obscuring the ice. She gladly accepted my offer. We walked to the car, which was left at the end of the sidewalk. I slipped on the icy sidewalk, fell, and hit my right wrist on the edge of the sidewalk. I heard and felt the crack and the pain. My first thought was: *It's broken; I'll have to wear a cast and will be unable to work for six weeks.* The sisters took me to the emergency room. Yes, it was broken badly.

The surgeon was in the building. He was called to the ER to evaluate the extent of the break and direct the procedure. Normally the patient with a badly broken wrist would be taken to the operating room. But the surgeon decided to do it right there in the ER. He applied a blood pressure cuff to my upper right arm and injected Novocaine into the vein below the elbow, which numbed the lower arm immediately. The nurse pulled my upper body in opposition to the doctor pulling my hand and wrist until he extended it far enough to let it go back into normal position. Another x-ray was taken to see if it was properly positioned. It was perfect. The cast was applied from fingers to middle upper arm. I was released with instructions on care of cast and ordered not to work for six weeks. *Great.*

Now what would I do to subdue my grief? Why had this happened on top of everything else? I did not realize at this time that God was being merciful and trying to deal with me to prepare me for good things to come. He was allowing a sequence of things to happen to help me realize the truth about Him, the God I did not know, about my neighbor, and myself. I felt alone, deserted, forsaken, and beaten at every effort I made to deal with uncomfortable circumstances. Every attempt to find peace and happiness was squelched. The kindness, goodness, and mercy of the sisters did not have the power to soothe and heal the wounds inflicted by the losses and disappointments. Where was all this leading? I saw no escape. No one could speak the right words of comfort to my distressed soul.

Sister brought me home from the hospital late that evening. I was groggy from the pain medication. Undressing was difficult and upsetting. While trying to get comfortable in bed with the cumbersome cast, I was constantly reminded of my mishap, and I cried myself to sleep.

I awoke the next morning hoping this had all been a bad dream. I struggled with my awkward cast just to get out of bed. Getting dressed was no less a challenge. Making my own breakfast gave me good reason to consider a forty-day fast. In desperation I gave in to tears. I sat down on the couch and opened the floodgates. My little dog, Schnitzie, came running, jumped on the couch by me, and cried with me in doggie fashion. I was grateful to be alone, since I couldn't bear to have anyone watch me crying—in other words, feeling sorry for myself.

I remember crying out loud, "God, wherever you are, don't you care? Help me!" I was angry, miserable, and rebellious. I refused to go to church or to pray. *What good did it do?* was my attitude. *This is what I get for living a good life and putting up patiently all these years with the most trying tests of obedience to my superiors. What a wasted life!*

Suppressing my bitter feelings was the best I could do. The weight of my misfortune discouraged me from even attempting to pull myself out of the dark hole. I was physically and mentally drained.

Then Sister Agnes, my director of nurses, called me to say that due to the long time I would have to be absent from work, she would have to appoint a new supervisor in my place permanently. This did not lift my already battered spirit. I got up from my chair and started practicing with my left hand, doing everything my right hand (the broken one) normally had to do. All day long I practiced writing, handling pots and pans, washing, ironing, slicing bread, and all the other daily tasks. I would have to become adept in starting blood transfusions and IVs. The IVs would be especially tricky.

At the end of the first week, I went to the hospital to attempt this difficult challenge. It proved successful. I called my doctor and told him I was ready to go back to work. After hearing my story, he lightened my sentence by four weeks. The cast was no longer a threat to me, just a clumsy appendage. I returned to work.

In six weeks the wrist was healed and the cast removed. Physiotherapy and hydrotherapy combined hastened to straighten out my elbow in the next three weeks. Although I could ward off the anger and bitterness a little better, the depression continued to dull my enthusiasm, reminding me that all was not well with my life. When the grief would not remain tethered any longer, my mind would refuse to function normally. I would recall the tragedies more and more until I would sob uncontrollably. How long would I be in this condition? Grief therapy as a specialty wasn't developed yet. I didn't know what to expect or what was normal in these situations. I didn't know if I would ever be healed from this pain. While I didn't want to live like this, I didn't know what to do for myself.

No one seemed to know what to say or do about my grief. I was sorry for talking to God as I had, and I confessed it. The following months did not change my condition much. I cried out to God to help me through. I wondered if He would ever forgive me because I had questioned His goodness and mercy. Yet He seemed to be the only one who would be able to help me. My mother had taught us that He knew our needs for He is almighty, omniscient, all-powerful. She had also taught us that He is a loving Father. But I did not know how to pray except to repeat the Hail Mary and the Our Father, wondering while praying them how they could help. I thought there must be another way of approaching God in prayer, but I didn't know what it was.

The month of May arrived, my favorite month. May brought a sense of hope, new life, strength, and excitement to me as spring would bring forth buds on the trees, warmer weather, and preparations for new beginnings. This season was a promise of new life.

One Saturday in late May, we six sisters were having our monthly meeting at our house four blocks from the motherhouse, discussing our economic situation. We had done well the past month, and we agreed we needed to continue holding tight the reins of spending.

All of a sudden I opened my mouth and started saying something I had not intended to say. "Sisters, do you mind if I get permission from Reverend Mother to make a private retreat with my brother Father Joe in Nebraska?"

Where had that come from? The idea made no sense. I never got along with Father Joe. We had always locked horns, especially in matters of religion. Why had I said that, and where had it come from? The sisters looked at each other and seemed perplexed but mercifully agreed I should go.

The next morning I wasted no time in going to see the Reverend Mother. She was as astonished at my request as were the sisters the night before. She asked me why I wouldn't consider making one of the three retreats at the motherhouse, the first one starting in three days.

I answered, "Reverend Mother, I don't know why, but I must go to Nebraska to make this retreat with my brother."

She did not argue any further.

I went home and wrote to Father Joe asking him if he could fit me into his schedule. In only three days I received his answer. Father Joe was so delighted at the thought of being the director of my private retreat that I worried while reading his letter. He scheduled the five-day retreat for June 6, 1971, Monday through Friday.

Thoughts raced through my head: yes, it would take five full days to straighten me out. I was live bait! That is the happiest letter I had ever received from him. But various doubts nagged at me. Why was I doing this? What had prompted the thought in the first place? I said to myself, *It's all settled; I am going.*

I started packing since I was leaving in the morning. I had to travel seventy-five miles to Minneapolis to board the plane to Hastings, Nebraska at 11:00 A.M.

I arrived at the airport in Hastings at 4:00 P.M., where Father Joe was waiting to take me to the monastery. I was surprised by Father Joe's broad grin; he was usually stern faced and quiet. Our ride to the monastery seemed short as Father Joe did most of the talking. I had never seen him like that.

As we stepped out of the car he informed me that he was taking me out to eat so we could be alone to visit. This was a first. We unloaded my two suitcases and were on our way to my favorite restaurant, The Golden Corral. Throughout the meal, Father Joe was smiling, joking, reminiscing about our childhood years on the farm. I was baffled by the obvious changes in my brother. He offered no explanations.

After dinner we went to see some of the spectacular sights, like the fountains and the Imex Building, one of three in the country. We returned to the monastery by 9:00 P.M. He had reserved the guest room for me. As I walked into the room I noticed a Bible and a paperback book on the bedside table.

Father Joe had some calls to make before retiring, and he said how happy he was I had come. He said, "Anne, something great is going to happen to you this week; you will see. Get a good night's sleep, but first, please read this book. He handed me the paperback *The Cross and the Switchblade* by David Wilkerson. He added, "I will see you at 9:00 A.M. for our first conference." I still had no clue to the unbelievable transformation in Father Joe. Maybe I would find out at the next day's conference.

Sleep came easily. The quiet, restful atmosphere of the monastery was welcome. I read the Wilkerson book. It was alive with love, strength, courage, victory, and fearlessness that nothing seemed impossible or too hard to endure when you loved human beings as Jesus does. Although tired when I had started reading, I was strong and lifted up when I finished it at 1:00 A.M. I longed for the same transformation in me no matter what I had to endure. For the first time in six months, I was hopeful. But I was more than hopeful, I was expectant. Something good was going to happen.

My Private Retreat with Father Joe

I bounced out of bed before any wake-up bell rang, happy and full of anticipation. I wondered what this first day would be like, meeting all the priests *at meals* (different from motherhouse retreats) but keeping silence the rest of the time, which I was used to. I thought, *I am in the right place.*

After dressing, I went to the chapel to celebrate the Mass with the priests and brothers. At breakfast I met the priests, who were cordial and true to their Crosier hospitality. They each had a good sense of humor and made me feel welcome.

Now it was time for my first conference. I prayed that it would be a fruitful experience since this would be my first private retreat, one on one with a clergy. I resolved to seek those aspects of my retreat that would bring me closer to God. I didn't feel that I knew Him or understood Him at all, based on the happenings of the last six months. Although I had come loose from my moorings, I believed new ones were available. I prayed, "Lord, I am sorry for all my sins. I have come here to get some answers. There is so much I don't understand. Please help me!"

I walked into the conference room, where Father Joe was already waiting for me. The same beautiful smile lit up his face as it had the day before when he had met me at the airport. His smile radiated love. He was glad I'd brought the Bible along, although he hadn't told me to bring it. I could see he was eager to start.

I seated myself opposite him at the table. We began with a prayer—the likes of which I had never heard before—asking God to be in our midst throughout the conference and asking the Holy Spirit to inspire and guide us both that the truth of God's Word would become my source for all I need for salvation. Where had Father Joe learned to pray like that? The

Father Joe Smerke, OSC

189

words of the prayer were not memorized; they had come from his heart. (The typical Roman Catholic prayer would be the Our Father or Hail Mary.)

Before I could make any comment, he proceeded with the following statement that I will never forget. "Anne, I want you to remember one thing. Jesus loves you more than the whole world put together, so place Him in the center of your life and never lose sight of Him."

The rest of the conference was an explanation of that statement: the attributes of God, His constant love and forgiveness when we repent of our sins. We can grow spiritually only if we show our willingness and desire to know Him, to accept Him as our personal Savior, and to follow the leading of the Holy Spirit who will teach us all things. Father Joe stressed a personal relationship with Jesus.

I said, "This is fine and good, but how do you explain the last six months of my life? Where was God when I needed Him?"

Father Joe caught the reason for the questions immediately. He said, "You still do not accept Father John's death, do you?"

"Right, and Mother Yvonne's and Sister Mark's! My three greatest friends!"

He immediately responded, "Could it be the great trial you have been experiencing and still are facing is God at work proving you?" He continued, "Look at Deuteronomy 8:2, where God proved an entire nation to find out what was really in its heart."

We read it together. It says, "Thy God led thee these forty years in the wilderness to humble thee, and to prove thee, to know what was in your heart, whether thou wouldst keep his commandments, or no."

He continued, "Believe me, God has a plan for you. He needs you to trust in Him, lean on Him, not people, to carry out His plan for you in this life. Be ready to obey Him in all things. Remember that God is omniscient, omnipresent, almighty, all-powerful, loving, forgiving; He is a true Father who loves all His children. You are His child and He wants to take care of you and He is waiting for you to turn to Him and ask for His forgiveness and accept Jesus as your personal Savior. He knows how you have been hurting. He wants to console you, comfort you, and bring you to a place of peace, love, joy, and rest. If you follow my instructions, you will see this happen before this week is over."

I was ready to do anything to escape my misery. I said, "Joe, if you knew how unhappy I have been these last six months, you probably would have hesitated to make that last statement."

Father Joe replied, "Let's talk about Jesus and get happy!"

The conference lasted an hour and fifteen minutes. It was unlike any religious activity I had ever attended. I had never heard anyone speak with such eloquence, enthusiasm, and genuine love for God as this. I came back to my room, sat down, and remembered everything we had talked about.

Father Joe had quoted the Bible frequently. I had asked him why he had, and his answer was, "The Bible is the Word of God. Everything you need to know to attain salvation is right there, God's own Word."

Naturally I had asked the next question, "Why didn't our parents, pastors, and nuns teach it, then?"

He explained that the teachings of the Roman Catholic Church did not include Bible teaching as a central tenet of the church, as the teachings of the Protestants did. A difference of opinion and tradition existed among different denominations, and, therefore, Roman Catholics needed more study in Scripture. (Since Vatican II, the Roman Church has encouraged more Bible study.) He explained that even in seminary the Bible was taught but not to the extent it should have been. Bible study was considered a personal choice. He ended by saying, "I advise you to start studying the Bible now, and don't ever quit."

No mention was made of our numerous arguments about religion in the past. My fears about a repeat were allayed. Father Joe was a changed person. He used to be dull, stern, and judgmental. Now he was interesting, full of fun, outgoing, and loving. I was eager to discover how this change had happened, but I decided to let this mystery unravel on its own.

I didn't know how to tackle the Bible. I started reading Genesis. The problem was not that we didn't know numerous important tenets about the faith. For example, I remembered our pastor at home had told us God made everything: the heavens, the earth, waters, stars, moon, and sun. I knew that Adam and Eve were our first parents. Our mother had told us about the first sin in paradise, the punishment, and our inheritance. We had learned, as children, about Mary, the mother of Jesus. We understood that He came to redeem us from sin by dying on the cross. We had learned the Ten Commandments of God. We had been taught our prayers, the Apostles' Creed, the Our Father, and the Hail Mary. We had said the rosary with our parents every night and prayers before and after meals. Every Sunday we had attended Mass. We understood that daily Mass, if possible, was highly recommended.

We had worked hard and attended church regularly because we believed our salvation depended on these things. More than all of this, however, was the example of living out the Christian faith, provided by our parents. Nevertheless, Bible study had not been part of our childhood or our church life, nor had it been part of my religious activities in the convent. Why, all of a sudden, had the Bible become so important? Some of the Protestants talked about "being saved." What did that mean? How do you know if you are saved or not? Was everything we had learned at home wrong? Was it incomplete?

I opened my sack of questions at the evening conference. Father Joe listened patiently. He calmed me down gradually as he answered one question after another. No, all we did in faith was not lost because we were seeking to please God. Those who seek Him sincerely will find Him. He will see to that. Again Father Joe was quoting scriptures which made perfect sense to me. I found it hard to believe the answers were there all the time in the Bible, which until now was to me only another book in the library.

In the Bible I would find the answers I was looking for. I could now hope for my future and a new beginning, late as it was, in my lifetime. I resolved then that I would study the Bible daily. Father Joe showed me the concordance and how to use it. I wondered if anyone else was using the Bible (the *one* copy) at the convent library and how difficult it might be to procure it. I would face that problem when I arrived at the library. Despite the nearly whirlwind changes occurring in my entire structure of belief, I was consoled by the knowledge that all my hard work for these many years was not in vain. I had done what I thought was most pleasing to God. He knows everything, including what was in my heart. I felt secure in His forgiveness.

I was feeling very energetic, excited, and full of anticipation when I entered the conference room the second day of retreat. After a short inspiring prayer we launched into the discussion of "being saved."

Father Joe felt the need to remind me of God's love to prepare me for the commitment. He began with, "Anne, I want you to know that God loves you very dearly and understands you better than anyone else in the world. So place Him in the center of your life and never lose sight of Him. Believe in Him, for He is your salvation. Jesus is not a million miles away. He is right here in you. He wants you to trust Him, to lean on Him—not on people—and accept Him as your Savior. We are all sinners, so ask Him for forgiveness of your sins, for He is merciful. Ask Him to help you start a new life in Him. Talk to Him as your best friend, when things go well and when things go wrong. Begin to praise Him daily for all the blessings you received in the past and are receiving now. Thank

Him daily for good parents, teachers, and friends, physical and spiritual health, life itself.

"Remember, He took our sin and suffered rejection that we be accepted," Father Joe continued. "He came down from heaven to redeem us from sin and hell; He was rich, but for our sakes became poor, so that through His poverty we may be rich" (2 Corinthians 8:9).

As he quoted this scripture, peace came upon me and a gentle calm soothed my mind and spirit. I no longer questioned having come here. My request the other evening, "Sisters, do you mind if I go to Nebraska to make a retreat with Father Joe?" was God calling me to come to meet Him here, away from the confusing atmosphere I was in. He could talk to me now and let me know how much He loved me and wanted me to be His disciple.

In that moment I realized how selfish I had been. As though he knew my thoughts, Father Joe said, "To follow Jesus' way of life is a way of love. Jesus is 'the Way, the truth, and the life. No man cometh unto the Father but by me.'"

In other words, when Jesus came down from heaven to save us from sin and hell, He showed us how to live a life of love, joy, and peace. We learn humility, meekness, patience, long-suffering, and perseverance. We learn to deny our fleshly desires daily and to empty ourselves of all selfishness, and we thereby make room for Jesus in our hearts, so we can serve as Jesus served. To accomplish all this we need to study the Word, meditate on it, and apply it to our daily living.

Father Joe showed me the scripture 1 Timothy 2:5: "For there is one God, and one mediator between God and men, the man Christ Jesus. . . ." He also showed me John 8:31–32 where Jesus said, "If ye continue in my word, then are ye my disciples indeed; and ye shall know the truth, and the truth shall make you free." John 5:24 says, "He that heareth my word, and believeth on him that sent me, hath everlasting life, and shall not come into condemnation; but is passed from death unto life."

Reading these verses gave me plenty to think about for the rest of the day. I studied them most of the afternoon in the quiet of my room. The afternoon passed quickly.

No doubt remained in my mind. Today was the beginning of a new life for me. The weight of my problems was beginning to fall off my shoulders. Praise God!

Although I do not remember the conferences in their sequence, the progression planned by Father Joe brought more inspiration, understanding, and anticipation than I could have imagined. One day as Father Joe and I talked, the death of Father John came up unexpectedly. Father Joe was speaking of the obedience of Jesus to the will of His Father at all times during His short life on earth. We discussed the difficulty we have in accepting things we do not understand.

I agreed and said, "Like Father John's and Mother Yvonne's deaths."

Father Joe admitted he had been shocked too, but he read Isaiah 55:8–9 to me: "For my thoughts are not your thoughts, neither are your ways my ways, saith the Lord. For as the heavens are higher than the earth, so are my ways higher than your ways, and my thoughts than your thoughts." God sees the whole picture; we see only part of the picture. He is infinite; we are finite.

What intrigued me was that Father Joe was able to answer my questions with portions of scripture. This was a welcome discovery. The comfort and instruction of scripture had been missing in my life. Here too were all the answers to my questions. These realizations gave me hope for the future. Now I would no longer feel alone, helpless, or forsaken by God when things went wrong.

The third day Father Joe introduced me to the Third Person of the Blessed Trinity, the Holy Spirit. I had never learned what the Holy Spirit does. Because of my unfamiliarity with scripture, my religious beliefs contained many loopholes, and my understanding was limited. Therefore, my problems had no solutions. My ignorance had allowed my worries to flourish. I believed I had to work my way through worries and problems on my own strength. I was alone with no one to help. Life was confusing, and I did not know who was causing the confusion.

According to my religious beliefs, the devil was in hell (he is not in hell, he is here on earth), God was in heaven, and we were here on earth trying our best to earn heaven. The Holy Spirit is the Third Person of the Blessed Trinity and the rest was a mystery. But there is only one God, that much I knew. Father Joe was keenly aware of my ignorance of basic Christian tenets. I didn't know the truth that could set me free. He patiently reviewed Tuesday night's lesson on Life Forever.

Again I was fascinated by the scripture text he quoted about our identity—the sons and daughters of Adam and Eve. We are all sinners, falling short regardless of how hard we try. We cannot *earn* heaven. Jesus, by leaving His throne in heaven, coming down to earth, and becoming God-with-us, was the only one who could make it possible for man to be saved. He showed us how to live a godly life through His example and His teachings. He taught us and showed us that we attain salvation through Him. But Christians are left with considerably more than a good example. Through His sending of the Holy Spirit, we are empowered to live a better life and to do what we know we ought to do.

Jesus even showed us how to deal with Satan's lies as he tries to trick us into sinning. He allowed Satan to tempt Him while He was here on earth. Satan is forever trying to win us over to his side. With his lies and deceitful ways he tries to trick us to rebel against God by giving in to our fleshly desires, which are in direct opposition to a godly life.

Jesus said, "If any man will come after me, let him deny himself, and take up his cross, and follow me" (Matthew 16:24). We have to resist the devil when he tempts us, remembering that the devil used scripture in his efforts to tempt Jesus. Jesus resisted him with scripture: "It is written, man shall not live by bread alone, but by every word that proceedeth from the mouth of God." Twice more the devil tempted Him and twice more Jesus spoke words from scripture and defeated Satan. The devil left Him, and angels came and ministered to Him.

We must know the Word of God so we can defeat Satan. Satan has to flee then because he cannot tolerate the name of Jesus, Jesus' precious blood, and the Word of God (scripture) spoken by believers.

In St. Paul's letter to the Romans we read, "For all have sinned, and come short of the glory of God" (3:23). We have all sinned because from childhood we desire to please ourselves and deny ourselves nothing in the flesh. In this condition we open the door for the devil to come and tempt us to sin. We turn away from God and feed our self-centered flesh whatever it desires. God must come first in our lives or we cannot help but sin.

Sin is (spiritual) death. In Romans 6:23 we read, "For the wages of sin is death; but the gift of God is eternal life through Jesus Christ, our Lord."

Jesus also said, "Most assuredly, I say to you, whoever commits sin is a slave of sin" (John 8:34). Once we commit a sin we are weakened and, therefore, have a tendency to repeat that sin and other sins. We may eventually become habitual sinners because we have inherited sin through Adam and Eve.

But God's love for us is so great that He demonstrated His love toward us "in that, while we were yet sinners, Christ died for us" (Romans 5:8). The power of sin held humankind hostage until Jesus paid for our release with His very life. Because He ransomed us, we no longer have to live under the power of sin. In Romans 10:9 we read, "That if thou shalt confess with thy mouth the Lord Jesus, and shalt believe in thine heart that God hath raised him from the dead, thou shalt be saved." What comforting words! Praise the Lord!

This study of the truth, the Word, helped me to realize God's immense love for mankind and realize my own shortcomings. But now we have someone to lead and guide us after we commit our lives to Jesus. That someone is the Holy Spirit. We must believe because faith unlocks our understanding of God's Word and faith releases the power of the Holy Spirit in our lives. Our obedience to God is what brings blessings to us and to others. The only way to know God is to know Jesus because Jesus is the only way to God. In fact, Jesus IS God because He is of one substance with the Father. We may choose whether to believe this or not. We must choose to believe if we are to have a personal relationship with Him. "But without faith it is impossible to please him: for he that cometh to God must believe that he is, and that he is a rewarder of them that diligently seek him" (Hebrews 11:6). Belief in Jesus Christ is the key to eternal life.

Father Joe continued his discussion on the Holy Spirit, starting with the death of Jesus on the cross. Before His death, He told the apostles why He was leaving. He was returning to the Father. Jesus promised to give every Christian a "Helper," the Holy Spirit, who is the Intercessor, Comforter, Advocate, and Counselor of all believers. When we receive greater understanding from scripture, when we see the truths we have not seen before, this is the work of the Holy Spirit. He gives strength to endure the hostility of the world system.

Jesus did not leave us alone in the world. Believers have an invisible Helper, the Holy Spirit. What a joy to know that the word *paraclete*, which comes from the Greek word *parakletos*, means "one who comes along side to help" and is used to mean an "advocate" for someone. The Holy Spirit is our Comforter and Counselor. Thus Jesus, who is our paraclete (1 John 2:1) refers to the Holy Spirit as "another Counselor." The Holy Spirit is another Jesus!

Thus Jesus, through the power of the Holy Spirit, will be multiplied and live in millions of believers simultaneously.

Thursday, the fourth day of the retreat, Father Joe asked me, "Are you ready to commit your life to Jesus?"

I answered quickly, "Yes! This is the answer I have been looking for! I know I am a sinner, and because I am a sinner I am condemned to die (spiritually) because the 'wages of sin is death' (Romans 6:23). I understand that God loved me so much that He gave His only begotten Son, Jesus Christ, as my substitute, who bore my sins and the sins of the world, and died in my place, because 'without shedding of blood there is no remission' (Hebrews 9:22). So what do I do now?"

Father Joe said, "Say after me, 'Oh God, I am a sinner. I am sorry for all my sins. I repent. Have mercy upon me and save me for Jesus' sake.'"

I repeated after him.

He then quoted another scripture: "For whosoever shall call upon the name of the Lord shall be saved" (Romans 10:13). He continued, "Take Jesus at His Word. Believe, and you shall be saved. No church, no lodge, no good works, *no one* but Jesus only can save you! Claim your salvation. Do not trust your feelings—they change. Stand on God's promises—they never change."

I sat back, relaxed, and closed my eyes. At that moment I felt a washing of my whole body, a cleansing and washing away of all my doubts, fears, anxieties, and guilt. I felt so clean, light, energetic, and filled with a peace I had never experienced before.

I rose from my chair and said, "Father Joe, I feel so wonderful. I have obeyed your every command. May I go to town and do some shopping?"

Without a word he handed me the keys to his car and gave me directions to the mall. "Go and enjoy yourself," he said with a big smile.

I felt light as a feather as I went to the car and then easily found the mall. Going into a store, I greeted everyone I met and selected some clothes. I was happy our community of sisters had changed the rule two years before about what we were allowed to wear.

Suddenly I was aware of a group of people gathering around me. One person said, "I have never seen anyone so happy! Where are you from?" They were surprised I was from Minnesota, the "cold" state. We all chatted for a while, and I noticed my usual shyness was completely gone. As we moved toward the cash register, I told them I was making a retreat at the monastery with my priest brother. I told them about my salvation experience, concluding with the suggestion, "If you want genuine happiness, make that retreat."

I left the store still knowing the same peace and joy, and as I started walking toward the car I suddenly felt as though I were floating. I drove to the highway, praising and thanking God for the good buys, when I suddenly began speaking in a strange tongue. With this event came such great joy that I burst into tears. Of course they were tears of joy and the beginning of a healing process.

Neither at my mother's nor my father's funerals had I wept. My anger kept me from weeping at both my brother's and Mother Yvonne's funerals. This beautiful healing recalled to me the separations, and I wept in the joy of the Lord. "His will, not mine, be done" was on my lips.

Friday was a day of rejoicing for Father Joe and me. We prayed, sang, and wept together in the presence of our merciful God of Love. Now it was time for me to go home.

I asked Father Joe, "Now what will happen? Nobody at home will understand this."

With a carefree shrug he answered, "Just let it happen."

Now I knew what had caused that miraculous change in him. Praise God!

An hour later I left for the airport a changed person. Where I had lived before, a new creature was living; I was born again. I had experienced my spiritual birth from above. All the confusion, doubt, and anger had been washed away to make room for a new beginning. Eagerly I anticipated what God would do next.

CHAPTER 6

A New Beginning with Manifestations

I went back to work as evening supervisor of the hospital the day after my retreat with Father Joe. The sisters saw the tremendous change in me and wondered what had happened. I answered their questions carefully. I realized they would not understand nor believe if I told them. For a while I just let them enjoy the new me.

The first week back at the hospital was exciting. One evening I was caring for a forty-year-old man in Room 119 who was dying from bleeding ulcers. He was unconscious, and the staff expected that he would die that night. I went to his room and checked all the machines that were keeping him alive. Thoughts about his three little children haunted me. Despite the fact that I did not know how to pray without a prayer book, I began to pray anyway, in a clumsy manner, asking God to have mercy on him, his wife, and children.

My beeper interrupted my efforts, announcing a four-car accident with ten people severely injured. They were coming to the emergency room. I was asked to come quickly. I did not want to leave the man in Room 119 at that moment, but the announcement was repeated. I had to go, so I just cried out loud, "Lord, heal him!"

With that I left for the ER. The injuries from the car crashes were extensive. We finished at 1:00 A.M.

As we were cleaning up, the doctor of the man in Room 119 came walking through. He announced, "Would you believe that I just turned off the machines and stopped the blood transfusion on Louis in 119?"

Someone said, "So he died."

Quickly the doctor answered, "No, he is up walking around telling everybody how good he feels. It's hard to believe."

Unable to speak, I froze in my tracks. In the center of my shock, the realization formed: God had heard my prayer and healed him! The heavenly joy I had felt at my retreat came over me and I wanted to dance, sing, and clap my hands, praising God for answering my prayer. This healing was the first of many more miracles.

Our hospital had become a satellite of the Sister Kenny Institute in Minneapolis, Minnesota. Little Falls had been chosen as the ideal place for a kidney dialysis unit. Kenny Institute sent us their machines to use because they were remodeling and putting in new ones in their large hospital. In a short time we had a full schedule of kidney dialysis patients, who were very happy about the availability of these complex and irreplaceable machines. Now the dialysis patients didn't have to travel one hundred miles to Minneapolis three times per week for the four-hour treatment. Patients whose kidneys fail to function have to use these machines to sustain life until they can receive a kidney transplant. The two kidneys, one on each side of our lumbar vertebrae, consist of tubes and tubules lined with cells which separate water and waste products of metabolism from the blood brought to the kidneys and excrete them as urine through the ureter to the bladder.

One evening as I made rounds of all the departments, I checked the equipment in the dialysis room. Two patients were scheduled to arrive in thirty minutes. I glanced toward the bedside table of the bed in the far corner of the room and noted the absence of the oxygen mask that belonged under the oxygen outlet on the wall. Then I noted the other bedside table had none either.

I said to the nurse in charge, "Where are the oxygen masks?"

He answered, "Come to think of it, we haven't had any the last two days."

With irritation in my voice I said, "You go to the supply room and get them now. I will stay here until you return." He left and was back in three minutes. When he returned I gave him the short lecture he needed: "Never start dialysis on any patient without checking the equipment and supplies. The oxygen masks must be at the bedside before you start dialysis on any patient."

Anything can happen during dialysis, and the machines we were using dated to the first dialysis therapies. They did not always perform as they should. If they failed in the middle of the dialysis, the patient could die. The machines literally replace the patient's failed kidneys. The patient's blood passes by IV through long tubing, leading to the machine, which contains the purifying solution, and back to the patient. At any given time, half of the patient's blood is in both the tubing and machine. Cleaning the patient's blood takes at least four hours for each session. These patients usually have a hemoglobin count of 4, whereas the normal range is 11–13. They are pale and extremely tired.

The patient this evening was a schoolteacher. She taught grades 5 and 6. She was always tired, not surprisingly, when she came in for her treatment. I had great respect for this devoted teacher. I started the IV in her arm and connected her to the machine. I left the room and left her in the care of the nurse. All was working well and the patient fell asleep as usual after a tiring day at school.

About an hour later my beeper alerted me with a scream, "Help! Dialysis!" I was on the second floor, dialysis on the third. I dropped the chart I was holding and flew up the stairs to dialysis. The patient was gasping for breath. The tubing had collapsed and no blood was going anywhere.

I yelled, "Hit gauge 3," and grabbed the oxygen mask and applied it to the patient. She was barely breathing. The tubing was still collapsed. I screamed, "Jesus, help! Only you can fix this!" The tubing started filling up, the machine started working, the patient began to breathe better, and she finally opened her eyes. She removed the mask and asked what time it was. I assured her she could sleep another two hours.

I had just witnessed another miracle. The Holy Spirit had made me aware of the missing oxygen masks. If we had not replaced them, the patient would have died. The Holy Spirit pointed out gauge 3 to me, but there were two other gauges that could have failed. I had no idea gauge 3 was at fault. Interestingly, gauge 3 never failed after that, not while I was there. The other two failed occasionally, but we knew what to do if they did fail. The nurse told me he had to hit number 3 three times before it started to work.

God had intervened; this was clear to me. Tears of gratitude for God's intervention flowed freely as I relaxed and let His love surround me and the patient who was again breathing normally, sleeping peacefully, unaware of her brush with death. I left the room, somewhat numbed by the experience, but doubly sure of God's protection and help. I was calm, secure in my work, and at peace. God cares what is happening in our lives and is available to us if anything goes wrong. Knowing His presence brought me such relief from fears of being alone, facing daily problems of life and death.

After two weeks of unusual blessings I said, "Lord, if I can't tell someone pretty soon, I am going to burst! I am a woman; I have to tell someone. The sisters are not ready to hear this, and I want to tell the world all the wonderful things you have done."

I thought of Yvonne. I had told her what had been happening and the dilemma I was in. It so happened that her sister Charlotte wanted to meet me, and we were invited to her house that evening for coffee.

When we arrived at Charlotte's, I was introduced to her friend, the pastor's wife of an Assembly of God Church in town. After we became acquainted, our conversation turned to God. I related my experience of loss, grief, and depression following my brother's death in December. I described my retreat with Father Joe in June. Halfway through my story, the pastor's wife invited me to give my testimony in their church the following Sunday. Imagine, a Catholic nun speaking in any church about anything, especially supernatural events! At no time did I worry about differences in doctrine or theology. Here was another answer to prayer.

I said, "Yes, with my superior's permission," and, "Thank You, Lord!"

The year before, in November 1969, I met a lady in the hospital who was a patient on the surgical floor. As I made my rounds one day I helped her deal with a problem that caused her great anguish and fear that she was displeasing God. The next day she left the hospital. I did not see her for the next six months. I had seen her later in the bank where she worked the day before I left for Nebraska. Somehow I knew she would play an important part in my life. We became close friends. On my return from Nebraska, she took me out to dinner one day. I told her of my experience with Father Joe as we rode along. She surprised me by saying she had spoken in tongues since she was fourteen years old. Wonderful! I found someone who understood my Nebraska experience. *Thank You, Lord!* She was an Assembly of God Christian, too, and she supported me along the next path, and many others, down which the Lord was leading me. Her name is Yvonne Saulter.

First Testimony

My schedule at the hospital allowed me to have every second weekend off. I was off the following Sunday. As a Catholic and a nun, I had never in my life entered a Protestant church. I remembered my days at my first mission in Elk River, which was 75 percent Protestant. I recalled how I was attracted to the kind and gentle demeanor of the Elk River Protestants. I knew they had something in their church that I wanted. What was it? Maybe this would help me find out.

I thought I would feel guilty going into a Protestant church, but I did not feel any guilt accepting this invitation to their service and sharing my testimony. The idea of any opposition from some convent authorities did not bother me. Prior to this invitation, I would have asked permission of the Board (of several sisters) before beginning any unusual, new experience. But I believed I was being obedient to the Lord's leading and that He was directing my footsteps with a definite purpose, for my good and the good of others.

I had obtained the permission of the Mother General to follow God's lead in this new endeavor. I was grateful that new regulations were in favor of this. I now was free to give glory to God for all the fruits of His blessings.

Sunday came in with its glorious autumn splendor. A few twinges of fear pricked my mind, but they were minor. All my life I had been afraid to speak in front of a group, especially in the presence of higher authority, like speaking in front of a class or facing my superiors in disagreement.

I dreaded stuttering (as I had in grade school) during my testimony. How would a Protestant group relate to the thoughts and experiences of a Catholic nun? Was this acceptable just because the minister's wife had invited me? Maybe a few generous souls would be willing to listen to a Catholic nun. Would they believe what she claimed happened to her? Why would God even allow this strange turn of events in a Catholic's life? From childhood I had been aware of the rift between Catholics and Protestants, mainly from the pulpit and from my parents. Was it possible that we were merging in our beliefs? Questions were mounting in my mind that I could not answer. I prayed that somehow the meeting would go well that evening.

My friend Yvonne came to my rescue. As we drove to the Assembly of God Church, I told her of my fears. Quickly she convinced me there was nothing to fear because God had provided this opportunity for me and, therefore, He would help me to minister to the group. At her words of encouragement, strength and courage dispelled the anxiety.

Everyone greeted me with that same warm friendship that I had experienced in Elk River the first time I ever spoke to a Protestant. The usher seated Yvonne and me in the second row in front. Catholics were not allowed to speak in church before services. If you had to speak, you went outside to converse. I was hesitant to answer questions or hold a conversation with some people who wanted to meet me and in their kindness express their happiness to hear my testimony. I tried my best to be sociable in spite of my training.

The pastor introduced me graciously. He stated he was astonished at the work of the Holy Spirit in the Catholic Church, and he felt honored to be the first Protestant pastor in that town of ten thousand people to welcome a Catholic nun to minister to his congregation. In fact, it was the first time a Catholic nun had ministered to *any* congregation in any church in Little Falls, Minnesota. With that introduction, he called me to the podium.

I went to the podium feeling much better than I had all day, until I turned to face the people. The church was packed—an occurrence I had not considered. But the smiling faces as I looked down on them brought back my courage. I was ready to give them my testimony. Their pleasant and attentive faces made me feel unusually comfortable while talking for ninety minutes. I felt like I had done the impossible with the help of the one who had arranged it all. This was the first time in my life I had spoken to an audience. The people in this church showed their appreciation with applause and many kind words after the service. They reminded me of the first Protestants I had met in Elk River, Minnesota. They accepted me with love and respect. God bless them.

More Testimonies

During the next week I received several invitations to give my testimony in neighboring churches. I scheduled one every second weekend that I was off from work at the hospital. In three weeks I was scheduled at churches in Minnesota for three months in advance. I refused no one. I wanted to spread the Good News wherever I was invited. God had opened the door at my request, and now it was time to do my part.

Yvonne was my constant companion on all these trips, providing transportation, meals, and motels at her expense. We were a team, chosen and brought together by God's divine plan. A Catholic nun and an Assembly of God Christian: who would ever think of such a plan? Only God could make it work! Time was needed for me to surrender completely to the Will of God for my life. I was trying to see the plan He had for me, but all I could do was "just let it happen" as Father Joe had suggested. I trusted God to lead me at the right pace, to the right place, to the right environment, and to the right people. How patient He is! One day at a time according to His Will was the only way to walk this highway to surrender.

In three months I was scheduled every second Sunday in towns and cities all over Minnesota, Wisconsin, and North Dakota. This was my schedule for two and a half years. My superiors were puzzled but did not interfere. Permission was granted for these excursions. Within the first year of testimonies, Father Joe was invited to speak to all the sisters. His teaching was received graciously, but only a few really wanted to change.

Nursing Director at Onamia Hospital

Within these two and a half years (1976 and 1977) I had completed my work as evening supervisor at the hospital in Little Falls and was assigned the position of Director of Nursing at the

Community's hospital at Onamia, Minnesota. Yvonne had bought a house at Onamia prior to my transfer. Because the sisters' house was already full, permission was granted to me to live with Yvonne as a renter. That, I am sure, was divinely planned.

The first few months at Onamia Hospital were a little difficult. I was sent there to prepare the place for Joint Commission (on Accreditation of Hospitals) inspection, which was due in six months. After one month of checking, I realized they had no written guidelines for isolation procedures nor for victims of spills of hazardous wastes, which were occurring more frequently. The main highway from the big cities, where transportation of these wastes was carried almost daily, was close to Onamia Hospital. Victims of accidents involving hazardous wastes would be brought to Onamia Hospital.

I started a manual that included every department in the care of handling these contaminated patients' bodies, clothes, and baggage to prevent contamination of the caregivers. Strangely, I found it difficult to convince the administration and doctors that this was necessary. In six months the manual was completed. Two days later the inspectors came. To everyone's surprise, the first request from the inspectors was "Where is your Isolation Manual?" I had just given it to the administrator the day before to review. The manual saved the day. The rest of the day went smoothly. The nursing part of the inspection received an A because the inspectors admitted they could find nothing wrong.

This was the work of God. My first experience as a director of nursing was a success, but the headaches that go with the job made me eager to leave the job to someone else. I longed to return to bedside nursing.

Christmas preparations were underway. The flu was on the loose. It was hard enough to juggle the schedule as employees, one after another, called in sick. Finally, all the nurses fell victim to the flu at one time. I was the only well nurse for two days and nights. Few aides were on the floor. I had to take charge of the whole hospital of thirty-eight patients with no one to relieve me. I had worked twenty-four-hour stretches before, but this was a new challenge. The first day and night were not too taxing, but to continue for another day and night seemed impossible.

I went to the chapel to plead for help from the Lord. I needed relief to rest. Even an hour would have helped a lot, but no one was able to come. This flu lasted two or three days, leaving one weak and unstable. I prayed again, "Lord, if I can't get relief, then give me your strength so I can continue." I left the chapel knowing God would help me one way or another.

As the day wore on I felt stronger and able to cope with the demands of the patients even better than I had the day before. An extra aide came in the afternoon after recovering from the flu. This help brightened my day, and things went very smoothly. God was answering my prayer throughout the day in different ways. Father Joe was right. God hears our prayers and answers them in a perfect way. The next morning one of the nurses felt strong enough to resume her schedule as day nurse. By noon other nurses were calling in. The schedule was back to normal. Despite my susceptibility to flu in the past, I was spared any sickness. All I needed was some sleep to gear up for the next crisis.

God's Voice, Guidance, and Healing

Christmas came and left before all activities could return to normal. The first three weeks of January were rather quiet and peaceful. On January 20, I was sitting in the living room praying. I closed my eyes and kept still for a while. I was surprised to hear a voice saying, "I want you to quit your job at the hospital." I knew I was alone because Yvonne had left for work half an hour ago. No one else was present. The voice must be God's. I waited quietly, hoping to hear some explanation. None came.

I was determined to obey the command. I left for work and as soon as the administrator came in I went to his office and asked to be released from my job. He refused.

I said, "My work is done here. I only came to help you get through the Joint Commission inspection." The discussion ended there. One month later he let me go. I would still be responsible for thirty days as counselor to the nursing staff, while the hospital used this time to find a replacement.

Two days later I was praying alone in the same place when I heard that soft and gentle voice again. "Now I want you to start planning on leaving the convent." This was the same voice, I knew, that I'd heard before. God was speaking to me; I had no doubt of this.

This time I started to argue. "But I don't have a job! How can I, at age sixty, take care of myself? You know my past: sickly, no knowledge of the world, ignorant of so many things!"

"Don't you trust me?" He answered. Pause. "I will take care of you. Lean on me. I want to take care of you. Do not fear."

End of conversation. Although it was possible, since the Second Vatican Council, to receive a dispensation from Rome from vows made for life, many monastics and lay Catholics looked down on the renunciation of vows as the act of a quitter or a person lacking courage and perseverance. But I knew God was releasing me from my vows. I truly had nothing to fear. He said He would take care of me. This command was not urgent like the first one had been. If He wanted me out of the convent, He would provide the right circumstances at the appropriate time. Again I said to myself, *I'll just let it happen.*

My last thirty days at the hospital were up February 21. I came home from work for the last time. I wondered how this could all happen with a good ending. I felt restless at times and then peace would come, and I refused to worry.

Two days later I woke up with a strange feeling that something was going to happen. I looked outside and noticed ice on the steps and on the road. I turned on the radio; the weather report was scary. The report said a strange weather progression had occurred during the night: the temperature had warmed up, almost raining, and then the temperature had taken a plunge to freezing.

Yvonne had to go to Little Falls that morning—a forty-mile drive. Hazardous driving warnings were out. As soon as she left I sat down to pray. As I was praying I suddenly saw in my spirit her head jerking as though she were being tossed around. I knew then that she must have had an accident. I kept on praying, listening for the phone to ring. In about twenty minutes it rang; the woman on the other end, twenty miles away, told me of the accident.

A truck driver coming from Little Falls spotted the car in the ditch under the bridge. He went to investigate the crash and found Yvonne unconscious in the passenger seat. He checked her pulse and found it strong and regular. He came to a nearby house for help to transfer Yvonne to this home and call the ambulance. She had a broken collarbone and multiple bruises. She had awakened enough before the transfer to tell the EMTs that her right shoulder was hurting. Carrying her up the icy slope to the house was a laborious task. The ambulance was on its way to take her to the hospital in Little Falls. I was instructed not to attempt going to see her until the roads had been cleared.

The next day was warmer with the bright sun melting the ice. The radio announced the icy roads were clearing. Traveling was possible, but cautious driving was recommended. By noon I felt safe making the trip to Little Falls to see Yvonne.

Yvonne's left knee was swollen to twice its size and bruises covered her body due to the car rolling over several times. She received physical therapy during her hospital stay of ten days. According to new hospital regulations, she had to be discharged and continue therapy on an outpatient basis. Her collarbone was not healing well, and she had to be discharged with relaxants and pain medications. The doctor's orders stated she had to have a nurse twenty-four hours a day because of her inability to care for herself and because of the medications she was taking. I was chosen to be her nurse.

One month prior to Yvonne's accident she had come home one evening with a puzzled look on her face. She said, "Now why did I do that?" she asked no one in particular.

"Do what?" I asked.

"My insurance man from AAA came to see me and talked me into taking out more insurance. Lord knows I have plenty of insurance! I am so gullible. I was so busy, we had to talk in between customers, and I don't remember what it pays for. Oh well, it's only $3.00 a month extra. What's done is done. Let's change the subject." She left it at that.

I received permission from the Mother General to take care of Yvonne. The question she asked was "Does Yvonne have insurance?"

I replied, "I know she has some insurance, but I do not know what it covers."

She was somewhat reluctant to give me permission at first but then conceded, realizing that Yvonne had been good enough to let me rent from her when no room at the sister house was available. Some of the sisters lived according to their respective individual service; we who lived apart from the Franciscan Convent were required to say all the prayers that our sisters said, as though we lived together in a group setting.

By this time sisters were employed singly in Minneapolis, Minnesota; Washington, DC; Kentucky; Texas; and other places. One sister was employed in Lebanon. The convent life I had entered years before was changing fast into a much more liberated way of living. Because of the changes concerning life vows after the Second Vatican Council, all religious convents and monasteries experienced an exodus of nuns and priests. Vocations to these institutions dropped to almost zero. The rules and regulations had to be modified to a great degree to receive any vocations. Today, my Community is happy to receive one vocation per year. During the time of my entrance in 1937, the Community received twenty to twenty-five vocations per year.

About a week after Yvonne came home I received a call from the insurance adjuster. After discussing the reasons for my care of Yvonne, he offered me $115 per day for my services. I was astonished at this offer since I had little or no experience with real-life economics. (My first check came after I decided to write to Rome for dispensation from my vows.) This was far better than working in the hospital. My answer from Rome approving my dispensation arrived two weeks later. As soon as I received my dispensation I was free of my obligations to the Franciscan Community.

God was taking care of me, far better than I had dared to imagine. What a wonderful Father we have! I was free, dispensed of my

Anne at age 60 in 1977 after 40 years in the St. Francis Convent, having received her dispensation from Rome.

vows to the Franciscan Community. My new assignment from God was to nurse Yvonne back to health and follow God's leading from there on. He was now my Shepherd, my Savior, my Counselor, and my All!

Weeks passed, but Yvonne's collarbone would not heal. Finally in June the doctor made his decision. If it did not start healing in two weeks, he would have to operate. This news was discouraging; Yvonne was worried and disappointed. She had to continue wearing a sling to keep the right arm immobile so she would not injure further the area of the break in her collarbone.

Yvonne went to bed early that night, tired and hurting. At midnight her sobbing awakened me. I went to her room and sat down beside her. "You are worried about the surgery, aren't you?" I asked. She nodded and continued sobbing. No more was said. I placed my hand over the area of the break and prayed for healing of the collarbone. I felt heat spreading through my right hand as I prayed. I had never experienced this before. I was not sure what it meant.

Two weeks later we went to see her doctor for an x-ray of her collarbone. Shortly, he returned from developing the film, grinning and excited. He announced, "I can hardly believe this! It's 75 percent healed!" He asked me what I had done. I told him I had prayed for healing. All he could say was, "Here is proof God heard your prayer!" What a relief! We were so elated we praised and thanked God all the way home.

During the first week in June 1976 I received a call from the Full Gospel group in Duluth, Minnesota, inviting me to come and minister to their group again and to the surrounding churches for a week. I was a little hesitant about leaving Yvonne with someone else. Yvonne was now able to provide more of her own care. She felt I should go. We arranged for her physical therapy sessions on a daily basis and for someone to stay with her and cook her meals. Friends are such a blessing! They were both Christians and reliable people.

In Duluth I stayed at the home of Carol, the leader of an intercessory prayer group. They met at Carol's home during my visit, and I attended the meeting. We prayed for many members of their congregation. This meeting provided my introduction to the hateful activities of the devil in the world and how easily we fall prey to his deceitful snares. I had always been told the devil is in hell. I had no idea he was roaming around seeking whom he could lead into sin in his loathsome, sneaky ways. I became aware of his presence in the world as a destroyer when I heard the intercessors pray with authority over the devil, casting him out of their presence.

A pause occurred in the praying. Before I realized what I was doing, I was kneeling in the middle of the group saying "Please pray for me. I have a big decision to make. I need to know what steps to take because I feel I will have to make a big change." No one knew I was leaving the convent and was taking care of Yvonne. The future was shaky in spite of my financial blessing.

No questions were asked. Instead, words of wisdom and knowledge came to me from several members. One said, "The step you are about to take requires cleansing, faith, and determination. I, your God, shall lead thee; be obedient."

Another said, "The Lord is saying, 'I will meet you in the cool of the evening,'" referring to my age (sixty).

Another said, "The flower I have planted in your bosom will blossom in the desert."

Carol, sitting next to me, was praying in tongues. She reached over, placed her hand on my head, and asked God to give me a word of knowledge. Instantly I knew that God wanted me to be *free* so He could use me. Everything became clear at that moment. As they prayed over me I felt the stripping of the bondage of slavery from me to freedom of spirit that could now soar to heights unknown. In my heart I knew He would lead me and guide me in wisdom from above. I must allow Him the freedom to shape circumstances that would lead me to the right decisions. Praise God!

The rest of my visits to churches and meeting places proved very interesting. One day we had a prayer meeting at a woman's house. I gave a short version of my testimony so we could spend more time in intercession. A young mother with two little girls came up to me, visibly disturbed. She knelt down and begged me to pray that she receive the gift of tongues. She stated she had been praying for two years, but she just could not understand why she wasn't getting results. I started to pray in tongues, but shortly I realized she needed something else first.

So I said to her, "I feel you are to receive something else first." I barely finished my sentence when she started to sob so hard her whole body shook. Still sobbing she looked up at me with the most beautiful smile on her face. I said to her, "That's what you needed, the gift of tears. Keep on smiling, praising, and thanking God." She nodded and continued smiling and crying.

The Holy Spirit knows what we need to pray for. Sometimes we pray for something we want badly instead of what we need badly at the time. I met the young woman, still smiling and crying, outside a couple times after prayer. Every time she said, "I feel so good! I feel like a ton of bricks fell off my shoulders." What a transformation! God's light had broken through the darkness in only a moment and birthed a joy she had never known before.

Father Frank's Story

The last night I spent in Duluth, I was scheduled to give my testimony at a Lutheran Church. The congregation was large. Pews were lined up in the middle section and on both sides with aisles in between. Every seat was occupied.

I began my testimony as usual. About halfway through I was speaking of the need to take time to speak to whomever happens to come our way. We never know who needs just a kind word or a smile to help them through the day.

Suddenly I stopped. My brother Father Frank came to mind. He had told me once of a strange incident. I felt urged to tell that story right then. This never occurred in my testimony before. Somehow I knew I had to tell it.

Father Frank had been on his way to Europe on sabbatical. In Chicago he had a two-hour wait for his plane to Kennedy Airport in New York. He had taken his suitcase and walked up to a bench in the middle section of the airport. At the other end of the bench sat a man, dressed as though he was poor, staring at the floor with a hopeless expression, looking like someone who did not wish to be disturbed.

After a few minutes my brother began a conversation, hoping to visit with the man just to pass the time away. At first he got no response, but he kept on. Then he told the man a funny story (Father Frank's forte in any situation). The man listened and seemed to enjoy it. My brother kept talking and soon won the man's attention. The two-hour wait seemed short. The man got up and thanked my brother for the visit. He commented that he had particularly enjoyed my brother's interest in astronomy and his explanation of the universe.

Father Frank went on to his plane and finished his journey to Europe without any difficulty. He returned to his mission in New Mexico a month later and continued in his work as a parish priest.

About two years later, he received a large package in the mail. The package had no return address. He had not ordered anything. Puzzled, he started to unwrap the package, and to his surprise the wrappings contained a large, beautiful telescope. Who could have sent this to him? he wondered.

A piece of paper was tied to one end of the telescope. It was a note of explanation. Quickly he looked to see who had sent the telescope. The paper had no name, so he read the letter.

Dear Father Frank,

I don't know if you remember me, but I will never forget you. About two years ago we met at the Chicago airport. You were on your way to Europe. You came to sit on the bench with me while you were waiting for your plane to Kennedy Airport in New York, which would arrive in two hours. You were so kind, but I was in no mood for talking. You started to talk about the creation, how God created the universe, and you started explaining the beauty of the creation and how He created man on the sixth day, and that God wanted to share His creation with man. You were so interesting. Something happened inside of me.

You see, I was on my way to committing suicide. After hearing you speak I changed my mind. When we parted I made note of your address on your suitcase because I wanted to thank you someday for befriending me. I had made up my mind to go out and find a job and make a change in my life. I found a job that same day with a company that made parts for telescopes. Today I am the president of that company, and I am rich. I will be eternally grateful to you for saving my life.

I do not want you to know my name because I do not want you to feel obligated in any way. I just want you to enjoy the gift.

I finished my testimony that night, wondering why I had to tell that story. I soon found out. One of the ushers told me that a lady wanted to see me. She seemed very disturbed and insisted she must see me. He led me to the lady.

The lady was probably in her early thirties, a nice looking lady, shy, but ready to unburden herself. She said, "I am a nun like you, but so unhappy. I really don't know why I am this way. I am not living with the sisters right now, because Reverend Mother thought it would help me to make up my mind to stay or leave the convent if I was away from the sisters for a while to think things over. I came here tonight to see what you were going to talk about. When you told your brother's story I, too, decided not to commit suicide."

That was why the Holy Spirit had wanted me to tell that story! We spent the next thirty minutes together, after which she resolved her problem and decided to go back to the convent and be honestly open with the administration concerning her problems with Community life. She seemed eager to go back and resume her duties. God works in mysterious ways.

My task at Duluth was finished. I returned home with a happy heart. I felt so much closer to God after witnessing these experiences, marveling at His tender mercy and the abundance of His love He bestowed on all the people I had met.

I had only two more appointments to take care of when I came home. My two-and-one-half-year schedule of testimonies would then be complete. Yvonne was doing well. We continued her therapy through the next two months. By August 22, 1977 she was able to go back to work. Her two middle fingers of her right hand were still numb, and she walked with a limp. More time was needed for all this to return to normal. However, this would not prevent her from resuming her duties at the bank.

About one month later the bank's insurance company called me requesting a statement of all I earned so far from my care of Yvonne. They would pay 80 percent of the total. The amount was $25,200. In two weeks I received another check from AAA Insurance Co. for $20,160, which totaled $45,360 with the previous check. God had promised He would take care of me, but this was beyond my wildest dream. When He made that promise in January I had thought He meant spiritual help only. Now I realized He was concerned about physical means also. I was still equating spirituality with poverty. It became clear to me that God had created heaven and earth, and they belonged to Him. I was a child of the King of heaven and earth, and poverty would no longer be a part of my life. Praise God!

Suddenly the requests for my testimony stopped. Had I done something wrong? Was I failing to please God? I was distressed about this, but in my heart I knew I had made these talks to churches to glorify God. After two and a half years, my scheduled talks were completed. I waited for an answer.

The rest of 1977 was a period of rest and quiet, a time to reflect, a time to start preparing for my future in a world I did not know. I was stripped of my fears knowing I had a God who loved me deeply and cared for me and heard my prayers. I would let Him lead and guide me as I started my walk leading to the surrender of my life to Him.

A Big Move

The year 1978 would be a new beginning but not in Minnesota. The prophecies given me were to be fulfilled in Texas, fifteen hundred miles away. Knowing that God would do the planning and I would do the obeying made the transition much easier. I never felt alone in the events as they were presented to me. Yvonne was doing very well now.

In May 1978 I was in the living room studying my Bible when suddenly I was struck with the knowledge that I was going to leave Minnesota. I said, "Lord, where should I go?"

The answer came quickly: "Go to Marfa, Texas." In my spirit I saw Father Frank, my brother, sitting in his living room in Marfa, Texas by the phone. He seemed to be waiting for the phone to ring. I knew clearly that Marfa was my destination. A team of horses could not have held me back from going to the phone at once to call him.

He was surprised when I told him I wanted to come to live in Marfa, but he was happy and ready to do anything to help me.

I said, "Are there any houses for sale? I also will need a job. Is there a hospital close by?"

He was not sure about a house, but there was a sixty-bed hospital in Alpine, twenty-six miles away. He offered to go and secure me a job first. He was quite sure the hospital had a shortage of nurses, especially registered nurses, to work in these rural areas. He was excited about my coming to Marfa because we had been separated for so many years. We had hours of catching up to do.

Father Frank went to Alpine that same afternoon to see the Director of Nurses at the hospital. That evening I received a call from him informing me that I had a job as supervisor of the whole hospital waiting for me. I could hardly believe this was happening so fast. He then told me that there was no house for sale in all of Marfa. However, he assured me he would keep looking until he found one suitable for me.

At this time I was not sure if Yvonne would follow me to Texas or not. She needed to know if this was what God wanted her to do. Also she would have to sell her home in Onamia, which might take a while. She was doing well at the bank. Would there be a job for her in Marfa? Her whole family was living in Minnesota. They were a close-knit family, and she had never lived in any state other than Minnesota. Her one brother and five sisters were very dear to her. I did not pressure her. This decision belonged with her and God. I told her she was welcome to join me any time she wanted to. I was not leaving until a house became available in Marfa.

The next evening at about 9:00 P.M. the phone rang. Father Frank greeted me with an exuberant "Cheerio" and quickly told me his great news. "Anne, I have a house for you! My friend Harold, who lives across the street from me, was here last night to tell me his sad story. He owns three or four houses here in town. He came through the door mumbling something about 'too many lawns and not enough time to take care of them.' I asked him what his problem was and he blurted out, 'Frank, I have to sell my house on Columbia Street. I can't keep up with all this work; I'm too old!' I said to him, 'It is sold. My sister from Minnesota is coming here and wants to buy it.'"

"Anne, I'm sure you would like it. You might want to change some things. It has two shops he used for his antiques. The place has a lot of potential. How about coming down to see it first?"

I asked Yvonne to come along and help me evaluate the property, as I had never done anything like this before. She was delighted at the chance to go.

That same weekend we flew to Marfa, Texas. We landed in Midland, Texas and called Father Frank. "How far are we from Marfa?" I asked.

He said, "One hundred and eighty miles."

We were lucky. A small airline had just established a daily flight from Midland to Alpine two weeks before. In one hour we were winging our way to Alpine, where Father Frank gave us the big welcome to Texas and took us to Marfa. I was enamored with the gorgeous mountains, oohing and aahing as we drove to Marfa. My childhood dream was coming true.

Ever since I had read the story of *Heidi* in grade school I dreamed of living in the mountains some day. In Minnesota there are no mountains, just hills. All the forty years in the convent I remained in Minnesota without any hope of ever living in the mountains. Coming to live in Texas was truly miraculous. We arrived in Marfa late that afternoon.

Marfa is a quaint town of about twenty-five hundred people. The courthouse, almost one hundred years old, stands proudly in the center of town as a statue of justice for all its citizens. Many of the buildings on either side of Main Street leading up to the courthouse had a Mexican accent of art, adding a touch of beauty to the town.

Yvonne and I were touched by the welcome of the people, waving to us as we drove to Father Frank's home a block away from the courthouse. We passed a beautiful three-story building with an enclosed courtyard. It was named El Paisano Hotel. In the front window we saw pictures of Rock Hudson, James Dean, and Elizabeth Taylor who starred in the film *Giant*, which was filmed in Marfa and surrounding ranches in 1956.

We finished eating supper with Father Frank and his housekeeper, Liz Pavlik, at about 8:00 P.M. We were beginning to feel the Texas climate that was different from Minnesota's. A big change from humidity to dry took its toll. By 9:00 P.M. we were sound asleep.

After a nourishing Texas-style breakfast, we were ready for a first look at our possibly new home in the near future. We drove three blocks north of my brother's house and waited anxiously for my brother to stop somewhere. He drove up to a long white wood-frame house with a spacious yard in which grew a dozen barrel cacti in full bloom. I never knew that cacti had such rich colored flowers. Next to the cacti were the two shops he had mentioned on the phone.

We met Harold, the owner, shortly and the renter who had just made arrangements for another month's stay. The front part of the house still had the equipment and space for a beauty salon that Harold's wife had operated for many years before her death. The adjoining rooms were small. The bedroom was next and two bathrooms. Next to the bedroom was a den leading to the kitchen. There was no carport. The whole building was long and in need of expansion and remodeling. For some reason or other I fell in love with the idea of some day remodeling it to our taste, and Yvonne felt the same way. The property was fenced in for privacy as are many of the homes in Marfa.

We both agreed the place had potential, but it had to be remodeled. I would return in August after settling all my affairs in Onamia, Minnesota. This would truly be a new beginning starting at the bottom and gradually working upwards as time and money would allow. I knew this was what God had planned, and I felt secure in His plan. Yvonne had more to contend with in Minnesota than I did before she could be sure of God's Will in her life. Family, job, sale of the house, and separating from all her loved ones, which was not going to be easy. This would be her first move far away from home. We placed it all in God's hands. Somehow it would work out.

We returned to Minnesota the next day. I started planning my exit, releasing the things I treasured because I would be traveling by car to Texas. Yvonne and I went to Brainerd to look at cars. I drove home that afternoon a proud owner of the first Honda Accord LX. It took me to Texas three weeks later with all my possessions in the back seat, except my new piano. I had no idea when that would follow.

On August 12, 1978 at 5:00 A.M., Yvonne and I started our trip to Marfa, Texas. We did not make many stops because by

10:00 P.M. that evening we were on the border of Texas. We were so proud of ourselves! It couldn't be far now. We did not know how very large the state of Texas is in comparison to Minnesota, the only state we knew. We did not realize we still had 750 miles to go. By 8:00 P.M., after driving all day we came to Ft. Davis where the sign read, "21 miles to Marfa." That was the longest twenty-one miles I ever traveled. By 8:30 P.M. we arrived in Marfa. Then I recalled that August 15 was my father's birthday. Oh, how we celebrated his birthdays at home until the wee hours of the morning. He always enjoyed celebrations. Well, I had reason to celebrate too! This was something I had only dared to dream about. *Today it is reality!* I thought. *I'm going to live in the mountains of Texas where I would regain my health and strength and start a brand new life according to God's plan.*

We drove up to my brother's house and, after all the welcoming, quickly unpacked my few belongings. My brother kindly offered me his extra bedroom until the renter moved out of our new home on Columbia Street. I accepted with no hesitation since that would solve my first problem.

The next day, Wednesday, I drove Yvonne to the airport in Midland so she could return to work in the morning. On my way back through Alpine I stopped at the hospital to find out when I was to report for work. The director of nursing was very understanding. Because of my long trip, she would schedule me for Monday morning for my first day at Big Bend Memorial Hospital in Alpine, Texas. I was surprised when she told me that I would be the only RN in the building. They had just hired an RN from Canada for the evening shift a couple weeks before. An LVN was in charge of the night shift. RNs were scarce in rural areas in Texas.

The rest of the week I rested and visited with my brother and Liz, his housekeeper. It was many years since we had gotten a chance to visit. He lived on missions in Texas and the Southwest, and I had lived in the frozen north. This was a happy reunion long overdue. We relished every moment. He introduced me to many people in town and helped me in many ways to get started in that new environment.

Sunday morning I met many of the Catholic people who attended Father Frank's Mass at his private chapel next to his home. Many of the people attending were Mexican-Americans. They were friendly, glad to add one more member to the small town of Marfa.

Marfa, at an elevation of 4,688 feet above sea level, is surrounded by majestic, unspoiled mountain country that rises in spots to more than 8,000 feet into clear sky free from pollution. Its citizens support themselves by ranching cattle, sheep, and goats and by working in allied industries serving the area. The town had a bank, an independent weekly newspaper, television cable reception, a modern, lighted airport, a city park, a swimming pool, a library, a museum, fine churches and schools, a state university (within easy commuting distance), and a hospital twenty-six miles away in Alpine.

Marfa and the surrounding area have been the scenes of several movies. *Giant, High Lonesome, The Andromeda Strain*, and *Sylvester* being the most notable. Marfa also has the first solar-powered government building in the Southwest, the U.S. Border Patrol Headquarters. They patrol vast areas of the U.S.–Mexico border from Marfa.

Marfa also has the highest golf course in Texas at a cool 4,882 feet above sea level. The biggest attraction, however, are the Ghost Lights of Marfa. They are still as mysterious as when they were seen by early settlers driving their herds into the area in 1893. What makes the lights? Where are they really located? How long ago did they first begin to shine? The mystery is no closer to being solved than it was in the endless days and nights gone by.

Wildlife is abundant in the Marfa area. Deer, antelope, javelina, dove, and quail live in the area and make for good hunting.

Marfa is also well known for soaring because of its excellent flying weather, among the best in the world. It has been the site of several state, regional, national, and world championship soaring events. These events are fascinating to watch.

Monday came quickly. I had to be at work at 6:45 A.M. I received no three-day orientation. I soon found out that this sixty-bed hospital was the busiest place I had ever encountered in my nursing career so far. We had a staff shortage for the sixty patients. I was told I was head nurse of the medical floor and supervisor of all nursing departments, including nursery and emergency room. I was on duty for only twenty minutes when I was called to evaluate the progress of an obstetric patient who had arrived an hour before. She was ready to deliver. I learned then I was expected to assist with every delivery.

As head nurse I made rounds with every doctor, administered all medications on the medical floor, and monitored the care of the babies in the nursery. I also helped on the surgical floor with any difficulty the surgical nurses might encounter, like starting IVs or blood transfusions, inserting nasogastric tubes, and solving equipment problems. I had one LVN in the ER who seldom had a break during the day. One LVN was in charge of the surgical floor. Aides assisted the LVN with baths and keeping the patients comfortable. I had a ward clerk on the medical wing, which helped greatly. I still had to do all the doctors' orders. One LVN was in charge of a four-patient ICU on the medical floor. I was responsible for the welfare of all these patients. Across the hall from ICU was a large room for pediatric patients.

My first day on duty was a review of all I had ever learned in training about nursing. We had no time to stop for coffee break—ever. The noon meal break was supposed to last thirty minutes. Later I would learn that I would usually be called out during those thirty minutes, sometimes never finishing my meal.

I came home at 5:45 P.M. that first day, wondering what all had happened. Was every day like this? Would I be strong enough to endure this pace? I loved every minute of it, but I had to eat a bigger breakfast in case I had to skip the noon meal. I went to bed at 9:00 P.M., exhausted.

The next day, I was up at 4:30 A.M. I had a breakfast of steak, fried potatoes, carrots and peas, applesauce, and two pieces of buttered toast. I was on my way to work at 5:15 A.M., feeling well fortified and prepared for anything. This was my routine every morning until things got better. They never did.

With the winter months came the severe flu, and we had to set up extra beds in the hallways for the seriously ill patients. When Christmas came, the doctors sent as many patients home as possible. We had ten empty beds when I left for home December 24. By morning when I returned, they were all occupied. It seemed impossible to keep a bed cool and empty for a day. This was real nursing care for me. Never had I felt so happy and satisfied by the end of the day.

All areas of my training were challenged daily, including public relations. In this profession I believed I was truly serving God's people who were afflicted with pain, depression, sorrow, and hopelessness. Yet so much joy came out of surmounting these miseries with patients in prayer and medicine linked together, giving them hope until they reached the shore of health again. Every day was blessed with challenges and victories because God supplied me with the strength and health I needed for each day. My nights were never interrupted by sleeplessness, and by morning I was thoroughly rejuvenated for a repeat performance.

On February 10, 1980 I awoke from a dream. I looked at the clock. It was 2:30 A.M. "No," I said, "I have to sleep two more hours before my new day begins." As I said that a familiar picture started to develop in my mind. I was standing at the front door of my house trying to see what was within. I opened the door and was surprised to see a large room with a brick fireplace at the right. I could see into the bedroom that was enlarged too. There was only one bathroom. The den and the kitchen appeared as I knew them. What had happened to the other bathroom? I saw it changed into a walk-in closet adjacent to the first bathroom. All the floors were carpeted. All the walls had beautiful paneling except the bedroom, which had wallpaper.

I was puzzled. A little voice said to me, "This is how you will remodel this house." I also saw something else in the living room up toward the ceiling. I did not know until later that it was the equipment for central heating and air conditioning. The next thing I remember was waking up to the buzz of the alarm clock. I do not know when I fell asleep again, but I remembered everything I saw.

That evening I called Yvonne and told her about it. We both agreed I should start remodeling right away. I convinced her to come down for the weekend so we could talk about the changes we would make. We had many things to discuss. I told her I would meet her at the airport in Midland on Friday evening at 10:30.

Yvonne came as planned. The weekend was just what we needed to catch up with the news in Minnesota and Texas. Neither of us had had time to write, so when our bag of news was full, it was time for one of us to call the other, whoever got to the phone first.

We made our plans, and Father Frank talked to Foxworth Lumber Co. of Marfa to do the remodeling. A week after Yvonne returned to Minnesota the plan was put into action. The house needed total rewiring and new plumbing, among other things. Deteriorated parts and windows were removed; ceilings and walls came down. The living room was enlarged by the removal of three small rooms. We added the red brick fireplace. The beauty parlor at the front entrance became my office with an adjoining utility room for washer and dryer, furnace, and water heater. One wall of the utility room had cupboards and two sinks which were left intact.

By the middle of May Yvonne was ready to leave Minnesota and join me. I was thrilled! I flew to Minneapolis on my birthday, May 22, and after a day of rest, we started out for Texas in her Thunderbird. My brother kept an eye on the remodeling proceedings while I was gone. All went well.

We returned to Marfa two days later, happy to be together again. Since two people had more than enough to do, Yvonne refrained from accepting any job until after the renovation was completed. A new shop was built, the two existing shops were carpeted, paneled, and air-conditioned and a carport was added in the back of the house. A cement block fence enclosed the property. The last touch was the red brick outside which added protection and beauty. Everything was completed by October 9, 1978. A housewarming brought many people to congratulate us and wish us well. The transformation was truly amazing for people who had frequented the beauty parlor.

All those months I had been working at the hospital in Alpine. After the first few months I became used to the pace, which never let up. We never seemed to have enough help to adequately meet the needs of every patient entrusted to us. We managed to maintain good standards for the inspection in March.

In 1974 Sul Ross State University had established a nursing school for licensed vocational nursing at the hospital. All classes were held in the classroom in the basement of the hospital. About twelve students per year took the course, with one RN teaching all ten subjects. She was director, instructor, and counselor for the program. This course provided a one-year program with bedside nursing care from August until the next August, at which time the students were prepared to take the state board exams.

In November 1979 I was asked by Sul Ross to take over that job teaching the nursing program because the preceding director was moving to another area of Texas by the end of November. I was the only one recommended. After some deliberation I took the job for there was very little time left for introduction to the program. To me this was a sacred trust; I did not take it lightly. This position was a responsibility that would test me as much as my students. I was known as a critic, a nurse that never seemed to be satisfied, always finding fault with a job that was done any way less than perfect because I remembered what I had been taught: The patient comes first.

Would I, a two-year grad in nursing, be able to inspire my students to do the same with respect, love, and sense of duty? I would do my best. Living twenty-six miles away could be a problem, since my students would be assigned to different shifts during the year. If any problem arose concerning a student's behavior, I would be notified, day or night.

Changing teachers in the middle of a course is difficult for both students and teacher. Less than halfway through the second week of teaching, one of the students who had worked at the hospital the past two years brought up an event concerning me that occurred the second month I was employed at Big Bend Memorial Hospital. She broached this subject very cleverly. We were studying pharmacology. I had mentioned that when a doctor orders drugs for a patient, a nurse must know if he has the dosage and strength correct as well as the route to be given, the frequency, and the length of days. We discussed this issue at some length when this particular student, who was not too fond of me as a teacher, asked me, "If a doctor orders a treatment for a patient, and you do not agree, do you still have to give it?"

Immediately I recalled the incident she was referring to. I replied, "If you do not agree with the doctor's order, you call the doctor and discuss it with him, but be sure you know why you are disagreeing. A treatment or a drug ordered by the doctor may not be right because of allergies unknown to the doctor or other circumstances. Very rarely is it necessary for a nurse to object to a doctor's order. A meeting of the board of directors (all doctors) is necessary to counteract a doctor's order by a nurse."

The student was not satisfied. She asked me to explain the incident. I knew she had been misinformed, and I needed to put the year-old incident to rest. By this time the curiosity of each student in the class was aroused.

I began to relate the incident. One wet autumn morning I came to the hospital, unaware of a motorcycle accident the evening before which caused a young man, twenty-seven years old, to be brought to the emergency room in serious condition. Many x-rays had been taken to determine how many bones were broken and whether he had internal injuries or not. He did have numerous broken bones, and his neck was broken. The doctor on call was summoned and came to evaluate his condition. The patient was still on a stretcher in the x-ray department when I arrived at 5:30 A.M.

A nurse and x-ray technician accosted me as I came past the door. "Anne, can't you do something? This patient has been vomiting the last hour; he has a broken neck, so we can't turn his head to vomit. He has to swallow his vomit. The doctor refuses to let us suction him because he is going to die anyway."

I didn't ask any questions. I went to the phone and asked the doctor if I could insert a nasogastric tube and hook up the patient to a suction machine. I heard the same answer:

"No. He is going to die."

I said, "Doctor, he may die, but I will not let him choke to death."

The doctor again said, "No."

I went to the administrator's office and told him briefly, "I am going against the doctor's orders on the motorcycle accident patient of last night because it is my duty as a nurse not to let the patient choke to death."

He said, "Anne, you do what you know you have to do. I will call the doctors in for a meeting. I support you."

I went quickly to the x-ray department and relieved the poor man. When I finished the procedure I checked the results and looked at the young man. He was crying and trying to get hold of my hand.

He said, "God bless you; you are so kind. Thank you, thank you." I'll never forget that moment. I knew in my heart I had done the right thing, and I was so happy. I could lose my license for having disobeyed the doctor's order. Yet I would know for the rest of my life that I had helped a dying patient suffer a little less agony knowing that some nurse was willing to put her license on the line because she cared for his comfort.

Before I left for the day I went to see how he was doing. He was resting quietly with eyes closed. The prognosis was very poor, but at least he was comfortable. The doctors had been in meeting from early morning to after dinner. What was the report? I did not know. It didn't really matter. I still had at least an hour of charting to do on this patient. I was prepared for a lawsuit, so I wrote my nurses' notes in detail for the hospital's protection and mine. I slept very well that night.

The next morning I made rounds with the doctors. When I finished I was called to the conference room regarding my actions of the day before. To my surprise no questions were asked. The chief of staff commended me on my quick decision and action in this case. The words he used in the name of all the doctors were, "Anne, you did the right thing. We are all proud of you for we realize what you were up against. We will all stand and support you in case of a lawsuit. Please do not worry about this at all."

I thanked them and went out to enjoy my daily routine of duties.

Six months later I was called to the administrator's office. The only reason for anyone being called to his office was either to be fired or to be confronted for some offense. I did not have any reason to fear, but this was unusual so I did stop and examine my conscience once more in case I had forgotten something. I knocked and entered at his response.

He pointed to the chair and said, "Please sit down." He smiled as he proceeded. "Do you remember that motorcycle accident last year? The twenty-seven-year-old patient who died from it?"

"How well I remember!" I responded.

"Well, you saved the hospital a million dollars. The family is suing the hospital and the doctor each a million. When the lawyer saw and read your charting, the case against the hospital was dropped. The hospital and I thank you! All of Alpine thanks you."

I was rather numb, but I managed to get out a short, grateful response. "Thank you for letting me know," I said. "I tried my best, and I am grateful that I had a chance to help not only the patient but also the hospital." Another chapter closed and another lesson learned. I thanked God for my good instructors in nursing school who had taught us our duties to the patient so well.

In the classroom, at the conclusion of my story, the room was totally silent. Remembering one of the most well known axioms of teaching, I now had their attention and took advantage of it.

"Nursing is more than passing medications, charting a few notes, and clocking out," I said, breaking the silence. "You must have standards to go by when you must make decisions. You cannot depend on others to make them for you. The patient comes first and you will be put to the test. Are you making this or that decision for your convenience or glory, or are you ready to place the patient's needs first and risk a few wagging tongues and a possible lawsuit? You might not be understood, as I wasn't, or called names for doing the best for the patient. Are you ready for that? Think this over. If you want to be a good nurse, you will have to prove to me that you understand the above or you will not be allowed to pursue the nursing career. I won't let you."

The hour was up, and the class dismissed in total silence. I was glad that someone brought up the subject. This student's mother was the DON of the hospital at the time, and the DON was not happy with me for having disobeyed the doctor. This student was disruptive in class, and I reprimanded her several times with no success. I had to refer her to the psychiatrist at SRSU. If she refused to see him, I would not accept her in the classroom. So many nursing students are not prepared adequately for the sacredness of caring for and healing the sick. Book knowledge is only a taste of one ingredient of this profession. Nursing requires love for mankind, gentleness, temperance, humility, the forgetting of self, and bearing a joyous nature. It is a godly profession. Anything less makes you fall short of its calling.

This test of my teaching ability was put to rest for good. The students were determined to show me that they understood what I had said. Their grades went up, their bedside care was impeccable, and I gave all the tests from there on. The rest of my teaching career went smoothly. The students passed their state board exams and many of them have gone on to become registered nurses, holding very responsible positions in hospitals and nursing homes. By my third year in teaching I realized the burden of this job was taking its toll on my health.

I felt uneasy about quitting four months before the end of the class year (August 24) when I met a lady in a neighboring town who would become my spiritual mentor for the next phase of my nursing career. Another friend of mine from Marfa introduced me to her.

After we visited for a while, she said to me, "Anne, you look so tired. What kind of work do you do?"

I said, "I am a registered nurse. I have been teaching the nursing class for Sul Ross. I am glad you brought up the subject. I feel I need to quit this job because I fear for my health. I would like confirmation on this before I make my final decision."

After I filled her in on more details, she looked at me and said, "You must protect your health, for your body is the temple of the

Holy Spirit. You have served God many years. I know He approves of your decision." Puzzled at what she said, I wondered how she knew I had been in the convent.

She smiled and said, "When you walked through the door I saw you wearing a nun's habit."

I said, "How did you know?"

Again, she smiled and said, "God has given me the gift of knowledge" (I Corinthians 12:8). She continued, "You go on a long vacation. You need it badly. God has given you direction; you are following His orders. I assure you, He will bless you for your obedience."

This is what I had needed to hear. This was the confirmation. I felt the hand of God in blessing and instruction. I was very relieved to hear that the leading I felt was from the Lord.

I needed an extended rest, but only after the university agreed to provide extra help to the next instructor. This job was too much for one person. In May 1981 I was relieved of my duties. That summer, Yvonne and I drove to Minnesota to see our friends and relatives.

Private Duty Nursing

We returned to Texas on August 1, 1981. I was ready to go to work, for I was well rested. About 7:00 P.M. I was unpacking my suitcase when the phone rang. The caller was Helen Mitchell, an eighty-three-year-old lady living on a ranch two miles out of Marfa. Her sister was living with her mainly for companionship because her husband had died several years before. Helen was a delightful lady with a keen mind. My brother had introduced her to me shortly after I had arrived in Texas.

Helen was calling from the hospital in El Paso two hundred miles away. She had suffered a stroke two weeks prior and would soon be released from the El Paso hospital to the hospital in Alpine for a couple weeks before she could return to her home. She could leave in a day or so if she were able to procure a nurse to care for her since she was unable to walk; the stroke had left her with partial paralysis. She wanted me to fill that position. Would I do it? It didn't take me long to check with the Lord. My answer was "Yes."

I explained to her that I was free to do so because I was no longer teaching the nursing program. Helen was wealthy and could afford private duty nursing, so we would have no problem working out a healthy schedule for three aides and myself. We were all paid well and were happy with the arrangement. I knew in my heart that God had provided me with this job. I also knew that it would change my life somehow. I said, "Your will be done, Lord. Help me to change according to your plan."

Caring for Helen was my first experience meeting all the needs of an elderly person who is totally dependent on those entrusted with her care. At the same time I became aware of the wisdom that the elderly possess. They have had many years of experience in many areas of life, good and bad.

Helen had been married to an intelligent man who loved ranching and shared all his experience with her and taught her the buying and selling of livestock for profit. His success was visible in the elegant furnishings of the house. It was remarkable. I was happy for Helen. She could still enjoy this beautiful home in his memory instead of living in a nursing home where the residents' independence is almost nil and the atmosphere usually drab.

This schedule was much less demanding than all my hospital work and teaching up to this point. I had time to begin planning how to utilize our three shops that we had remodeled three years ago. Until now they had been just storage areas. In 1979 when Yvonne came to Texas, all our furniture, including my piano, had been brought down by the Bekins Van Line. Included also were all the antiques we had collected from Onamia, Minnesota.

Birth of "Anne & Yvonne's Treasure Chest"

I decided we should sell whatever we could not use in the house. The money would be welcome. Yvonne was working full-time at the courthouse as secretary to the judge. She agreed with my plan. We started labeling the items and separated them from the things we would keep. We finally had our sale. We entered it in the weekly paper. Much of the larger furniture was placed on the patio between the shops and the house.

Saturday morning at eight we were already swamped with customers. We could barely keep up with the sales. I handled the patio, and Yvonne covered the shop. As I was going in the house to answer the phone, I noticed Mary, one of our friends, standing by a couch. She said to me, "Anne, I want this couch."

I said, "I'll be right back," while dashing into the house for the phone. By the time I returned, Mary was standing by the couch, defending her claim to the couch, telling a man she had been there first! I jumped into the fray as quickly as I could and tried to appease the man.

"I can get you an almost identical couch next Saturday from El Paso." I offered.

The man was happy with that promise, saying it would match his carpet. I promised him he could come the next week to pick it up. Mercifully I found the couch, and he bought it the next week.

This incident sparked the idea of starting a furniture business. The name of our business was "Anne & Yvonne's Treasure Chest." That first Saturday sale acquainted us with the people of Marfa, their needs, and their tastes. We had to limit our store hours to 6:00 P.M. to 9:00 P.M. because we were both gone during the day. We started our business with supplying bedroom sets, dining room sets, chairs, dressers, outdoor furniture, etc. In two months we had to expand into kitchenware, including freezers, refrigerators, dishwashers, stoves, and microwaves because of many requests.

In two more months we emptied our third shop and with some additional wiring equipped it for an electronics shop.

We did not advertise except for that first sale. To our surprise, we waited on people from El Paso, Midland, Odessa, Ojinaga, Mexico; Presidio, Balmorhea, and Ft. Stockton. By Christmas we were well established and making many Marfans happy. Small town stores tend to be more expensive because of the expense of hauling their ware from large cities by truck. We did our own trucking every Saturday. We bought a large van, then took all the seats and other aperture out. We did the unloading. We managed very well and had a wonderful business partnership. This business proved to be a worthwhile venture.

A few times, however, we had to stop and take care of other problems. Shortly after we started our business, Yvonne was called home to Minnesota. Her sister Charlotte, only fifty years old, had died of a heart attack. Charlotte had made it possible for me to come closer to the Lord in giving my testimony to many people. This had been my first attempt at presenting God's mercy and love publicly. Charlotte was a person who had no selfishness in her heart. She put everyone else first.

We continued our business from 1983 to 1991. Because we were antique collectors, we had customers from many different states. Numerous customers from this time still look us up and buy whatever we have on hand.

In 1983 Helen had another stroke. Her relatives from New Mexico came and decided to take her back with them and place her in a nursing home. Helen realized their concern and agreed to go with them. About a month later she died. She must have realized that she did not have much time left for this world.

Caring for Helen had been an enjoyable experience. We had had many interesting discussions on many subjects. She had helped me monitor my finances because I had acquired considerable money from the time in her employ and from our successful business. At the time, I was unaware of what my relationship with Helen was doing to me. It made me more secure and in control of my affairs. I was aware, however, of where my financial blessings were coming from. God was keeping His promise to me as long as I leaned on Him for my provisions. But something else was happening in my heart. I no longer wanted to work in a hospital. I no longer wanted to teach. God used this opportunity to let me taste a new dimension in nursing.

Caring for Helen created a new desire in me to use my nursing expertise in a nursing home. This desire exploded in me during prayer one day. When it came, I started to laugh. I remembered what I had told some sisters at the convent who were curious about where I wanted to work as a nurse. I had answered, "In a hospital, of course! Certainly not in a nursing home! Never!" Only God can make a stubborn Slovak eat her own words. And eat them I did. I would work in nursing homes for the rest of my nursing career—and love it!

In March 1983 I had a sudden desire to buy a van. We were going to El Paso on Saturday, so I looked at some GMC vans. Despite the large variety of vans, I had little trouble selecting one. I chose the GMC top-of-the-line Vandura, and ordered many special features, such as a couch that rolled out into a bed, a sink with five-gallon water capacity, a place to hang clothes, a television, and four chairs. The price was $25,000. The van was promised to arrive June 16. All went well until I came home.

I had never had large amounts of money to spare before. Hadn't I been a little extravagant? I searched my soul and wondered why I had suddenly become so carefree in spending. I told myself that the deed was done and tried to forget about it, which worked for a while. In the middle of April I called to see if things could be speeded up a little. I asked my agent if it would be possible to have it by my birthday on May 22.

He laughed and said, "Anne, you are asking for a miracle! No way can it be completed and sent here from Arlington before June 16. Even that is pushing it. Sorry."

Getting an answer like that spurred me to say to the Lord: "Lord, if you really want me to have the van at all, I would like to have it on my birthday." I put my mind to rest about the van and felt relieved.

On May 21, I received a call from my agent. He said, "Anne, what kind of prayers do you say?"

I answered cheerfully, "Prayers that get results."

He laughed and said, "Your van is here. I don't know how you could have done this, but this is a miracle."

I chuckled and said, "God wants me to have this van!" I was so relieved to know that God Himself had honored my prayer. I had so much to learn about stewardship since I was no longer in bondage to poverty. I was learning that God blesses His people in every need. If I am God's child, poverty has no place in my life. I will cast off all my fears and lean on Him. What riches He gives me I will use with discretion. I will look to the guidance of the Holy Spirit.

We drove to El Paso the next day and proudly drove my new van home to Marfa. After fourteen years, I still have it. This van has taken us all over the U.S. as we traveled from North to South, East to West. Every summer we took a three-week vacation to see another part of our wonderful country. The comfort of the van lightened our trips for we never seemed to get tired. It still looks like new, without a scratch, even after driving from 162nd Street on Broadway in New York to 41st Street where our hotel was. That was a nightmare!

What a blessing this van has been to Yvonne and me. We have worked hard, but it was worth it. Every summer we shook off the worries and hard work by a three-week journey to another beautiful spot in our big GMC van. We came back rejuvenated, renewed in mind and spirit, ready to tackle whatever was to come. Our God protected us on our trips and provided beautifully for all our needs wherever we went. He watched over us at work in the same way.

Back to Bedside Nursing

The following Monday after Helen's funeral, I went to the Alpine Nursing Home, which was only a half block away from the hospital I had worked in five years before. I remembered some of the remarks made by the doctors and nurses at the hospital about the delinquent care of the residents at the nursing home. Maybe I could help in some way to make it better. I went to the director's office and applied for a job.

In 1983 an LVN was allowed to be the director of nursing in a nursing home. This changed in 1991 when the state dictated differently. Since 1991 the DON has to be an RN. At the time I applied for a job, an LVN was the DON. I told her I wanted to be a bedside nurse. I specifically added, "I do not want any position. I want bedside nursing."

The DON said she had an opening for me in two days because the 2:00 to 10:00 P.M. nurse was leaving for her two-week vacation. She assured me a three-day orientation. She asked me if I had any nursing home experience.

I said, "No." It was settled. I was hired for two weeks as charge nurse on the 2:00 to 10:00 P.M. shift. I was elated at the thought of bedside nursing again.

My first day on the job was spent meeting all the patients, mentally placing them in the room to which they were assigned and at the table where they ate in the dining room. The nursing home had fifty-nine patients, many in wheelchairs. About twenty of them had to be hand fed. I also had to remember the names of the aides I worked with. There were five aides, two of whom worked only until seven at night. Medications were passed to certain patients at four and five in the afternoon. At half past five while the residents ate supper, at least eighty pills had to be passed to different residents. In addition, the home had five bedridden patients, whose trays were brought to them in their rooms. The amount of work for one nurse was overwhelming. But I loved it! I also found out that many pain medications were required in between meals for arthritic patients and patients with numerous conditions, aches, and pains, whenever they needed it.

And then we had to supervise and second-guess the smokers! We had to watch how much they smoked and where, so they wouldn't burn the place down. Keeping all these residents comfortable and happy was a real challenge! It took good working relationships with the aides to keep things rolling smoothly.

After supper most of the residents wanted to go to bed. We began the bedtime routine at 6:00 P.M. and by 8 P.M. all were in bed, some watching television, others sleeping. At this time on the evening of my first day at the home, I needed to chart on many of the patents, but I had no time. At eight at night I had to do the treatments on about twenty patients. Some had rashes, cuts, and skin tears, and some had acquired bedsores or raw areas on their bodies. Treatments were completed at half past nine. I sat down to chart and the night nurse walked in. I gave her a report on all the patients and completed my work by 10:30 that night. What a relief! I still had to drive twenty-six miles to Marfa. Sleep came easily that night. I woke up at nine the next morning. I thought about my first day at the nursing home. I had learned so much that first day.

Yes, it was a new dimension in nursing. The needs of these precious people were different from those in a hospital setting. Most nursing home residents have lost their independence totally, bringing out many difficult emotions like anger, despair, and bitterness. Caring for these residents often evokes verbal abuse of the attendants, sarcasm, lack of cooperation in care, loss of appetite, and depression. They often beg for death to end it all. To me this is the ultimate nursing challenge. Alleviating these problems requires dedication, perseverance, careful, watchful, loving attendance, and the forgetting of self to the point of exhaustion.

For a Christian nurse, these apparently hopeless conditions presented a true picture of nursing. Patience, extensive knowledge of bedside nursing, and watchful attendance to every need of the elderly resident were the requirements for this branch of nursing. I believed that positive goals could be implemented instead of an attitude of minimal maintenance. For four months these fifty-nine residents had my undivided attention. Bedside nursing is such a joy. Making these residents happy was sufficient reward for me. They were lacking so much physically but less was offered to help their spiritual needs. The spiritual hunger was there but never satisfied. Much room for improvement was visible. For now it was up to me to supply as much love as I could pour out to these precious people in an attempt to heal their minds and bodies and to provide some meaning to their lives despite their circumstances. Love was the only medicine that could cover this vast desert of pain and suffering. I prayed that the employees working with me would cooperate with me.

In two weeks I was asked to accept the charge nurse position on the day shift from six in the morning to two in the afternoon. I gladly accepted. I would have more opportunity to meet relatives and friends of the residents, whose help I needed to establish all-around health care for their loved ones. My daily round of duties on this shift was beyond belief. The administrator of the facility was a lady who had great concern for the residents. She was very helpful and open to suggestions. We had many discussions of the problems and some ideas of solving them. By the end of the first month we had established some goals and some corrections.

The next two months went very smoothly. The yearly state inspection was due any time. The inspectors do not notify the facility when they are coming. In fact they arrive at any time, night or day, whenever they wish, to inspect a facility for any reason without notification. Later in October they arrived at five in the morning. Being so new in nursing home work I had no idea what to expect. I soon found out how intense the inspections are. You really have to know your job from A to Z to pass the test.

Four or five inspectors usually come for the annual inspections. Each one inspects his particular department—maintenance, nursing, drug pass, administration, and dietary. Sometimes two nurses come. The majority of our patients were on Medicare, which is a very carefully inspected area because of so many instances of Medicare fraud. The inspectors are meticulous in their inspection of drugs and drug passes. The action of a nurse (LVN or RN in a nursing home) who sets out all the drug doses and gives them to the residents is called a drug pass.

The pharmacist inspector never leaves your side during a drug pass. He watches the nurse prepare the medications in individual containers with a card for each medication for each patient. Some medications are liquids, others are pills or injections. Some are given before meals, some after meals, and some between meals. Various rules cover the preparation, dispensing, and disposal of medications. The inspector watches every phase of the dispensing of medications, including where the nurse leaves her cart.

They scrutinize every detail of nursing including washing of hands, especially in giving treatments, gloving, disposing of dressings and gloves used, isolation techniques, and on and on. The safety of the patients is a big issue. Patients' rights have to be a priority in care giving. You cannot force a patient to do anything. The inspectors stay as long as it takes to check everything. I did my best. No hospital inspection was this severe. They spent three entire days checking.

The outcome of the inspection was devastating. The state inspectors were unhappy about the total picture. They fired the director of nursing on the second day and the administrator on the third day. On the fourth day they told me I had to take the director of nursing position or they would close the doors of the nursing home. The amount of paperwork for every incident required a keen, alert mind to handle the loads of documentation to rightly protect the facility, residents, and caretakers. Unlike patients in a hospital who stay for a few days, these residents were not leaving until death claimed them. And as their bodies weaken with age, nursing home patients have many illnesses.

I did not want the DON job. I felt inadequate. Having been a DON in a hospital was bad enough. I would not consent to their demands and gave them every reason I should not be the DON. The inspectors argued every point I had made and finally won by saying, "So you really don't care if these people are taken care of properly or not."

We came to an agreement. I would try, inadequate as I was, until the inspectors came back in two weeks to check on the progress or lack of it. I begged them to keep the place open for the sake of these residents whose relatives were close-by. I did not want to see the residents go through the added suffering of a transfer to a facility far from their loved ones. I would do my best to correct the mistakes made, but I needed everyone else there to help me. They promised me their complete support.

The nurse investigator promised to call me every morning at nine to discuss any new problems that might arise or any old problems needing her expertise for solving. Before leaving she called the acting administrator in for a conference; I was there as well. She made it plain that he had to supply everything I needed to solve the existing problems. She also told him what my wages should be. He agreed to all the demands.

The next morning at nine sharp she called me. She was very helpful. She taught me how to be a good caretaker of the elderly in a nursing home situation, which is very different from a hospital setting. The main goal in a nursing home is prevention, which can be accomplished by adequate staffing.

In turn, I taught the nurses and the aides all the things they needed to watch for as they were doing their daily round of duties. I was impressed with the cooperation I had from all the employees and other departments. Every day at 9:00 A.M. the nurse investigator's call came as she had promised. I was happy to give her some good report every day. The doctors were cooperative in doing their part of the paperwork. After the first week everyone was happier, including the residents.

By the time the inspectors returned, many treatments had been eliminated because the patients' wounds had healed. Even residents' appetites had improved. More activities were initiated for them, which brought about better interaction among the residents and the employees. The overall picture improved so much that relatives wanted to visit and volunteered their help to improve the home. Family members started decorating the rooms with pictures from home. They brought televisions and radios for loved ones. We passed the second inspection with flying colors.

I had no doubts that God's love for the elderly prevailed against all the odds. He blessed the efforts of all the willing workers to bring about a new energy into the lives of the residents. That blessing touched all of us. While absent for a long time, happiness now permeated the home.

Four months flew by quickly. Things were back in order, paperwork was on schedule, and I was very tired. I had accomplished all I had promised to do and needed rest. With no regrets, I asked the administrator to relieve me of my job and let me return to bedside nursing. I could be of more help without jeopardizing my health. We had a skilled nurse with DON experience who would be ideal for the DON job. She was a capable LVN. The administrator granted my request and offered me the night shift if I would consider being the consultant for the facility. (A consultant was required by the state if the DON was an LVN.) I agreed. This would be a much lighter load.

I continued working in this capacity for about a year. The new DON was doing very well carrying on the program with great interest and enthusiasm. She took corrections well and had new ideas with plans to incorporate them into the existing program. It was a joy to be her consultant.

Early the next spring, the ownership of the facility changed hands. The new administration, for reasons unknown to me, fired the DON and replaced her with an inexperienced LVN who was incapable of management. A big mistake had been made, and it was evident to me. I was told to continue as night nurse and consultant.

My worst fears were developing into reality. My weekly consultations revealed the worst decline in nursing care I'd ever seen. The director of nursing in a nursing home is critical to its operation. Obviously the new DON wanted the position for its own sake and didn't have a heart for service. She refused to listen to any advice and never carried out corrections. The place began to crumble from the beginning of her tenure in response to her neglect. The careless attitude she projected spread among the workers quickly, and the nursing home was soon on its fatal downward plunge.

My heart bled for the residents. They stayed awake at night to tell me their miseries. The meals were inadequate, so I would feed them at night. A trip to the store was necessary many times for milk, bread, and whatever I could acquire before going on duty. The kitchen was inaccessible at night because it was locked. I felt so helpless. How long would this heartless management continue?

In three months the place was in a shambles. Residents were losing weight and falling back into depression. Bedsores were becoming numerous because of the poor diet and lack of sufficient fluids to drink.

Evidently enough complaints reached the state inspectors from relatives of the residents. One day at dinnertime the inspectors walked through the front door and saw for themselves the state of affairs. The two nurse inspectors were new. It did not take them long to assess the situation. For three days they worked late into the night. Again the administrator and the DON were fired, and again I was called to take over as DON. I agreed to do it for three months. It was a repeat of two years prior. The inspectors would be back in two weeks to examine the conditions again. If not improved, the home would be closed.

Two weeks later they were back. I had spent all my time retraining the aides so the residents would be taken care of properly. I had to leave the piles of paperwork uncompleted until I had time to tackle them. I was reminded of this kindly. The inspection was short. They were satisfied with the turnaround, and I agreed it was time to catch up with the forms and reports to the state officials.

For the next eight years I continued in that same capacity to watch over Alpine Nursing Home. In that length of time I worked with six different administrators. Although it was difficult to work with such insecurity, with God's help we provided good care for His special people, the elderly.

On August 31, 1985, I was driving to work at 9:30 in the evening. I was asked to help the newly hired night nurse get acquainted with her job. On this cloudy evening the visibility was poor. As I approached the underpass next to Alpine, the bright lights of two cars coming toward me blinded me. Unknown to me, a horse had gotten out of the pasture onto the highway. The drivers of the two cars were trying to keep the horse to the side of the road to avoid an accident by shining their lights on the horse. I could not see because of the bright lights, and I am sure the horse was in a panic because of all the lights in front and in back of him.

As I slowed down to a crawl, I heard a clip-clop sound, like train cars above. I looked up through my windshield to see the train and came face to face with a horse's head. I was thrown with a jerking motion into the passenger's seat. I felt a stabbing pain in my left lower back. Although conscious, I could not move because of the pain. The ambulance came and attendants asked me where I hurt. I answered that I thought I'd broken my back. The car had been slammed against a high rail on the right so the attendants could not open the door. They retrieved my keys by climbing through the back window up to the front. Putting me on the stretcher was time consuming and difficult because of my pain and the crowded situation. I was driving a Honda CRX, a two-seater. The attendants took me out of the car on a stretcher, through the right window upside down, feet first. I still marvel at this unique operation.

After arriving at the hospital I spent all my time in the x-ray department. The soreness in my back increased by the minute. Finally the doctor came, checked the x-rays, and stated, "You are a lucky gal; no broken bones! I just saw your car. It's totaled. The top is smashed down past your steering wheel." Someone else asked about the horse. No one had found him yet.

The police walked in then and told me the rest of the story. The horse was found two miles away from the scene. He had a six-inch tear in his left hind leg but was doing fine. By the looks of the car the horse hooked his left hind leg on the corner of the car when he tried to run past me and that caused him to fall on top of my car on the driver's side—all two thousand pounds of him! I had felt the scrape on the left side of my head as I was thrown to the passenger side. My left forehead and face were black and blue for two weeks after.

I was relieved and grateful beyond words that I could go home that evening. Yvonne had arrived with the van by this time. The pain was becoming intolerable. The doctor gave me pain medication, and we left for home. As we drove past the accident area, I saw my car. Chills came over me. The car was a broken heap. How could anyone survive an accident in a car so banged up? And with no broken bones. I rehearsed the accident in my mind: the bright lights, the horse's head, the scrape, the breaking glass, and the terrible pain in my back. In only a second or two all this had occurred. In my spirit I saw a dozen angels working rapidly all around me, the car, and the horse. I realized that Satan had been out to kill me that night. He was trying to put a stop to my care of the elderly at the home. I realized I had been saved by a miracle.

At that moment I felt certain my guardian angel was still watching closely over me and for months after, while driving in the dark to work, I could see angels clearing the road, chasing the deer off the road, back into the woodsy mountains. The angels were always smiling. God was watching over me, and He wanted me to know that. I felt so drawn toward God in these moments that I felt lifted out of this chaotic world.

That night I slept fairly well after the pain medication took full effect. In the morning I called my prayer partner and told her of the accident. She has the gift of knowledge from God. "Wisdom and knowledge is granted unto thee; and I will give thee riches, and wealth, and honor, such as none of the kings have had that have been before thee, neither shall there any after thee have the like" (2 Chronicles 1:12). I was in great pain and I needed someone to pray over me.

As I was describing the accident, she asked me if I had ever had a bone out of place. I replied that I had had a bone out of place for years, which impaired my walking. Doctors refused to operate.

"Why do you ask?" I inquired.

She asked, "Is it in your lower left back?"

I said, "Yes, and it is so sore there I don't feel comfortable standing, sitting, or lying down. I am miserable."

She chuckled and said, "Well, God did surgery on you last night, and the bone is back in place for good. The area looks red hot and must be very painful." She then prayed for complete healing of the area.

I felt better already. Another miracle had taken place. What a good, caring, loving Father in heaven we have! This night made me search deep into my heart. I had immersed myself so deeply into my work that I had put aside my search for God in His Word. Again He had rescued me from the jaws of death. He showed me I needed to search deeper into the Word of God if I genuinely wanted to know Him and serve Him (in addition to caring for the elderly).

I had to find time to better know this God who loved me so much. What had happened to my personal relationship with Jesus? Had I replaced my caring, loving God in heaven with the god of work? Had I grown lukewarm? I concluded that my spiritual life needed a thorough overhaul.

Father Frank, who still lived in Marfa, was found dead in bed the day after Christmas 1986. He died of a heart attack and possible stroke. I will never forget his Christmas Day sermon. It was a plea to the congregation to "love your neighbor as yourself" (Romans 13:9). Father Frank said Christmas was a time to bring peace into our lives and the lives of others by forgiveness before it was too late.

Father Frank Smerke, OSC in street attire; time and place unknown.

"Life is too short to bear grudges. Bring joy to those around you as Jesus did, for you know not when God will call you." He seemed to know this was his last sermon.

I handled the funeral arrangements, following instructions given to me by phone from the authorities at the monastery in Hastings, Nebraska, where he would be buried. The funeral Mass was held at the parish church of Marfa, for the benefit of the people of Marfa who had known him for fourteen years and loved him dearly. Then he was flown to Hastings for burial.

In January 1991 I was approached about taking the job of DON in Ft. Stockton, Texas, ninety miles away from Marfa, where a new nursing home was being built. The company's administrator was scouting around in Alpine and Marfa for a DON and assistant DON.

I asked for prayers regarding this from my prayer partners. The answer was in the affirmative, even though it meant being away from my home in Marfa. Yvonne also encouraged me to take the job. My commitment would be for one year. By that time they would be able to find someone to replace me because my assistant and I would have established the groundwork for smooth operation of a 120-bed nursing home. It would have four wings, with one wing for Alzheimer patients. It provided private rooms and double rooms. The building was beautiful. Upon entering the front door, you wondered if you were really in a nursing home. The place looked like a chalet.

The building was completed and ready to accept residents by mid-March. We were excited to welcome our first resident to this brand new facility. He certainly got everyone's attention and the best of care.

The number of residents grew steadily until it came very close to 120. This large nursing home was different in several ways from the small one I'd come from. Family closeness, which comes naturally in a small home, is harder to maintain in a large home. Nurses did not know their patients as well. The paperwork alone was time consuming because more detailed documentation was expected as time went on. On the whole, things went quite smoothly. Soon my year was up, and I returned home to Marfa.

I was asked to help at the Alpine Nursing Home again in whatever capacity I wished. I did so with the understanding that I would only do bedside nursing. I enjoyed the remaining years of my nursing career in this capacity with as great enthusiasm as when I first began.

Now I was able to help the residents in every category of nursing expertise. The spiritual side was much more important to me than ever before. I was seventy-three years old, but my enthusiasm was higher than when I was sixty. I was experiencing a new dimension of spiritual growth due to the daily study of the Bible. My prayers became more intense and effective as I prayed with these precious people. The joy and peace that I could bring them through prayer at their bedsides was from God Himself and far more effective than any medication. This was of primary importance to me. I started to think more and more of doing only that—bringing comfort, joy, and peace to destitute people. How this would come about was in God's hands.

I was still attending the Catholic Church and obeying the rules of the Church. My priest brothers admonished me to remain true to my Catholic upbringing. Protestants made it look too easy to live a Christian life.

Father Frank's sudden death brought me again to thoughts of both mortality and my present spiritual life. Only three of us in our immediate family were left. And I was having serious thoughts about remaining a Catholic. My spiritual life was empty, my spiritual hunger unfilled. I found myself being drawn into worldly thinking and living. No one seemed interested in studying the Word of God. Attendance at Mass and confession of sins to the priest were the paramount spiritual acts. What part did God have in this? It brought nothing but turmoil to an already confused mind. The repetitious prayers were monotonous like vain babbling. I couldn't see how this was building a foundation for real relationship with the Lord, for me or for anyone.

I clung to the remembrance of the glorious praise and worship of our Lord on the many times I had given my testimony in Minnesota, Wisconsin, and North Dakota after I had been saved during my retreat with Father Joe. I wanted more of that. I was looking for a closer relationship with Jesus, who saved my soul from sin and hell. I wanted to know Him again like I'd known Him for that time after the retreat. I was seeking an intimacy I'd already known. I prayed for guidance because that was all I knew to do. I also knew that God guides each individual differently. He is a personal God and knows all our needs and circumstances.

Having been a Catholic all my life I never went to any other church for services. Where would I start looking? I needed His direction.

Roads Leading to the Truth

About three days later I received a call from a lady in Ft. Davis who attended a church in Marfa on Sundays. She wanted to know if I was interested in playing the organ at the Episcopal Church in Marfa. I knew immediately that God was gently leading me somewhere new where I could begin to break the bonds that were separating me from Him. I accepted without hesitation. I enjoyed this change for the next three years. A change of jobs in 1991 made it impossible for me to continue as organist.

While in Fort Stockton I was invited to attend a nondenominational church service with a friend. I liked it very much. The music was inspirational, although the band was very loud. They seemed to have something special. The music was heartwarming. Their sincerity reached to everyone they knew or didn't know. The theme I picked up was "We are all God's children, let us rejoice and be glad." Although I was a total stranger to everyone, I was accepted and loved as one of the believers.

I attended several times, but my schedule at the nursing home prevented me from worshiping with them on a regular basis. Being on call every second weekend and trying to get home to Marfa on other weekends did not allow much churchgoing in Ft. Stockton.

When my year of service as DON was up in February 1992, I began my search for a church home in our area of Marfa and Ft. Davis. I attended different churches like a lost sheep for about two years. Something was missing in all of them. I even attended a nondenominational church in Ft. Davis one Sunday. It did not have what I was looking for, either. I almost gave up searching. I began to wonder if there was any church on earth that would satisfy the hunger I had for praise and worship like I had experienced in Nebraska with Father Joe.

About six months later I felt drawn back to the nondenominational church in Ft. Davis. I told Yvonne about feeling persuaded to try once more at this particular church. She had no objection. We would go the following Sunday.

At this time I was giving Chelation Therapy in our home under supervision of a doctor in San Antonio. A couple from Ft. Davis requested it and soon others applied. The couple from Ft. Davis informed me that the nondenominational church had a new pastor. Something quickened in me. I sensed, "Yes, you must try again."

Sunday came and Yvonne and I drove to the church in Ft. Davis. I had such high expectations of finding the answer here and now. We were a little late, and the singing had already begun. The seats were almost all taken. It was shortly after Christmas. We joined in the singing, although no one had hymnals. Everyone followed the words on a large screen up in front. The leaders of the singing and instrument playing were in the sanctuary in front. Everyone was keeping time with the music by clapping. It sounded so happy! The people all smiled. When the song ended, the congregation was lifting their arms and praising God! I could hardly believe I was seeing and hearing what I had been searching for so long! This was the place. This was the moment that I had waited for. "Seek and ye shall find" came to life.

The praise and worship was finished when a lady shared a word from the Lord. The message spoke so strongly to me as though I were the only one there: "Focus on Jesus." Hadn't that been Father Joe's first sentence to me at my retreat? I knew for sure now that this was the right place, the right church for me. He had also said to look to Jesus when times are good and when they are bad. Jesus should be the center of our lives.

A gentle peace came over me as the new pastor walked up to the podium. Every word he spoke seemed directed at me. I knew in my heart that my search for the God I wanted to know and serve was answered.

This Church in the Mountains, twenty-one miles away from Marfa, opened its arms to Yvonne and me, covering us with the gentle peace of Jesus, welcoming us with a love and acceptance we could not resist. We began attending in January 1994. It is a small church with a small congregation. As I took part in the songs I became increasingly aware of the prophecy I had heard spoken over me years before: "Anne, I will meet you in the cool of the evening." It was being fulfilled at this moment. I felt the quickening of the Holy Spirit with such heavenly joy that I burst into tears, but with no embarrassment. I felt at home!

Jesus had been preparing me for some time for this breakthrough. I realized how patiently the Holy Spirit had led me through all the different churches, so that when I returned to this one I would know for sure without any question that this was the secret place of the Most High. I would abide here under the shadow of the Almighty, my God in whom I trust. Psalm 91 spoke to me as never before. Never was I so sure of myself as at this time. His presence was so assuring. This was worth my seventy-four-year search. Thank You, Lord!

The nursing home in Ft. Stockton had rehired me in 1993 to help with the paperwork. Documentation was of the utmost importance, and the inspectors refused to accept any leniency in examining reports on any individual problems of the residents. I would go early in the morning every Thursday and work a double shift of sixteen hours and come home the next morning. The ninety-mile trip to Ft. Stockton seemed long at first but less boring as time went on.

All went well for a year. The paperwork was accepted, and I was happy I could help. In January 1994 I found my happiness in the Church in the Mountains at Ft. Davis. Things could not be any better. I felt healthy and spiritually secure. The winters are mild in Texas, so traveling ninety miles to work was no problem.

In the beginning of May 1994 I was finding it difficult to work my regular schedule. My bones and muscles were aching almost continuously. Extra rest helped but little. I was overdue for a routine checkup.

At my checkup, a polyp was discovered and a specimen sent to pathology for examination. Many blood samples were taken, but the reports were negative. The cervical polyp specimen report came back positive with unidentified abnormal cells indicating a possible cancer problem. The doctor told me he would have to find out where it was, so he would follow with another surgery, a dilatation and curettage of the uterus. If that specimen showed abnormal cells, we would proceed with a total hysterectomy. He also prepared me for chemotherapy and radiation, if they became necessary. I became more frightened with each report because these results were quite indicative of the dreaded disease. The uncertainty of the future was depressing.

June came but nothing certain was revealed. The only person that knew my problem was Yvonne. No one at work had any idea what was happening to me. I continued to work as usual. I prayed and asked God to cleanse me of anything diseased or unhealthy in my body. I prayed with difficulty, unable to verbalize my feelings. I had not learned yet how to approach God when I wanted to pray for my health. Satan was the author of sickness and disease, I knew. God gives health, even restores health in time of sickness.

The second surgery showed the same results. A complete hysterectomy was in order. My doctor scheduled me for surgery a week from then on July 23, 1994 at noon.

I went to church services that Sunday as usual. Our pastor asked anyone needing prayer to come up to the front. Three people went up and I followed. I was scared, depressed, and shaking with fear.

Although I had prayed for others' healings many times, I had never been prayed for myself.

After I explained the reason for needing prayer, the pastor took my hand and put me at ease by saying, "We believe that you will come through this ordeal healed in the Name of Jesus. You put your trust in Him and believe. It will happen."

During the rest of the week I prayed, believing and declaring that I would come out of this like a new person. But on Thursday Satan attacked me with all kinds of doubts, trying to make me believe I was too old to recover, that at age seventy-four I should be more mature and realize this was asking far too much favor! He tried so hard to depress me. I fought with all my might.

Finally I cried out, "Jesus, help me!" I started to sob in fear. Then I wiped my tears and said, "Jesus, I believe in your mercy and power. I will be healed!" At that moment I saw in my spirit a piece of flesh, healthy pink, with many dots of sick cells on it. Then slowly they were being washed off from the top down to the bottom. A great burst of joy came over me. He had heard my cry for help! I had nothing to fear. I knew in my heart that the operation would bring good news.

The next day I had the surgery as scheduled. I was happily surprised and overjoyed to see my pastor and his wife enter my room an hour before surgery. In all my seven major surgeries before this I had never had this privilege. My dear friends, Jay and Anna Beth Ward, were there also. My very dearest friend, Yvonne, brought me there early that morning and took care of all my needs as she always does. Pastor Koch prayed again for total healing. All present joined in prayer! A new strength and courage came over me. All these priceless friends had driven over a hundred miles to be with me in my hour of need and later stayed all day until I was awakened after the surgery. *God bless them richly*, I thought.

Pastor Koch and his wife, Ina Rose, are true shepherds of their flock. They sacrifice their time for everyone who is in need. They support their flock with sincere concern in prayer and good deeds like the Great Shepherd. I thank God for this treasure of God's goodness in our midst.

Now the time for surgery was here. On my way to the operating room I saw in my spirit angels escorting me. As I lay on the operating table I closed my eyes. I saw an angel with the anesthetist, one with the nurse, and two with the surgeon. I was relaxed and at peace. In a short time I was given the anesthesia.

The anesthetist awakened me back in my room. All my friends were around my bed, including my surgeon, who gave me the best news one could hear. "Anne, you have no cancer. Two large fibrous tumors were causing all your troubles."

What wonderful news! My friends rejoiced with me for a short time for I fell asleep quickly.

My recovery was remarkably quick. By the next morning I was walking up and down the halls with no difficulty. I was eating well and gaining strength quickly. I knew Yvonne would be back to see me on Sunday afternoon. When the doctor came to see me that Saturday evening I asked him if I could go home with her to Marfa. I didn't see any reason why I should stay any longer. He checked me over and decided I could be discharged and leave on Sunday.

Five days later, Yvonne and I left for Minnesota, 1500 miles away, for her family reunion. On the way we made a detour to Branson, Missouri for three days of fun and entertainment which was good for both of us. We arrived in Minnesota in time for the reunion and surprised everyone. We had not notified them because of my illness. My heart was full of joy and gratitude to God for restoring my health again in such a beautiful, quiet way after all the worry and frustration for so many months. I felt better and stronger every day. Thank You, Lord!

Upon my return to Texas that summer of 1994, I resumed my work at the nursing home. This was a happy day for me, back at work, feeling well and strong, doing what I loved, serving others.

Back in December 1990 I had bought a house across the street from where Yvonne and I are living. I had been led to check it out and buy it. The house needed considerable fixing. The renters had left about six months before and now it was for sale.

One day, the yard keeper was mowing the lawn, so Yvonne and I went over to talk to him. He had the key to the house and let us in. No prospective buyers had looked at it so far. The house was small inside. The kitchen and dining room were small, but the ceiling was of wood, giving it class. The living room was more spacious, and it also had a wooden ceiling. As I walked into the bedroom, I had a sudden desire to buy it with the intention of remodeling and adding a couple rooms.

I had no obvious need for an extra house, but I knew that I should buy it. I asked the Lord if this would be the right thing to do at this time. That urge came again. The house would be for His benefit. That was enough reason for buying it. The owner lowered the price so much that I knew God was paving the way for something special. I bought it.

In May 1991, six months later, I was able to procure a carpenter to remodel it and add two rooms. Walls came down and the kitchen grew to twice its size. All the old paneling, linoleum, and carpeting were replaced. A large Jacuzzi room was added with a shower and bathroom. The other new room was a utility room. We enlarged the patio by taking down one storehouse. We furnished the whole place with new furniture. We enclosed the entire property with a wire fence. We were proud of it.

A couple days later I was looking over the improvements we had made. I stood outside on the patio and without realizing it, I said out loud, "That is good!" as though it were a new creation. So I asked the Lord, "Why did I do this?"

Instantly He replied, "For prayer meetings and more."

I wondered how this was supposed to happen, since I did not belong to any prayer group. (In 1991 I was still a practicing Catholic.) No more information came. I realized I had to be patient and let God lead me wherever He wanted to. I had no idea what was going to happen. In the meantime I used the place to house Yvonne's relatives who came down for a vacation from Minnesota. They are used to the cold weather from January through April or May. Sunning one's self and wearing shorts in January is a miracle to them.

The first year they came was the beginning of a yearly migration southward to Marfa, Texas to get a healthy tan and warm up their bones. It was such a treat for us to have them here with us. We felt the blessing of God upon them and us. Their health improved while they were here. The first year their plan was to stay one month. The last time they stayed from December 29 to April 10, 1997.

I made the big decision in January 1994; it was not sudden. I left the Catholic Church permanently and joined the congregation at the Church in the Mountains in Ft. Davis, Texas.

In October 1994, after my surgery and healing, I was invited by members of the Church in the Mountains to join the Intercessory Prayer Group. We met every Tuesday afternoon in Marfa at the home of a family about two miles away. Being a new church member and working full time had given me very little time to get acquainted with church members. This was a wonderful opportunity to do just that.

One afternoon about three weeks later, after our intercessory prayer session was over, one of the members asked me how I had become filled with the Holy Spirit. I related the exciting experience as though it happened yesterday. I also revealed my forty years in the convent, God's command to leave the convent, His promise of provision, and how He had accomplished these promises. As a result, I was asked by my pastor to give my testimony to the congregation. I was happy to do this on November 23, 1995. This was a first for this congregation to hear a former nun tell her story. It was well accepted and it brought me closer to all the church members.

Through the second year of prayer meetings there seemed to be a special outpouring of the Holy Spirit. This outpouring of the Holy Spirit fell upon each member of the team. The hard-working ranchers who came to the meetings every Tuesday inspired me. These men joined in with the praise and worship of our loving Father, who protects and provides and blesses in such abundance. The gifts of knowledge and healing were made manifest. I began to see and understand diseases and sicknesses better than I had in my whole nursing career.

One Tuesday afternoon of the second year of my attendance at prayer meetings, the lady of the house told me she and her family would be out of town for two weeks. Would I consider having the prayer group meet at my house?

I said "Certainly. I am honored to think we would have it at my house." My heart skipped a beat. What God had told me about the purpose of our second house was coming true. This is what He had wanted when I bought it and remodeled it. Perfect timing and a perfect way of establishing it for the good of everyone. At this time He also urged me to open its doors to missionaries who come to minister to the congregation and might need a place to stay. How beautiful are His ways.

I consider it such a privilege to be a part of the prayer group. The presence of God is with us as we are gathered in prayer, and the Holy Spirit manifests His presence as He guides and leads our thoughts so we can see with God's eyes and hear with God's ears in solving the problems presented to us. God's anointing has touched each of us. God's love has united us as brothers and sisters of the Lord. How I treasure this fellowship!

I agree with David in Psalm 133:1: "Behold how good and how pleasant it is for brethren to dwell together in unity." Also, "For where two or three are gathered together in my name, there I am in the midst of them" (Matthew 18:20).

Believe me, we feel His presence when we pray in unity. There is power in the name of Jesus, and when we ask the Father anything in Jesus' name, He will give it to us (John 16:23). Jesus says, "Verily, verily, I say unto you, whatsoever ye shall ask the Father in my name, He will give it to you" (Matthew 18:26). I shall never stand alone again as I did in the past. When difficulties come my way, which come from the devil, I take my stand on God's Word and believe with all my heart that what I ask of the Father in Jesus' name I will receive.

My faith was put to the test in December 1996 and all the way through March 1997. Yvonne was diagnosed with breast cancer. All through December and January she had continued tests and examinations which included a mammogram, a biopsy, and a bone scan. She had a mastectomy on February 14, 1997. She withstood the surgery well, and in three days I took her home and cared for her according to the doctor's directions. The specimens sent to the pathologist would reveal if the cancer had been sufficiently removed.

One week after discharge from the hospital the doctor removed the drains. He had received the pathologist's report and it was not good.

During this whole time, our congregation held us up before the Lord in prayer asking for strength and healing and removal of all the cancer. Our pastor and his wife were there the night before the surgery and most of the day of surgery. The surgeon's report of successful surgery on February 14 was good, but no one can be absolutely sure until the pathologist's report comes back about a week later.

The news was a shock to Yvonne and me. After giving the news, the doctor vigorously promoted both chemotherapy and radiation. He was quite aggressive in spite of the fact that Yvonne protested. We had prayed for the doctor before and during surgery that his skilled hands would be guided by God to perform a successful operation. We knew God had heard our prayers. Why this turn of events? We also knew how deceitfully the devil works. He does not want to lose a battle he starts.

As a nurse, having witnessed the agony of patients taking chemotherapy and radiation, I could not agree to the doctor's direction. The destruction of healthy tissue in the process and the damage to the immune system does not invite participation in these procedures.

Yvonne and I talked about this and prayed for direction from Him who has all the wisdom and power to solve any problem. I knew several cancer patients who had refused this therapy and were doing well handling full-time jobs.

I thought of a missionary who comes every year to visit our congregation and of what he had told us about his cancer ordeal some years ago. He had prayed for healing and believed in his heart that God would heal him. His faith had been steadfast, not giving in to discouragement. It took a couple years before prayer defeated the cancer. He had ended his story by saying, "After you have placed it in God's hands, keep believing no matter how long it takes, and *stand*." He quoted Ephesians 6:11–19:

Put on the whole armor of God, that ye may be able to *stand* against the wiles of the devil. For we wrestle not against flesh and blood, but against principalities, against powers, against the rulers of darkness of this world, against spiritual wickedness in high places. Wherefore take unto you the whole armor of God, that ye may be able to withstand in the evil day, and *having done all, to stand. Stand* therefore, having your loins girt about with *truth*, and having on the breastplate of *righteousness*, and your feet shod with the preparation of the gospel of *peace*; above all, taking the shield of *faith*, wherewith ye shall be able to quench all the fiery darts of the wicked. And take the *helmet of salvation*, and the *sword* of the *Spirit*, which is the word of God: praying always with all prayer and supplication in the Spirit, and watching thereunto with all perseverance and supplication for all saints; and for me, that utterance may be given unto me, that I may open my mouth boldly, to make known the mystery of the gospel (emphasis added).

This scripture came to mind as we prayed for guidance. Yvonne and I agreed that destructive therapy was not the answer. God was the one that promised healing no matter what the disease. The medical profession could not promise that with their expensive, dangerous methods. We put our faith on Jesus, our healing Savior, and determined to *stand* on His Word: "By whose stripes ye were healed" (1 Peter 2:24).

In Isaiah 53:5, the prophet says, "But he was wounded for our transgressions, he was bruised for our iniquities: the chastisement of our peace was upon him; and with his stripes we are healed." We knew that Satan would try hard to put doubt into our minds many times in the future. When that happened we would reinforce our stand with the same scriptures and praise God for healing her. This happened several times with such force that, had we not been equipped with this knowledge, we would have succumbed to Satan's devious attacks. We would stand on the Word of God, praising, worshiping, and glorifying His Name.

Another scripture we used is Matthew 18:20: "For where *two* or three are gathered together in my name, there am I in the midst of them" (emphasis added). We prayed thus daily together, placing all our trust in Him who loves and cares for us so much that He came from His glorious heaven to this sick, sinful world to show us how to live righteously. He shows us how to battle the devil by speaking the Word (scripture). When He left earth to return to His Father in heaven, He sent the Holy Spirit to those who believe in Him, and the Spirit leads and guides us on the journey to everlasting life with Him in heaven.

Our congregation at Church in the Mountains *stood* by us on our decision with fervor and joy, praying with us as true brothers and sisters in the Lord. Their support stood as a wall of angels surrounding us, allowing no evil to touch us. We were truly strengthened as the power of God fell on Yvonne. The next week she went back to work half days and the following week full-time. She has not missed a single day's work since. Praise God! Yvonne and I have every reason to be thankful and full of praise to Him who keeps all His promises. "For the Lord is good; his mercy is everlasting; and his truth endureth to all generations" (Psalm 100:5).

Now, almost a year after her diagnosis of cancer, Yvonne is still employed full-time as a secretary to the county judge, a position she has held for eighteen years. We continue to stand with the same strength against Satan and his deceitful threats, and we will not give in. For we have "the word of God" which "is quick and powerful, and sharper than any two-edged sword, piercing even to the dividing asunder of soul and spirit, and of the joints and marrow, and is a discerner of the thoughts and intents of the heart" (Hebrews 4:12).

Jesus wants us to be healthy and whole. We have to fight Satan with all that is within us, for it is he who wants us sick and diseased. We have all the weapons: truth, righteousness, peace in our hearts, the shield of faith, the helmet of salvation, and the sword of the Holy Spirit. Jesus won all this for us by the spilling of His precious blood as He hung on the cross, dying so that we may have life everlasting. So let us fight for the good things God has given us power to receive. Repent, confess, believe, and trust in Him; study His Word and profess our faith in Him, for "If thou canst believe, all things are possible to him who believeth" (Mark 9:23).

In Romans 10:9–10, we read "That if thou shalt confess with thy mouth the Lord Jesus, and shalt believe in thy heart that God hath raised him from the dead, thou shalt be saved. For with the heart man believeth unto righteousness, and with the mouth confession is made unto salvation." And in verse 13, we read, "For whosoever shall call upon the name of the Lord shall be saved." Salvation is for everyone.

To obtain salvation, we must change from a life of sin to a life in God. Sin is something we do consciously against God, against man, or against ourselves, and sometimes it is all three.

God's final judgment against you will not be made only because you have committed sin, but because you have remained a sinner, because in your heart you have formed a life pattern—a way of life that is directed toward wrong. A fornicator develops fornication as a way of life. He does not want Christ; he wants his own way, removing Christ as Savior from his thoughts and becoming hardened. He, therefore, shall not come into the Kingdom of God.

God's heart is open to everyone. We choose to serve God or the devil. I choose God because His way brings peace, love, and joy into my life. Choosing the devil brings fear, hopelessness, discouragement, sickness, disease, guilt, and frustration. I will always choose happiness, which accompanies faith in God. I have experienced miracles in my life and in the lives of people who believed in God's love, mercy, and power to help them.

He is my only source of good. He is my strength when I am weak, and He is my protector and my provider. I go to Him in my every need. From the time I left the convent to this present day, He has kept His promise to me faithfully. I have not wanted for anything, whether finances, health, or spiritual growth. He has taken care of every physical and spiritual need beyond my wildest dreams.

There is one thing I realize now more than ever before. A person can know the Word of God and quote the Word brilliantly, but if that person is not walking in love, his faith won't work. I have heard it said that love is the "fire" that kindles faith and the "light" that turns hope into certainty.

In 1 Corinthians 13:13 we read, "And now abideth faith, hope, charity, these three; but the greatest of these is charity." While love is the most important of these three virtues, they must all work together to become effectual in our lives! There is no room for holding grudges, being envious, mouthing off to people, trying to outsmart your neighbor, being angry with someone. We must learn to forgive and go on. By refusing to forgive and forget, we will hinder our walk with God. We may not feel like walking in love when we know that persons are talking unkindly about us or trying to hurt us. We are still responsible for walking in love toward those people. If we are really walking in love, we will forget past hurts and mistakes. When someone asks you for forgiveness, you forgive and let it go!

Many people let their minds constantly dwell on the past. If they happen to see a person who has hurt them, they explode with anger inside them. That is not walking in love. No matter what someone has done to you, instead of talking about how he has hurt you, thank God that you can forgive him as Christ has forgiven you. That's walking in love! If you want to experience the power of God in your life in abundance, learn the value of hope and become a person of faith who walks in love!

Remember the advice of St. Paul in 1 Peter 5:8. "Be sober, be vigilant; because your adversary the devil, as a roaring lion, walketh about, seeking whom he may devour." He may threaten you to try to get you to fear and to relinquish your faith. We read in John 8:44: "The devil is a liar; he is the father of lies, and there is no truth in him." If you are in Christ and anchored in the Word (the Bible), the devil cannot do what he says he is going to do. If we have faith in God to perform, His Word can cause us to triumph. Faith declares, "God said it; I believe it; that settles it!" Faith will support us in trials, temptations, and the storms of life. It is a pillar of strength that keeps us grounded.

This is what I have learned and gained by my new life of commitment to Jesus Christ, my Savior. God is a good God. He wants only the best for mankind. Because of Adam's sin, the gates of heaven were closed. Adam chose to believe the devil (Satan), who is God's enemy. In order to open the gates of heaven, only God Himself could adequately atone for the sins of mankind. Jesus willingly took on your sins, my sins, the sins of every person in the world, and redeemed us from damnation by spilling His blood. He suffered the humiliation of a sinner by dying a shameful death on the cross, hated by the world of sinners who would not believe in Him as He spoke the truth, the Word of God.

Holiness cannot be put on like a cloak. It has to be lived. He gave us all the instructions to live a life of godliness in that one book, the Bible. It is the Word of God. It has spiritual energy. It is active. It is more powerful than a two-edged sword. Every word in the Bible is filled with the same power that resurrected Jesus from the dead. It is the same power that created the universe. The Word of God has the power to go beyond our conscious mind to the very core of our spiritual being and to cleanse, convict, and transform us. The Word of God can tear down strongholds of fear, failure, lust, and negativity and then build new habit patterns that produce life, love, and victory.

Believers not only have the Holy Spirit of God living inside them, but also they have Jesus interceding for them in the throne room of God. The very God of the universe not only cares about us, but loves us, saves us, and prays for us.

When we accept Jesus as our Lord and Savior, we are given a brand new inner nature, which delights to do God's Will. God completely transforms our inner being to set us free from *trying* to be good (in our own strength) to *wanting* to do right by the transforming power of the Spirit.

Only the shed blood of Jesus can remove sin. In Hebrews 10:16 we read, "This is the covenant that I will make with them after those days, says the Lord: I will put my laws into their hearts, and in their mind I will write them. Their sins and their lawless deeds I will remember no more."

There is healing in the Word of God. Proverbs 4:20–22 tells us, "My son, attend to my words; incline thine ear unto my sayings. Let them not depart from thine eyes; keep them in the midst of thine heart. For they are life unto those who find them, and health to all their flesh."

The Bible is the Word of God. Jesus is the *living* Word. The scripture is the *written* word of God. John 14:23 says, "If a man love me, he will keep my words: and my Father will love him, and *we* will come to him, and make our abode with him" (emphasis added). God's promise to us, that He is with us and in us, empowers us to separate ourselves from worldly ways and all evil and to place our trust in Jesus. We lean on Him in that trust, in every difficulty, believing in His Word and standing firmly, knowing He is the only one we can trust.

Governments may fall, people will disappoint us and turn their backs on us, but we can always count on Jesus. He keeps His promises to those who place their trust in Him. I am living proof of this.

As I complete this book at age eighty, I marvel at the grace of God carrying me through the many illnesses in my early years and completing my life with such good health as I have experienced in my latter years. What a mighty God we serve!

Glossary

chastity. A nun making her vow of chastity forswears marriage and family life.

convent. A community of nuns living under strict religious vows and rigid discipline.

novice. One who has entered a religious order but has not made any vows. The novice has a two-year period in which to learn about the three vows she may make at the conclusion of the novitiate (see below): poverty, chastity, and obedience. She may leave the convent if she chooses during this time.

novice mistress. A perpetually professed religious in charge of the novices. She teaches and trains them about the rules and regulations of convent living and prepares them for the vows they may take in two years.

novitiate. The two-year period of probation of a novice in a religious order.

nun's apparel. (These were modified by the Second Vatican Council.)

   1 *habit*: The name for the complete attire of a nun (also *garb*.)

   2 *coif*: A cap that fits the head and neck closely.

3   *guimpe*: A large white, heavily starched collar (later replaced by plastic).
4   *scapular*: A sleeveless outer garment falling from the shoulders and worn as part of the habit.

obedience. This vow is made to obey the rules and regulations of the Community and to live a life of service.

perpetual profession. After the three years of temporary vows, the religious makes the vows of poverty, chastity, and obedience for life. She may not break these vows. They are kept until death.

postulancy. The period of time a postulant seeks admission to a religious order.

postulant. A candidate seeking admission into a religious order.

Reverend Mother. A professed nun chosen by her Community to assume responsibility for the physical, emotional, and spiritual welfare of her entire community of nuns.

rosary. A string of beads used to keep count in saying a specific arrangement of prayers.

temporary profession. The period following the two-year novitiate. The religious makes her first profession of vows for three years. She may decide to leave the convent during this time.

vow of poverty. One of the three vows taken by a religious nun. She renounces possession of all material wealth and possessions and lives according to rules of her Community regarding poverty. She has no claim on anything given her. Everything she wears, uses, and sees is considered "ours," not "mine."

vows. Solemn pledges or promises, especially made to God, dedicating oneself to a service or way of life, such as a nun makes.

To order additional copies of

THE VEIL AND
THE VICTORY

send $14.95 plus $3.95 shipping and handling to

Books, Etc.
PO Box 4888
Seattle, WA 98104

or have your credit card ready and call

(800) 917-BOOK